Season of Rains
Africa in the World

STEPHEN ELLIS

Foreword by

ARCHBISHOP DESMOND TUTU

THE UNIVERSITY OF CHICAGO PRESS || *Chicago*

STEPHEN ELLIS is senior researcher at the African Studies Centre in Leiden and the Desmond Tutu Professor in the social sciences at the Free University of Amsterdam.

The University of Chicago Press, Chicago 60637
C. Hurst & Co. (Publishers) Ltd, London
© 2011 by Stephen Ellis
All rights reserved. Published 2012.
Printed in the United States of America

21 20 19 18 17 16 15 14 13 12   1 2 3 4 5

ISBN-13: 978-0-226-20559-5 (cloth)
ISBN-10: 0-226-20559-2 (cloth)

Library of Congress Cataloging-in-Publication Data

Ellis, Stephen, 1953–
    Season of rains : Africa in the world / Stephen Ellis ; foreword by Archbishop Desmond Tutu.
        p. cm.
    Includes bibliographical references and index.
    ISBN-13: 978-0-226-20559-5 (cloth : alkaline paper)
    ISBN-10: 0-226-20559-2 (cloth : alkaline paper) 1. Africa—Economic conditions—21st century. 2. Africa—Social conditions—21st century. I. Tutu, Desmond. II. Title.
    HC800.E45 2012
    330.96—dc23   2011030249

♾ This paper meets the requirements of ANSI/NISO Z39.48-1992 (Permanence of Paper).

CONTENTS

ACKNOWLEDGEMENTS

The idea to write this book came from Roel van der Veen, scientific advisor at the Dutch ministry of foreign affairs. In April 2008 he invited me to read a short paper to a seminar attended by government officials, and subsequently he suggested turning the paper into a book that might help people at the foreign ministry to develop some new approaches to Africa. I am most grateful to him for his invitation to carry out this study and for providing me with a research budget. I am also grateful to the minister of development cooperation at that time, Bert Koenders, for assenting to the original proposal.

It was clear from the outset of this project that I would have complete liberty of expression, and for this I am enormously grateful to all concerned. Chapter Six contains a reflection on the possible uses of European development aid that has been included in conformity with the original terms of reference of this study. This as well as other chapters benefited from debates with officials of the foreign ministry too numerous to list by name, although I must single out Maarten Brouwer, who among other things formally commented on a presentation of an earlier draft of this book. Nevertheless, the views contained herein are entirely my own.

Leo de Haan, then director of the African Studies Centre in Leiden, agreed to me taking time off from other duties in order to work on this project. He too deserves my thanks. I would also like to acknowledge my other employer, the Vrije Universiteit Amsterdam, and especially my colleagues in the southern Africa unit, Savusa.

In the course of travelling to gather material for the book I have contracted numerous debts of gratitude. I am particularly grateful to the following: Liu Haifang in Beijing; Ahmed Rajab and John Foster in Dubai; Adams Bodomo, as well as my brother David Ellis and my sister-in-law Susan Ellis, in Hong Kong; Richard Dowden in London; and Marja Hinfelaar in Lusaka. Sadly, one of the last people I saw during a research trip to Nairobi in 2008 was Tajudeen Abdul-Raheem, who was killed in a car accident just a few weeks later. It never crossed my mind that I would not see his cheery smile again. May his soul rest in peace.

Michael Dwyer, managing director of Hurst & Co., read an earlier draft of the manuscript and made many valuable suggestions. He is everything a publisher should be. I am also grateful to Daniel Branch of Warwick University for his comments on an earlier draft, and of course I am indebted to Archbishop Desmond Tutu for writing a foreword.

As always, I am grateful to my life partner, Gerrie ter Haar, for her help and support.

Amsterdam, July 2010

FOREWORD

Archbishop Desmond Tutu

I remember vividly the glorious day in 1994 when Nelson Mandela was inaugurated as president of South Africa—the first to have been elected by majority vote. His election drew a line under our history of apartheid and institutional racism and made us all look towards a better future.

I also remember the day in 1980 when Zimbabwe gained its independence. Many of us had similar feelings of elation at that time, but they have turned into deep disappointment.

When it comes to politics, we could say that these two stories summarise Africa's achievements but also its struggle to realise its full potential.

I have always had hope in humankind. I know what marvellous things people can accomplish. I have also seen what mistakes they can make. Worse, they can be guilty of corruption and wickedness. In my lifetime, Africa has had its share of all of these. Its recent history is a mixed record of both achievement and disappointment. I have no doubt that this is true of every continent as well, which serves to make the point that in the end, we Africans are like everyone else. We are capable of the best and the worst.

I believe that Africa will play an important role in our still-young century, for reasons that Stephen Ellis explains in this book. We have the people, we have the ability and we have unwavering hope in the future.

This book was written by a professor at the Vrije Universiteit in Amsterdam whose title has an interesting name—my own! I congratulate his university on establishing the Desmond Tutu programme, which cooperates with students and academics in South Africa. Most of all, I hope that you will read and enjoy this thought-provoking book.

Cape Town, July 2010

ACRONYMS

Africom	United States Africa Command
ANC	African National Congress
AQIM	Al Qaeda in the Islamic Maghreb
AU	African Union
BBC	British Broadcasting Corporation
BCCI	Bank of Credit and Commerce International
COSATU	Congress of South African Trade Unions
DRC	Democratic Republic of Congo
ECOWAS	Economic Community of West African States
EU	European Union
FARC	Revolutionary Armed Forces of Colombia
FDI	Foreign direct investment
GDP	Gross domestic product
ICC	International Criminal Court
IMF	International Monetary Fund
KGB	Committee for State Security, the security organ of the Soviet Union from 1954 to 1991
MEND	Movement for the Emancipation of the Niger Delta
NATO	North Atlantic Treaty Organisation
NGOs	Non-governmental organisations
OECD	Organisation for Economic Cooperation and Development
SADC	Southern African Development Community
UN	United Nations
UNODC	United Nations Office on Drugs and Crime
UK	United Kingdom of Great Britain and Northern Ireland
US	United States

INTRODUCTION

No one knows exactly when or where the billionth living African was born. The United Nations has calculated that Africa was home to 987,092,000 people in 2008, more than 40 per cent of whom were under fourteen.[1] With a population growing at 2.3 per cent every year, by now there are over one billion Africans.

Births in Africa since the middle of the last century amount to the fastest population growth over a substantial area in the entire history of the world.[2] When I first went to Africa, in 1971, the continent's population was probably less than half what it is today. A century ago, it may have been little more than an eighth.

In statistical terms, the billionth African is more likely to have been born in Nigeria than in any other country, since it is the continent's most populous nation with its 150 million or more inhabitants. There is also a higher chance of the billionth baby having been born in a village than in a town, although urban-dwellers are catching up fast in what has historically been an agrarian continent. The average African baby has about a one in seven chance of not making it to its fifth birthday,[3] although Africa contains middle class families and some immensely wealthy ones whose new arrivals have significantly better prospects than this. Poverty being relative, the poor always outnumber the rich, but one of the main arguments of this book is that well-to-do Africans are better networked and more influential than ever before.

This book is not written in the mode sometimes called Afropessimism. It does not argue that an extraordinarily high birth-rate is leading to disaster. It simply notes that Africa's growing population is one of the main factors that are changing the continent's

1

position in the world. Africa's history was for centuries shaped by the relative abundance of land and a shortage of labour, but that relationship is changing radically. One of its main problems today is not labour shortage, but unemployment.

The fact that there are more people in Africa also changes the historical balance of population between Africa and Europe, which now has fewer people than Africa for the first time, as far as can be traced. More people create a greater demand for goods, resulting in more trade. Given the rise of China to become the world's top exporter, this is leading to a new relationship between Africa and China. More importantly, Africa has many of the raw materials that China and other Asian countries need for their industries.

Many emerging features of Africa's new place in the world are neither surprising nor alarming. If they appear unexpected it is often only because outsiders so often think about Africa in the form of a few tired old clichés. This is not uniquely the fault of people who work in the mass media, including journalists, film-makers, novelists and many others. University professors and officials of governments or international organisations can be equally unoriginal, as we shall see.

Here are some examples of recent events concerning Africa that challenge many widely held assumptions. Mo Ibrahim, a Sudanese billionaire who made his fortune in mobile phones, is a philanthropist who is using some of his money to endow scholarships at London's School of Oriental and African Studies,[4] originally founded as a place where British officials could learn how to run their empire. According to a study by a business organisation, the Boston Consulting Group, 500 African companies have been growing at more than 8 per cent a year since 1998 and some are placed to do business worldwide.[5] In the religious field, Catholic priests from Africa now minister to the faithful in Italy, where there are too few vocations among the indigenous population to supply the country's parishes, while many industrial cities in northern Europe are experiencing a measure of spiritual regeneration through the activities of evangelical preachers from Africa.[6] The spectacle of a Christian mission in reverse—Africans travelling to convert the descendants of those who once ventured into the dark continent to save souls—has a certain irony to it. Africa's global connectedness has no better illustration than the havoc caused to farmers in Kenya by a cloud of ash from a volcano in Iceland that erupted in 2010. By disrupting air traffic, the ash prevented farmers from exporting the flowers that they normally send to the enormous wholesale market at Aalsmeer in the Netherlands and to other outlets. The hold-up cost the industry about $2 million per day and caused thousands of Kenyan workers to be laid off.[7]

The financial crisis—or perhaps more accurately a series of crises, each one provoking the next—that has overtaken the world since 2007 has offered many glimpses of Africa's new position in the world. Many aspects of Africa's new position have nothing to do with finance, but the emergence of new perspectives enables us to see all sorts of things in a fresh way, and this book will consider just a few of these. A leading economic historian judges that Africa has a better chance of economic success now than at any time in the last five centuries.[8] But this statement is not to be mistaken for one of those light-at-the-end-of-the-tunnel analyses that are oxygen to the development business, which has a vested interest in arguing that marvellous things are just about to happen. In reality, there is no good reason to believe that Africa is suddenly going to develop governments that are corruption-free and do their best to look after widows and orphans. Africa is heading neither to perdition nor to redemption.

The omens of the future are there to be interpreted. That is the reason for naming this book after a poem by the writer Simon Mpondo, who describes how when the rains arrive in his native Cameroon, causing the maize to flower, the swallow to migrate and the spider to spin its web, the signs that people read into these movements are always ambiguous.[9] In the end, the omens offered by nature at the start of the rainy season are unsure and tell us more about the season that is just past than about what comes next. The wish to look forward being a fundamental human trait, we feel obliged to read them nonetheless.

Africa's Prospects

Nearly twenty years ago, two leading economic historians speculated about the possibilities of 'a new form of post-imperial capitalism based upon a cosmopolitan world order characterised by the unification of diverse capital markets through competing financial centres, [and] the domestication of multinational corporations by hosts who have ceased to be hostages'.[10] If Africa were fully integrated into global financial circuits, they mused, bankers could feel as much at home there as they do in developed countries. Financial aid would be unnecessary other than in emergencies. National economies would be able to generate domestic capital and to obtain capital from abroad through efficient and well-integrated markets. From a conventional business point of view, this is the ultimate goal of development—an Africa as bankable as any other continent.

Africa has not got this far, or not yet. Africa—or more precisely the sub-continent consisting of the forty-eight sovereign states south of the Sahara, sometimes known as black Africa—remains the world's poorest continent. Nevertheless, before the financial crash that started in US mortgage markets in 2007 and went global the following year, the quality and density of Africa's financial institutions were fast improving. Foreign investment and trade were growing. They are already resuming, and have actually quadrupled since 2003.[11]

For China in particular, whose star has risen with the financial crisis, Africa is now of very great importance as the location of so many of the raw materials that it needs for its industrial future. Less widely noticed is the fact that the Chinese government also has a political interest in developing its relations with African countries, as it looks to them to provide it with votes at the United Nations and the legitimacy to assert itself in other international forums. Some authors even speak of a Beijing consensus,[12] the combination of authoritarian government and aggressive capitalism on display in China that has admirers in several parts of what used to be called the third world. In fact the Chinese approach probably has more admirers in Africa than anywhere else.

A crucial factor affecting how the world views Africa these days is that it has some of the world's last wide-open spaces, together with Latin America. Africa is said to contain some 80 per cent of the 250–800 million hectares of land suitable for agriculture that are currently 'available'—in quotation marks, because most land is claimed by someone or other, and availability is therefore hard to determine.[13] More than ten years ago, a government official from a town near Beijing was already canvassing schemes to settle Chinese farmers in Africa. 'The lease on land is usually 99 years', he pointed out. 'Maybe by then Africa will no longer need food aid from the UN. Its industry and technology will be developed immensely'.[14] Several Asian countries are now looking to Africa not only to grow food for their own use, but also bio-fuels for the world market. In the Middle East, some shrewd operators foresee rapid growth in trade based on African exports of raw materials and on its growing appetite for Asian consumer goods. An increase in demand of this sort could prove to be a huge stimulus to African economies. The commercial nature of China's interest in Africa, combined with the pragmatism of its government and its vast piles of cash, could conceivably stimulate African development in a way that a trillion dollars in aid never did. But it is not hard to imagine how Asian interest could perhaps more easily turn to Africa's disadvantage. An uncontrolled rush for commodities could strip Africa's subsoil bare in a display of what the French call *capitalisme sauvage*, 'wild capitalism'. Asian manufactures could destroy what little industry Africa has. As the veteran South African columnist Stanley Uys puts it, 'the Chinese [will] be like goats: after staying in a country for the required period, extracting the minerals they want, their legacy is—scrub, rocks and sand'.[15]

Whether these new circumstances will cause Africa to be better or worse off in ten years' time is impossible to say. No one can be sure of the future. What can be identified with some confidence, though, are the factors likely to have an influence on future outcomes. Population growth, high food prices, climate change and many other factors will all play a role, as we will see during the course of this short book about Africa's prospects in the twenty-first century world. They will constitute the circumstances in which, as Karl Marx famously declared, people make their own history.

If the new interest from Asia is to redound to Africa's benefit, the continent's political leaders and thinkers are going to have to show more perspicacity than they have generally demonstrated in the fifty years since most countries gained independence from colonial rule. It is sometimes regarded as bad manners to say so, but the

fact is that Africa's political elites—as well as various groups elsewhere in the world, of course—have actually profited from the
degree of their countries' dependence on the rich world and have
done everything to encourage it. Dependency is a sibling of the aid
and development business that for decades has been key to Africa's
relationship with the rich world, turning over the years into a veri-
table industry. Dependency enables people at strategic locations in
African bureaucracies to receive 'rents', as they are known in the
academic literature, payments that they do not really earn but that
come to them simply as a result of their official position. It is not
only government officials who may receive rents, but also businesspeople and even the personnel of humanitarian agencies and
non-governmental organisations (NGOs). Dependency has been a
joint venture to a greater extent than is often realised.

The development industry is peculiarly susceptible to the idea
that African societies can be shaped and reshaped as though they
were made of wet clay. At the same time development workers
from the rich world persist with a single, simple idea that has been
in existence for over 200 years—namely, that Africa needs to be
improved, and that Europeans and North Americans are uniquely
placed to ensure that this happens due to the superiority of their
technical knowledge, including their quasi-scientific insights into
how societies evolve. A century ago, Europeans had no qualms
about referring to their self-appointed role as patrons of Africa as
a civilising mission. These days, they generally use less arrogant-
sounding expressions, but whatever words are chosen, they always
boil down to the same conviction: that Africa is living in the past,
but that with a dose of technical know-how it can be brought bang
up-to-date.

There are shelves full of books and essays on the economics of
development and aid, but less attention has been given to their
effect on people's self-esteem. This can not be determined by statistics alone. In a policy world that is dominated by economists,
there is always a tendency to equate the elusive process known as
development with a growth in Gross Domestic Product. In a
broader sense, development has usually meant making the populations of poor countries more like those of rich ones in terms of
taste, behaviour and patterns of consumption. But development is

6

also a psychological process that is intimately concerned with self-respect and with a perception of being in control of the forces that shape individual and social life. Decades of civilising missions and development projects have left many Africans with something like an inferiority complex, unsurprisingly. Yet African traditions of thought have much that others can learn from. In a world that faces dangers from climate change and food and water shortages brought on by a consume-what-you-can mentality, it is helpful to think seriously about the ideas held by people who believe that the world is not just what we want to make it. It is in this field that the effusion of religion in Africa can usefully be seen, since it emanates from a worldview that is not based on a rigid separation between the material and the spiritual.[16]

Discussion of Africa remains in thrall to simplistic ideologies that are at least thirty years out of date. A great deal that is said and written about Africa remains rooted in mid-twentieth century notions that made some sense when countries were emerging from colonial control and when the highest priority seemed to be to furnish them with the accoutrements of a sovereign state. So crude is the level of much public debate that thoughtful suggestions risk being lampooned as either nationalist extremism on the one hand or imperialism and racism on the other.

A debate formulated in such stale phrases finds it quite difficult to cope adequately with China's spectacular entry into Africa. Much that is written in the Western press on China's role in Africa is unfair and even biased.[17] Strictly speaking, China's move into Africa is actually a re-entry, as China famously sent a vast fleet to the coast of Africa in the fifteenth century,[18] and East Africa has been integrated into an Indian Ocean trading system for 2,000 years. Officials from Beijing score with Africans by portraying themselves as coming from another developing country, historically uninvolved in imperialist adventures, that seeks only to do business. Chinese policy-makers seem to be without the concept of a civilising mission that sits so deep in the ideologies of Europeans and Americans when it comes to discussing Africa. China's pragmatic approach often appears refreshing to African politicians and intellectuals tired of being lectured by Western politicians who, away from the glare of the camera lighting, may actually be less interested in elevating the entire human race than in pursuing their own national interests or even just the interests of their own political party or faction. But the same pragmatism causes many Chinese businesspeople who are active in Africa not even to pretend concern for the rights of their African employees, nor for democracy or environmental standards, and Chinese diplomats show something close to contempt for human rights. Africans who have lived in China or who have worked with Chinese firms in Africa often complain of the racism they have encountered. It would be naïve to suppose that the Chinese connection will automatically bring a better life for Africans.

The various attitudes taken by people from different countries are to a large extent reflections or refractions of history, specific experiences that have been assimilated, consciously or otherwise, into stories full of meaning. The past weighs on the present, shaping the range of possibilities for action. Economists refer to this in the jargon of their trade as 'path dependency'. Chemists refer to a process called hysteresis, the change in its nature undergone by a substance when subjected to various types of treatment.

In other words, we might say, history matters. In the case of Africa it is a history that includes the slave trade, colonialism and more than half a century of development aid. A good place to start thinking afresh about Africa's place in the world, therefore, is by considering how it is situated in time.

1

AFRICA IN TIME

'The tragedy of Africa is that the African man has never really entered history', France's newly elected president, Nicolas Sarkozy, told an audience in Dakar on 26 July 2007 during his first trip to Africa after his inauguration. His speech provoked fury among intellectuals in both Africa and France. He continued: 'The African peasant, who for centuries has lived according to the seasons, whose ideal is to be in harmony with nature, has known only the eternal renewal of time via the endless repetition of the same actions and the same words. In this mentality, where everything always starts over again, there is no place for human adventure, nor for any idea of progress'.[1]

President Sarkozy and his speechwriters are probably not the only people who believe that Africa south of the Sahara never made any progress until Europeans proclaimed their formal rule over most of that vast area in the late nineteenth century and that even now Africans are reluctant to contemplate change and self-improvement. It is quite likely that many Europeans and Americans still hold fairly similar views, although few historians today would support views like Sarkozy's.

It is important to make a careful distinction at this point. What President Sarkozy, like many before him, was asserting is not that nothing ever happened in Africa before colonisation. Rather, he contended that earlier happenings did not constitute history in the modern sense, which is more than just a chronicle of events. According to a point of view widely held for at least two centuries by many Europeans, North Americans and others strongly influenced by emigration from Europe, 'real' history is a record of progress. Even if, as Sarkozy went on to do in his Dakar speech, Western believers in history-as-progress recognise the errors and brutalities of colonisation, they nevertheless regard the colonial moment as Africa's true entry into time.[2]

Colonisation came rather late to sub-Saharan Africa and arrived rather suddenly. Before about 1850 there were a few port-towns that had become European possessions years or even centuries earlier, like the four communes controlled by the French in Senegal and Portuguese settlements in Angola and Mozambique. Europeans had settled in the hinterland of Cape Town and at a few other points around Africa's southern tip. The descendants of slaves from North America had established a chain of precarious settlements on Africa's west coast, and in 1847 some declared themselves to constitute the Republic of Liberia. This and the ancient empire of Ethiopia were to be the only African territories that never came under the formal political control of one or other European country.

If anything has perpetuated the idea that Africa must be helped to enter real historical time, it is the concept of development. This has dominated everything said and done concerning Africa since the mid-twentieth century. The reality, though, is that old Africa was in constant mutation and its legacy is very much alive today, to the extent that it is illuminating to work out the relationship between what is new and what is old in Africa. Grand statements about what it all means, Sarkozy-style, are worth little if they are not based on a careful examination of the dynamics of change.

King Jaja and His Kind

Let us go to the hot, green, humid delta of the Niger river, in Nigeria. The name of King Jaja is widely remembered there. His career and subsequent events in that troubled region tell us something about how much has changed, and yet how much has remained the same, during the last 150 years.

Jaja was born into a family of slaves in the land of the Igbo people, to the east of the Niger river, in 1821 or thereabouts. It was one of the most densely settled areas of what, in those days, was a thinly populated continent. As was quite common in a region that was for two centuries a prime source of supply for the Atlantic slave trade, Jaja was sold to a trader when he was hardly past boyhood. He was taken to the port of Bonny, situated on an island at the mouth of the River Niger downstream from the point where it splits into the vast maze of creeks and islands that make up the Niger Delta. Unlike many others, Jaja was never loaded on to a slave-ship bound for the Americas.[3]

Bonny was home to some 10,000 people in Jaja's time. As the slave trade declined, the port continued to serve as a leading outlet for the produce of the interior, becoming a hub of the palm oil business that flourished from the mid-nineteenth century as British consumers began to buy soap made from the products of the palm tree. Since then, Bonny has switched businesses again, becoming an oil export terminal. 'Bonny light crude' is an oil industry standard, prized for its easiness to refine. They may not know it, but many American drivers ride on gasoline from Bonny. Today, the town has a population of some 100,000 although it remains unreachable by road, accessible only by air and sea. From slaves to palm oil to crude oil, Bonny has been a mart for international business.

Arriving in Bonny, Jaja was attached to one of the so-called 'houses' that were an important form of political organisation in the Niger Delta during the time of the slave trade and the palm oil trade that succeeded it. At the core of each house was a body of men sufficient to equip and paddle one of the huge canoes that were the main form of river transport. Together with wives, children and dependents, a house could include hundreds of people. Each such establishment was headed by an entrepreneur with the commercial acumen necessary to succeed in the import-export business that was Bonny's speciality, plus the political skill to build a clientele. Despite his slave origins, Jaja worked his way up to become head of the Anna Pepple House, absorbing a number of Bonny's other factions until he broke away to set up a new settlement at Opobo in 1867.

Now operating as a more or less independent ruler, Jaja saw the potential of his position as a middleman in the palm oil business.

He adopted an aggressive strategy, aimed at keeping British traders arriving by sea cut off from suppliers of produce in the interior of the country so as to create his own monopoly of export products. British oil merchants complained to their home government. After the famous international conference held in Berlin in 1884–5—the event marking the beginning of formal colonial control in most of Africa, when the continent was partitioned into spheres of interest associated with rival European powers—British officials claimed that Jaja's taxes were now illegal under the terms of international agreements. This was an early example of Africa's fortunes being connected to a set of rules that was held to be universally binding but that was largely of European origin. In 1887, Jaja was arrested by a British vice-consul and exiled to the West Indies. He died four years later at sea on his way back home to Africa.

Seventy years or so later, Nigeria's first generation of professional, university-educated historians saw Jaja as a patriot who had dared to fight against British imperialism. He has a place in popular memory. There are songs about Jaja and, according to one newspaper,[4] even a three-act opera about him in the language of the Ijaw, Nigeria's fourth-largest ethnic group.

As for Bonny, it is now situated in one of Nigeria's thirty-six federal states.[5] The Niger Delta has become notorious as the scene of complex struggles that are sometimes considered as a violent political contest, at other times as a low-intensity war, and quite often as an epidemic of crime. Every night, barges loaded with oil stolen by illegal tapping from pipelines chug downriver to rendezvous near Bonny with larger ships that take the oil out to tankers lying off the coast. Cargoes of stolen crude oil are paid for with arms, cash, and, some people say, cocaine. Very senior Nigerian state officials, military personnel and politicians have interests in this trade that may be worth a billion dollars per year.[6] These officials are stealing money from the state they were appointed or elected to serve. The guns are used in local conflicts. Some of the cocaine is trafficked to Europe.[7] The oil passes through various hands until it ends up on the international market. Whether by the oil companies, the traders or the smugglers, a lot of oil gets spilled. Over five decades, the amount of oil leaking into the Niger Delta has been about thirteen times that of the 2010 Deepwater Horizon spill in the Gulf of Mexico, as of early June 2010.[8]

Hostilities in the Niger Delta feature most often in news headlines when militants kidnap an oil worker or do battle with the Nigerian armed forces. The group that is most adept in the single most important technique of modern political-military contestation—presenting a bold image to international media—is an outfit calling itself the Movement for the Emancipation of the Niger Delta (MEND). Glossy magazines like to print high-quality photos of MEND's muscular young men, sometimes with torsos bared, wearing balaclava masks and military fatigues, cartridge belts draped over their shoulders, skimming over the creeks of the Delta in speedboats.[9] Oil company executives, prime ministers and presidents in the world's richest countries worry about the fact that the mysterious activists of the Niger Delta are sabotaging a sizeable portion of Nigeria's potential two million barrels a day oil production, putting further pressure on oil markets that are already volatile.

In 2009, the Nigerian government reached a peace agreement with some MEND leaders, but few people doubt that a new generation of young militants will take their place. A political solution to the conflicts of the Niger Delta is made exceptionally difficult by the factional nature of local politics. Particularly during election campaigns, politicians sometimes hire as thugs the very same militant leaders who at other times are officially described as crime bosses. These local and state-level politicians have connections to the highest levels of the Nigerian state, and in many cases also to some of the world's major oil companies. In recent years, governors in some of the oil-producing states of Nigeria's centre-south have been charged with massive corruption, accused of stealing millions of dollars of state funds. Although certain individuals and institutions make a more positive impression than others, it becomes impossible to make sharp divisions between the forces of stability and equity, represented by those who are officially pledged to uphold the rule of law, and the forces of disorder. Governance and politics in the Niger Delta are not conducted via a model bureaucracy, rule-bound and predictable. They still bear some similarity to the houses of Jaja's day in the sense that individual entrepreneurs who are able to carve themselves a position through the adroit use of commercial and political connections, in which violence is sometimes instrumental, can aspire to become major players in regional politics. Given the importance of oil, they can even gain national status.

Yet there is also a younger generation of sophisticated politicians who believe the area would be better served by more conventional forms of politics and administration. Prominent members of this cohort are former employees of one or other oil company. Sitting with dark-suited businessmen and bankers at a lunch-table in one of London's most elegant hotels, a new-style politician from the Niger Delta can be articulate, charming and persuasive.

The Past in the Present

If there is some similarity between the Niger Delta in Jaja's day and the same area now, the differences are probably more evident. There has been a massive change in the scale of operations in the intervening century and a quarter. The sovereign state of Nigeria is far bigger than Jaja's micro-kingdom. Market disruptions caused by events around Bonny now impact the price of oil worldwide immediately, and therefore the world economy. Local and global elements affect one another as the fine-grained societies of the Niger Delta adapt to changing international conditions of communication, commerce and diplomacy and, by the same token, heads of state and chief executives the world over are obliged to take account of the militias and money-grubbing politicians of the Niger Delta, however exasperating they may be. Violence in Nigeria is increasingly linked to world events, as when an attempt to hold the Miss World beauty pageant in Nigeria's capital city, Abuja, in 2002 led to violent protests in the north of the country in which over 200 people were killed.[10]

Among the tangled strings binding the people of the Niger Delta to world affairs is ethnicity. Ethnic factors play a political role in many of the world's countries, but they often seem to be particularly important in Africa. Clearly this has something to do with the way that its political boundaries are drawn. Nearly all Africa's national frontiers are of colonial origin and owe their ultimate paternity to the 1884–5 Berlin conference, a gathering of European statesmen that, in defining European spheres of interest in Africa, divided existing groups and obliged others to become neighbours with people they didn't particularly like. Nigeria is reckoned to be home to over 250 distinct ethnic groups as defined by reference to language and cultural traits. It was described by the colonial administrator Lord Hailey as 'perhaps the most artificial of the many administrative units created in the course of the European occupation of Africa',[11] while his contemporary Margery Perham, an academic specialist on African affairs, referred to Nigeria as an 'arbitrary block'.[12]

People often suppose that each ethnic group in Africa has a continuous history as a sort of mini-nation, with its own language, distinctive cultural institutions and political authorities surviving more or less intact over time in spite of the administrative arrangements imposed on them by outsiders. They therefore think that the fundamental error—sin, even—of the Berlin conference was to divide existing ethnic groups. This is not in fact true. It is inaccurate to think, as people both inside and outside Africa often do, that ethnic groups have existed there for centuries as political units. Every single one of the communities in Africa that are today designated by an individual ethnic label has been transformed or even created by the experience of bureaucratic government, in colonial times and subsequently. In the case of Nigeria, one of the country's largest such units, the Yoruba, nowadays numbering some thirty to thirty-five million people, easily enough to qualify as a nation, was essentially created by the experience of Christian evangelism closely followed by colonial rule.[13] To be sure, there were people called Yoruba even before the nineteenth century, but they had no more idea of political unity than the ancient Greeks. Like the citizens of the old Greek city-states, the Yoruba of old often made war with and enslaved each other while remaining conscious of their common cultural attributes. The style of political ethnicity that is such a distinctive feature of African politics, often described as tribalism,[14] is in fact a product of the very colonial government and nationalist politics that brought Africa into the legally constituted world order that is still with us today.

If ethnic labels did not have the same meaning in Jaja's day as they do in our own time, then Nigerian national identity is an entirely artificial innovation. The word 'Nigeria' was invented six years after Jaja's death by Flora Shaw, a pioneer female journalist

15

on the London *Times*, the most influential newspaper of its day.[15] 'Nigeria' appeared in print for the first time on 8 January 1897, when Shaw proposed it as an easy-to-remember term for the British protectorate on the Niger river that was then administered by a business concern, the Royal Niger Company, which had received a charter from the British crown. In 1900, the Royal Niger Company was wound up and its assets taken over by the British government, and two years later Shaw married Frederick (later, Lord) Lugard, a former army officer who had originally been hired by the Royal Niger Company and, since its demise, had transmuted into a civil servant. He went on to become an administrator of the jumble of colonial possessions and protectorates that Britain had acquired in the Niger valley and adjacent areas in the previous three or four decades. Aiming to merge these territories into a single administrative unit under his own authority, Lugard was able to count on his wife's influence to generate political support in London. On 1 January 1914, he announced the amalgamation of the British-ruled territories of the Northern and Southern protectorates to create a single colony and protectorate of Nigeria, with himself as governor-general. The scale of this innovation, creating a vast new country bearing a name coined just seventeen years earlier, has to be set alongside the continuities in local histories if we are to get a sense of how the forms of Africa's insertion in the world have changed.

Lord Lugard, the rigorous administrator, and Lady Lugard, née Flora Shaw, the brilliant journalist, were convinced that British rule was a destiny reflecting the moral superiority of British government. British interest in the region was driven not only by the palm oil trade but also by a national commitment to suppressing the slave trade, and it was the wish to have a naval base for its anti-slavery squadron that had led Britain to annexe its first territory in the region, Lagos, in 1861. Lugard wrote that the southern districts of the country he had created had previously been 'populated by tribes in the lowest stage of primitive savagery'. The western region, Yorubaland, he regarded as more advanced, although here too rulers had been addicted to 'many barbarous rites',[16] a reference to the ritualised killings that were a normal part of Yoruba politics and government. In regard to the north of the country, the dry savannah that bears no resemblance to the humid swamps of the Niger Delta, Lugard recognised that the previously existing states ruled by a Muslim aristocracy had 'an elaborate administrative machinery', but judged that this 'had become corrupt and degraded'.[17] Henceforth, rulers in all of these polities were to be guided by British officials and the governor-general would administer a single budget for the whole territory. Nigeria was created for reasons not even of imperial strategy, but of administrative convenience.

The ideology expressed by Lugard and other creators of European colonies in Africa has become almost as hard to understand today as the seventeenth-century doctrine of the divine right of kings.[18] Nevertheless, the European habit of regarding African societies as being in need of expert advice to navigate the modern age remains pervasive. It is often implicit in the language used to express the policies of powerful governments and in the attitudes of Western journalists and the wider public. Although no serious writer or politician today advocates the re-colonisation of Africa, items of colonial vocabulary and habits of thought that originated in colonial times continue to influence how Europeans, especially, think about Africa. In certain contexts, they even affect the way Africans think about themselves.[19]

Chronological Periods

For 200 years or more, Europeans, later joined by Americans, have generally believed themselves to be the possessors of the most advanced institutions and systems of government the world has ever seen. They have often thought these systems so good that they should in principle be applied everywhere.

Reasoning along lines dictated by a particular idea of progress, it was common until quite recently, and among the European and American general publics perhaps even now, to suppose that Africans are living not just in another continent, but in another time that Europeans outgrew long ago. When Victorian explorers noted in Africa the existence of social units that did not have an exact equivalent in their own countries, they reached for the concept of 'tribe', a word generally used until then in regard to Old Testament Israelites and ancient Romans but not modern people. Since Afri-

cans were thought to be living the type of life that Europeans themselves had abandoned long ago, it made sense to use an archaic
word to designate their social units. The replacement of 'tribe' by
the more polite 'ethnic group' since the mid twentieth century has
not really solved the problem of how to discuss social and political
entities that are of contemporary importance in Africa without
implying that they somehow belong to a past that ought by now to
have been superseded.

How we consider Africa's place in the world, then, is closely
associated with how we assess the relationship between present
and past more generally. This relationship is mediated not only by
the use of particular words, but also by institutions. As one generation passes on codes of behaviour and systems of knowledge to the
next, institutions become a medium for transmitting historical
experience. Many key institutions in Africa are of colonial origin,
starting with the states themselves and their national boundaries.
Only two of the continent's current states, Ethiopia and Liberia,
never had some sort of legal status as a dependency of a European
power, yet even they are only partial exceptions. Ethiopia was
occupied by Italian troops from 1936 to 1941, although Mussolini's
conquest never enjoyed full international recognition. Liberia was
colonised in a different sense. It began its institutional life in the
early 1820s as a territory settled by small communities of black
Americans, originally under the administrative authority of a body
called the American Colonization Society that was sponsored by
some of the most powerful white politicians in the USA, alarmed
by the growing number of free blacks in their own country and
keen to send as many of them as possible back to Africa. After
declaring themselves to constitute a republic in 1847, the small
band of African-American settlers, now calling themselves Liberians, gradually asserted their control over the far more numerous
populations of the hinterland who had never previously been subject to a single sovereignty.

In some cases, the colonial regimes inaugurated in the late nineteenth century had an immediate and radical effect on Africa's
people. In what is now the Democratic Republic of Congo (DRC),
the establishment of government by Europeans caused a catastrophic decline in population that remains a matter of hot debate

to the present day.[20] The Congo Free State, as the forerunner of the DRC was originally called, was run from 1885 as the personal estate of King Leopold of the Belgians. Leopold gained this outrageous privilege by manipulating a purportedly humanitarian organisation called the Association Internationale Africaine. Interestingly enough, therefore, both the modern Democratic Republic of Congo and the Republic of Liberia have their origin in a non-governmental organisation. The influence of non-governmental and humanitarian organisations in Africa is a thread that runs through the continent's history as far back as the Society for Effecting the Abolition of the Slave Trade that was established in Britain in 1787. British abolitionists were the founders of the settlement at Freetown that lay at the origin of yet another modern African state, Sierra Leone, settled by black loyalist veterans of the American revolutionary war.[21] By the same token, as we have seen, Nigeria began as a concern of a commercial company, as did several other British colonies.

While European rule was brutal and disastrous from the outset in Congo and some other areas, elsewhere it was at first so thin as to be almost invisible. Once the first generation of imperial officials had learned that metropolitan governments were not interested in investing taxpayers' money in military adventures or in colonial improvement schemes, governors resorted to working via indigenous intermediaries in the rural areas where the great majority of the population lived in those days. Many Africans in the age of sun-helmets and native bearers never even saw a colonial administrator, continuing to be governed by their own chiefs and potentates. Most Nigerians, for example, even in the 1940s had no concept of Nigeria.[22] This was why an eminent Nigerian historian once described the colonial period as 'one episode in the continuous flow of African history',[23] suggesting that its importance can easily be exaggerated, at least in the case of his own country. In other places, particularly where there was a large population of European immigrants, like South Africa, the impact of colonial rule was far more profound. Even where there were few administrators or settlers, colonial rule could be imposed by indirect rule via indigenous authorities and through market mechanisms transmitted by minted currencies and official demands for tax payment. It was often through these more insidious methods rather than through brute force that colonial rule made itself felt.

The Berlin conference of 1884–5, which indirectly caused the downfall of King Jaja of Opobo, is regarded as a historical landmark because, in inaugurating colonial government, it inscribed African societies into an international legal order. The paradox that an event of enduring significance may in fact cause little immediate change in people's way of life has given rise to a continuing argument about who bears ultimate responsibility for Africa's condition today. There is disagreement between those who tend to see Africans as the main agents in their own history and those who regard colonial rule as having introduced changes so basic to Africa's situation, by saddling it with states of a type foreign to its previous existence, as to have had overwhelming influence on everything that has happened subsequently. These positions lend themselves easily to political and ideological polemics.[24]

Ideology causes people to invoke history in such a way as to ascribe a meaning to events that contemporaries may have understood quite differently or that they were not even aware of. To call King Jaja 'the first Nigerian nationalist of the nineteenth century',[25] for example, poses a bit of a problem since he died before the state of Nigeria, the nation associated with it and the name Nigeria itself had actually come into existence. It is like calling Christopher Columbus an American.

It is even problematic to consider Jaja as living in the precolonial period since that statement, too, implies that he was living in the expectation of something that he can hardly have anticipated. The habit of thinking about Africa's history in terms of precolonial, colonial and postcolonial periods arose only after most African countries gained political independence in the 1960s. The precolonial period extends from the late nineteenth century backwards into infinity. At the near end of the spectrum, postcolonial history extends from 1960 forwards into infinity. Only the colonial period has a definite beginning and a definite end. The implication is that the entire history of the world's oldest continent, where people have been living for thousands of years, is given shape and meaning by a period of formal colonial rule that in most cases lasted for no more than two or three generations.[26]

'*Contemporary history begins when the problems which are actual in the world today first take visible shape*', an exceptionally far-sighted historian wrote in 1964.[27] By this standard, the nineteenth-century partition of Africa marked a clear rupture with everything that had gone before in one respect only: it placed the whole continent squarely in a global system of rules and conventions that was almost entirely of European origin but that purported to be international. Most other themes or problems that are prominent in Africa today had their origins at various points in time that bear little relationship to the conventional chronology of African history, represented as being dominated by the formal start and end of the colonial period.

If we follow the advice to search for the years when Africa's current problems first became apparent, we are led most compellingly to the Second World War.[28] The pre-war years saw the timid beginnings of a planned attempt by Britain and France to invest in the economic development of their African colonies, resulting in Britain's 1940 Colonial Development and Welfare Act. The outbreak of hostilities transformed Africa's place in the world, not least because 'one of [US President] Franklin Roosevelt's war aims, in addition to defeat of the Axis powers, was to dismantle the European empires',[29] a fact that is often overlooked. As Americans and Europeans came to a working understanding on the future of colonial territories, the need to adjust to the new situation both at home and internationally at war's end caused the leading colonial powers to take a new interest in their African colonies. They introduced central planning and systematic development plans directed by technocrats and backed with funds that were substantial by African standards. This was the start of the orthodox idea of development that is still with us today.

Although Roosevelt's successors moderated their hostility to European colonial empires in light of their Cold War interests, their eventual dissolution was part of a wider US strategy that took shape following the end of hostilities in 1945. Washington committed itself to a strategy of global economic expansion that was intended both to outflank Communism and to avoid the economic depression that had ensued after World War One. President Truman announced in his inaugural address on 20 January 1949: 'we

21

must embark on a bold new program for making the benefits of our scientific advances and industrial progress available for the improvement and growth of underdeveloped areas'.[30] Throughout the Cold War, the US used financial aid as a prime instrument of foreign policy, loaning or granting huge sums to its key foreign allies, most famously in the form of the Marshall Plan for Western Europe, but also in the $500 million it gave per year to Japan between 1950 and 1970, the near $13 billion in economic and military aid to South Korea between 1946 and 1978, and the $5.6 billion given to Taiwan.[31] By comparison, the US gave much smaller sums to Africa, leaving it to the former colonial powers, insofar as they could be relied on, to prevent the continent from turning pro-Soviet. Africa received from all sources perhaps a trillion dollars in aid in the sixty years after 1945.

So it was that modernisation and development came to dominate the formal agenda of African politics and policymaking, first under colonial administration and then under the rule of the African politicians and bureaucrats who took control of governments when so many colonial territories acquired sovereign status, encouraged by the US and the Soviet Union, between 1945 and the mid-1960s. Both colonial governments and their nationalist successors implemented programmes of social and political engineering that were designed to create economic growth and to expand markets. These policies had a precipitate and massive impact on people's lives, contributing to extraordinarily rapid population growth, a shift of population from rural areas to cities, and many other dramatic effects. All this coincided with a three decades-long post-war economic boom. In terms of everyday life, the 1940s saw the beginning of a new phase in African history that affected every single person in the continent.

Development in Context

The idea that time has an inherent meaning has roots in Judaeo-Christian theology, but it has gradually become detached from its religious origin. Early European visitors to Africa, especially Christian missionaries, often thought that indigenous societies could be uplifted by what was then termed 'civilisation',[32] a word designating a transfer of European technical expertise and Christian religion that, it was believed, could transform whole populations and bring them into the world of capitalist trade and within the orbit of the international concert of states. This Victorian way of thinking was the ancestor of the later notion of a modern, secular, technically-driven process of development.

Like many fields of knowledge exported during the global expansion of Europe, the view that history is full of meaning has become the common property of people in other parts of the world, who add their own twist to it, as people usually do when they acquire ideas from abroad. Among those who adopted the idea of history-as-progress more than half a century ago were the small number of Africans who received an extensive European-style education early in the colonial period. Like the colonialists themselves, the cohort of pioneering African nationalists who animated debates on matters of state in the mid-twentieth century attached great significance to the imposition of colonial rule. But, unlike supporters of colonialism, they generally attributed a negative sense to colonial occupation, which they experienced as humiliation and oppression.

There were African thinkers who argued that they should concentrate not on independence but on claiming equal political and civil rights with Europeans, but they were left behind in the post-war rush to decolonise. After 1945 it rapidly became clear that Africa was destined to take its place in a modern world that was being recast as a family of sovereign states. The remaining European colonies in Africa were soon perceived as nothing more than absurd relics, like valve radios and biplanes. The euphoria of liberation was to last until the election of Nelson Mandela as South Africa's first black president in 1994, widely (but not quite correctly[33]) considered the final act of Africa's political decolonisation. Nationalist aspirations were sustained by a conviction that former colonies, in achieving independence and undergoing programmes of modernisation and development, were taking a giant step forwards. International diplomats and writers generally assumed that with political independence, African countries were fully entering the modern world. Many people embraced the notion that former colonial territories could be modernised by the application of

23

known methods and technologies. 'The view prevailing for ten or fifteen years [c.1950–65] was that all you had to do was to pour in tractors, bulldozers, pipes, pumps and other machinery and money—the recipients preferred money, unfettered cash—and something called "know-how", a magic especially in the gift of the Americans, to put Afro-Asians on the way to becoming something like Canada' was how a cynical Australian ambassador to the UN remembered the atmosphere.[34]

The basis for faith in development was still the Victorian notion, now assimilated into nationalist ideologies, that Africa had previously existed in a different time-frame from Europe, as measured on an evolutionary scale. Moreover, this worldview was only one of many respects in which African nationalist thinkers appropriated colonial ideologies and techniques for themselves. Many of the underlying assumptions of colonialism did not disappear as Africa's last colonial governors packed their bags and mounted the aircraft steps, but became reproduced in nationalist thinking. These fundamental assumptions included not only the notion that the national elite should lead the masses to a better life—the civilising mission updated—but also the exceptional importance attached to the formal aspects of government expressed in legalistic form or, in other words, the idea that progress could be achieved by legislative and administrative fiat.

Looking back from the twenty-first century, the story of Africa's decolonisation needs to be told in a different way. For a start, it is apparent that nationalist thinkers greatly overestimated the power that went with formal independence, believing that the instruments of sovereignty were enough to transform Africa and its standing in the world. 'Seek ye first the political kingdom, and all things shall be added unto you', Ghana's first president, Kwame Nkrumah, told his followers, in mock-Biblical style.[35] In reality, it soon emerged that there were forms of 'soft' power that easily escaped formal control. Nkrumah and many others placed the blame for this on people they called neo-colonialists. Of course, there were European interest-groups that had profited from the colonial relationship and that now struggled to retain their influence, as interest-groups do. But neo-colonialists were not supermen, with naturally superior talent. The accusations made against them were often a reflection of the impotence of African nationalists who had misjudged what could be achieved by political will alone. By attributing every misfortune to neo-colonialist bogeymen, African leaders could deflect blame for their failure to deliver on their own extravagant promises, which was increasingly evident as time went by.

The related projects of development and national emancipation required Africans en masse to change their way of thinking about their collective future in relation to their past. In the golden age of modernisation, progressive thinkers tended to see tradition as an obstacle to progress. This, too, was a sign of how the Victorian belief in historical phases of evolution had become subsumed in the concept of development. Over recent decades, it has become clear that the acquisition of modern attributes does not always supplant older ones, and that innovation and tradition in fact always exist at the same time. Africans have enthusiastically embraced such new inventions as mobile telephones but often use them for purposes that are quite traditional. Twenty-five years ago, a Nigerian politician declared that phones were not for 'ordinary people'. In 2000, the country had only 450,000 landline users. By April 2010 it had 77.3 million active mobile phones, although these are used by only about 38 per cent of the population since many people have two or more SIM cards.[36] At the same time institutions and ideas that were long thought to be outdated or irrelevant have shown extraordinary dynamism, perhaps most importantly in the field of religion. The exuberance of religious practice in Africa is often misinterpreted as a revival of tradition or a return to the past, but it is more accurate to see it as an illustration of just how mistaken was the supposition, so widespread in the mid-twentieth century, that tradition had to make way for innovation in just about every field if Africa were to enter modern time.

Global changes too require us to rethink Africa's independence in a broader context. After all, the countries that colonised Africa were not Europe's only expansive powers. Russia was also a European state that acquired a colonial empire, using bureaucratic-rational techniques and scientific theories similar to those in vogue in other European metropoles and sometimes competing with them directly for territory and influence. Since the Russian empire in its Soviet form[37] existed till 1989–91, we can see with hindsight how inaccurate it was to regard the 1960s as the end of the European colonial age, as it has been conventional to think. The idea that the USSR was not comparable to other European imperial systems on the grounds that it was a land rather than a seaborne empire was correctly demolished long ago by a British colonial governor, who derided it as 'the salt-water fallacy'.[38] Britain, France and Belgium formally divested themselves of nearly all their African colonies in the 1950s and 60s, with Portugal following, but it now emerges that they did this at a time when the political logic sustaining the great European empires was not yet played out. Provided only that it was suitably camouflaged, empire could remain a viable form of domination for European powers, even until the late 1980s, later than most commentators realised at the time. This perspective throws an interesting light on the tendency of former colonial powers to continue using some of the instruments of colonialism throughout that period—the phenomenon that Kwame Nkrumah called neo-colonialism. France in particular performed a sleight of hand for decades under General de Gaulle (president, 1958–69) and his successors, granting formal independence to its African colonies while continuing until late in the twentieth century to operate a system with striking similarities to formal colonial control in political, economic, military and financial matters. France began to relax its colonial-style grip in Africa only as a result of a series of events including Côte d'Ivoire's decline following the death of President Félix Houphouët-Boigny in 1993, the devaluation of the CFA franc currency a short time later, the political debacle surrounding the Rwandan genocide of 1994 and the end of the regime of President Mobutu in Zaïre (now, the DRC) three years later.[39] A series of politico-financial scandals has also taken a toll on the credibility of the system widely known as *Françafrique*, a term coined by Houphouët-Boigny himself. The latest gossip is that President's Sarkozy's wife, Carla Bruni, having teamed up with the world's richest woman, Melinda Gates, to perform good works in Africa, is trying to persuade her husband to finish with *Françafrique* for ever.[40]

With the advantage of hindsight, we can see that the idea that Africa was entering a brave new world with its achievement of formal sovereignty, which acquired general currency in the 1960s, was dubious from the start. There was actually a great continuity between colonial rule in its last phase and the first years of African sovereign states. Postcolonial regimes that were presided over by Africans rather than Europeans continued to make abundant use of the practices, routines and mentalities of their colonial predecessors. Postcolonial states at first actually implemented colonial techniques and policies more intensively than ever, using them as a platform for a more ambitious form of political monopoly than anything their colonial predecessors could aspire to, while the former colonial metropoles were also pleased to make use of the continuities between colonial and nationalist rule for their own purposes. The discourse of development was used by both Africans and their foreign partners to give legitimacy to this edifice.[41] But this phase did not last long. Within a short time, various global crises and problems were producing pressures, external and internal, for the economic and political reconfiguration of these states. By the 1990s, some of Africa's polities had lost their quality of 'state-ness' to the extent that talk emerged of 'failing' or 'collapsed' states,[42] today more generally known as 'fragile' states. There was a renewal of informal politics as local societies adapted to the diminished presence of a bureaucratic state and the services it could provide.

In narrowly political terms, the postcolonial period in Africa in fact came to an end in the last quarter of the twentieth century. Therefore, many of the assumptions about Africa dating from before the later twentieth century now need to be reconsidered, although confusion arises from the fact that the term 'postcolonial' remains current in the academic world to designate rather vaguely a set of debates about the relationship between power, discourse and certain political institutions and practices.[43] Considering the postcolonial period in a strictly political sense rather than in a vaguely cultural one, it is apparent that postcolonial governments in most of Africa were undermined in the first instance by the global financial changes of the 1970s. These included notably the ending of the Bretton Woods system of currency stability provoked by the USA's delinking of the dollar from gold in 1971, the oil price rise of 1973–4, the rapid fluctuation of commodity prices and worldwide inflation that followed and an increase in debt as petro-dollars were recycled, becoming a formidable instrument of power,[44] to which could be added the development of information technology. In this context various actors took decisions that shaped a new financial globalisation. Key measures included market reforms undertaken by the Chinese government from 1978, the abolition of foreign exchange control in the United Kingdom in 1979, deregulation and tax cuts enacted by the first Reagan administration in the USA, the European commitment to creating a single European market, the collapse of the USSR, and India's move away from protectionism in 1991.

These major shifts combined with domestic factors to produce a clear watershed in most African countries. Although many Africans experienced the late twentieth century as a series of setbacks or even calamities, there were others who saw events as providing an opening for reform. But the opportunity for renewal was seized above all by the international financial institutions and other aid donors, who used their enormous influence to determine the tempo and content of economic reforms known in professional jargon as structural adjustment programmes. The determined, and highly ideological, campaign against big government led by the international financial institutions at the end of the last century actually resulted in the implosion of some African states and their literal dis-integration. Yet there is a further twist to this tale, since it now appears that an imploded state can be compatible with certain forms of capital investment. Often described in terms of a flow, capital investment can be seen in the case of Africa to have more of a tendency to hop, skip or jump, concentrating in certain strategic sites while it avoids others. This process is accompanied by new geographical patterns of order and disorder.[45] In countries where the state has no monopoly of violence and the rule of law is weak, mining companies can work in enclaves that are more or less cut off from the societies in which they exist, creating micro-environments of prosperity and security in an otherwise troubled landscape. The most extreme example is offshore oil-platforms, where expatriate personnel can live for weeks with little contact with the mainland.

Humanitarian organisations, too, often contribute to the rather patchy nature of political power in Africa, since they almost inevitably have their headquarters in capital cities and, like everyone else, they have to make strategic decisions about where to concentrate their efforts in countries where infrastructure, services and security conditions can vary greatly from one area to another. Humanitarian and other nonprofit organisations have become particularly important because foreign governments over the last two or three decades have often privatised their concern for wider political stability and for humanitarian matters in Africa by subcontracting their activities to private-sector and non-governmental organisations, causing security, development and aid to converge.[46] One consequence is that aid and development workers may become military targets in violent conflicts. Conversely, soldiers sent from donor countries to Africa are expected to behave like armed social workers.

I am suggesting, then, that the true postcolonial age came to an end in the last quarter of the twentieth century. Since then, Africa has entered a phase in its history that as yet has no name. (We can't call it 'post-post-colonial'.) This change has to be interpreted within the context of wider movements that characterise the contemporary phase of world history. Among the dynamic new factors shaping Africa's environment in recent years are a rapid rise in foreign investment in Africa, particularly from Asia, although Western countries are still the leading investors in Africa, and large-scale immigration by Chinese entrepreneurs. It is already apparent that Asian businesspeople and diplomats do not come to Africa with the same expectations as their European and American counterparts, nor with the same ideological baggage, and that they make different demands. Some aspects of 'state-ness' that Westerners regard as vital seem to have far less importance to Middle Eastern and Asian business operators more familiar with conditions in emerging markets. One South African investment strategist refers to the ability of Chinese businesses to 'hunt in a pack', as he puts it, simultaneously cooperating and competing with one another, and speaks enthusiastically of the Tata-ification of Africa, by reference to the Indian industrial company of that name.[47] As African societies respond to new demands and as people develop new strategies, new forms of insertion in the world are emerging.

2

A WORLD OF LIGHT AND SHADE

It is amazing how many foreigners think that Africa exists outside the political, commercial and social circuits that constitute the world's nerve system. In the Netherlands, where I live, people sometimes refer to Africa as *het verloren continent*, 'the lost continent', as though it had drifted off into the ocean and lost its mooring to a globalised world.

Nothing could be further from the truth.[1] The argument that Africa is a lost continent is actually an ideological statement. It is a continuation of the old idea that Africa exists in a separate time-zone from the rest of the world, with the added twist that it is doomed never to catch up. The Victorians and the colonial modernisers, although they generally believed that time had stood still in Africa, were at least confident that progress would come.

A large part of the reason that Africa is sometimes perceived as immobile is because its connections with the practices, networks and institutions that constitute globalisation are often made via their hidden side and in unexpected ways. Development itself is an example. This was originally seen as a quick way of catching up with the industrialised world, maybe within a couple of generations. Half a century ago, it was reasonable to suppose that development was helping to build efficient states governing societies with improving living standards, but this is no longer convincing. It has actually turned into a way of life. Development is like scaffolding that was originally put up around a house under construction. The scaffolding is still there and the builders still have not

31

finished the house. Thinking about this analogy, it becomes easier to see why many people may think nothing has actually changed.

In reality, it is not that African countries have failed to develop, but that they have developed in ways that no one foresaw and that do not register on most official measures. Many African governments can no longer articulate a genuinely national interest, only a factional one. Their objective is to generate income and other benefits for themselves and their supporters rather than to manage a whole society. They are often beholden to foreigners at least as much as they are accountable to their own people. Every rich-country government has a ministry or other administrative unit whose mission is to assist in the development of the world's poorest countries, many of them African former colonies of European powers. The policies of these development ministries inevitably reflect the politics of the governments that own them.

In addition to running their own programmes, development administrations also provide finance to some of the thousands of non-governmental development organisations that exist all over the Western world, and Western countries in recent decades have to some degree outsourced their Africa policies to humanitarian groups. The Comparative Nonprofit Sector Project at Johns Hopkins University estimated in 2005 that if non-profit organisations were a country, they would have the fifth largest economy in the world.[2] In 2006, only a third of the $325 billion in aid to the developing world (not just Africa) coming from countries of the Organisation for Economic Co-operation and Development (OECD) was provided by governments.[3] NGOs (as everyone refers to non-governmental organisations) working in Africa vary from reputable and competent organisations with clear goals to fly-by-night outfits that do little beyond funding their own staff. Alongside the older aid and development NGOs, there exist also personal ones, created by some of the almost unbelievably wealthy individuals who have emerged in recent decades. Bill and Melinda Gates, for example, have established the world's fourth-biggest philanthropic fund, with an endowment amounting to some $35.1 billion. In 2007, it paid out over $2 billion in grants, making it larger than the GDP of many UN member-states.[4] In effect, policy choices made by Bill and Melinda and their staff can have an outcome more significant than those resulting from the actions of many of the world's 193[5] sovereign states. So important has the non-government sector become that in many countries NGOs handle some of the conventional functions of a state. This is especially interesting in light of the fact that quite a few African states started life in the nineteenth century under the administration of humanitarian organisations and even private companies, like the Royal Niger Company that originally employed Lord Lugard.[6]

Travelling through Africa, it is not hard to find foreigners who have committed themselves to the continent in ways that command respect. I have met surgeons from Mexico and the USA who spend their holidays working in makeshift hospitals for medical charities, treating severed limbs and looking after malaria patients. They give expert attention to people who otherwise would receive no medical help at all. There are still old-fashioned Christian missionaries who live for decades in remote areas, appreciated and trusted by local people more than any other foreigners. But the aid business also has room for figures of breathtaking hypocrisy. Whether they are more or less numerous than in other businesses is not clear, but they certainly exist.

Tens of thousands of Westerners, ranging from sandal-wearing volunteers through to the highly paid consultants found in five-star hotels, would have to look for a new line of work if Africa stopped needing aid. They collectively constitute a key lobby in Western relations with Africa and are the lineal descendants of the merchants and missionaries who influenced British policy in the nineteenth century. Whether bright with sincerity or dulled by cynicism, workers in the aid and development business have become a key part of Africa's perverse integration[7] into globalisation.

This perversity takes many forms. Flight capital has for fifty years left Africa for tax havens and bank accounts abroad, sometimes even in suitcases stuffed full of banknotes, on a larger scale than aid flowing in the other direction. Illicit financial flows from Africa between 1970 and 2008 are estimated to have been up to an amazing $1.8 trillion.[8] There are many types of transaction that could be described as perverse or illicit. Some multinational companies routinely bribe officials to obtain contracts, and probably nearly all of them transfer assets between countries in a search for the lowest tax rates, channelling money through shell companies located in tax havens. Industrial companies in richer continents sometimes dump their toxic waste in Africa, although the boom product these days is old computers, to be stripped of the precious metals they contain. Sleazy businessmen from all over the world travel to Africa to sell weapons or buy 'blood diamonds' or even tankers full of stolen oil, a Nigerian speciality. Illegality and irregularity seem to be routine in all sorts of situations.

Meanwhile, Africans travel the world in substantial numbers. Some 30 per cent of African university graduates are said to live outside the continent. Some make outstanding careers in the professions or in business in their adopted countries. However, the many Africans who are not doctors or nurses, top engineers or brilliant footballers, may have to resort to subterfuge if they want to work abroad, especially in Europe. Some claim to be tourists and then overstay their three-month visas, or arrive as students and stay after their studies, while others risk their lives on leaky boats or on lorries that grind their way through the Sahara desert. Thousands die on the more difficult routes. The survivors draw on almost incredible reserves of psychological strength, like Sunday,[9] a penniless, thirty-year old Nigerian migrant whom I met in Spain in 2009. He left home at the age of nineteen and has been travelling ever since. He spent six years living rough in Morocco and lost both his legs in an accident. He took up wheelchair sports and won medals for javelin and discus throwing. Although he has now reached the European Union, without papers and without legs his chance of finding a decent job seems close to zero. He does not seem discouraged although he would like, he said, to find a good woman with whom he can share his life. Sunday told me that he spends hours of each day praying, and he radiates a spirituality that makes me believe him.

The latest destination for African migrants is China. The manufacturing city of Guangzhou has seen the number of African migrants increase by a third every year since 2003, and there are now an estimated 20,000 Africans legally resident there, predominantly West African, young, and male. Taking account of illegal residents and short-term visitors, the figure could even go over 100,000 people.[10] In May 2010, for the first time an African was

sentenced to death in China for drug-smuggling after being convicted of possessing six kilos of heroin.[11] The current rate offered
by African drug traffickers to a courier for smuggling a kilo of
narcotics internally, by swallowing small packages wrapped in
condoms, is just $3,500.[12] Fortunately, only a small minority of
migrants resort to such desperate measures. Nevertheless, the
existence of large numbers of Africans on other continents in conditions of semi-clandestinity, sending significant sums back home
to their families through informal networks, has deepened Africa's
perverse integration.

There are also refugees and internally displaced people who live
in camps, directly dependent on international organisations for
their daily sustenance. Some 20 per cent of the refugees assisted by
the United Nations High Commissioner for Refugees are in sub-
Saharan Africa.[13] Relying on an international bureaucracy for food
and shelter does not represent progress by any yardstick. At the
same time, it is hardly an index of marginality in regard to the
international system.

Pretence

Africa's odd form of insertion into global affairs has emerged over
decades. Colonial rule itself often depended on pretence, since
small numbers of Europeans could not really govern such a vast
continent without the complicity of some of the people who
wielded authority in African societies. It was largely in order to
make a system of government by bluff function that European
colonials insisted on their own status and dignity above all else; the
prestige of belonging to a master race was essential to uphold the
official version of reality, so insubstantial was their authority in
many respects. During the first part of the colonial period, it was
not too difficult to keep up appearances, as hardly anyone was
asking hard questions about what colonial rule was for. After the
Second World War, the next scene in the play was to act as though
rational, modern bureaucracies were rapidly supplanting every
other means that people might find to govern themselves and to
argue that development was just around the next corner as Africa,
allegedly, entered modern times at last.

Since the 1970s, the gap between the official and actual versions of reality in Africa has become increasingly obvious.[14] The official version is that which is prescribed by the law and government regulations, usually more or less in conformity with what foreign aid donors deem appropriate. Reality is what happens. The actual governance of African societies often bears almost no resemblance to the diagrams shown on consultants' Powerpoint presentations and has little to do with legal texts.

Ambitious people understand that there is money to be made by maintaining appearances while, in reality, doing whatever is necessary for success. When talking to a Western ambassador or a development worker, it is essential to use buzz-words like 'democracy', 'good governance' and 'gender' although these may not in reality be major concerns. The rulers of cash-strapped governments, having particularly sensitive antennae when it comes to money and resources, activate informal networks in such a way as to benefit from the privatisation of aid. Every thinking person in Africa is so accustomed to these forms of dissimulation that they appear almost as instinctive knowledge. The whole system is a breeding-ground for misunderstanding, artful manipulation and, for those with a moralistic turn of mind, charges of hypocrisy.

One of Africa's most dynamic leaders is Paul Kagame, president of Rwanda. He is a driven man, highly intelligent, determined to turn his small, resource-poor country into a hub of efficiency and progress that will be able to attract high-quality business from a wider area, Singapore-style. He seems genuinely intent on dispensing with the development industry, and yet he has been a donor favourite. Born in Rwanda in 1957 into an aristocratic family, he moved with his parents to neighbouring Uganda to escape political violence when he was little more than a baby. Growing up in Uganda at a time of political mayhem, including the reign of Idi Amin and the even bloodier presidency of Milton Obote, he joined a rebel guerrilla army in Uganda. His long experience of war has made him a true militarist, a person who believes in military solutions.[15] In dealings with the West his standard tactic, successful time after time, is to evoke the failure of the UN Security Council to halt the 1994 genocide in Rwanda and to play on feelings of guilt. Anyone who does not support him Kagame accuses of complicity with the genocide, direct or indirect. Anyone who asks about his government's own hounding to death of hundreds of thousands of Rwandan refugees in the Democratic Republic of Congo in the late 1990s—a matter that the UN has recently raised in a report[16]—or of Rwanda's repeated destabilisation of its giant neighbour, is treated with contempt. Asked about relations between Hutu and Tutsi in his country, President Kagame replies simply that these distinctions have been abolished. Kagame was particularly adept at manipulating the touchy-feely administration of Bill Clinton. Clinton's Africa team, which had NGO veterans and former solidarity activists in some key positions, for a couple of years touted Paul Kagame as one of a new breed of African leader. The 'new' African leaders were former left-wingers who had embraced capitalism and were said to have understood the need for rigorous administration and good governance. Among those who submitted to Kagame's mixture of steely contempt and cerebral charm were successive British aid ministers including notably the hapless Clare Short, secretary of state for international development under Tony Blair. As a leading chronicler of central Africa's wars remarks, 'it is amusing that the most enthusiastic supporters of the New Leaders paradigm were both former Leftists like Short, with a soft spot for what they saw as a modern reincarnation of their old beliefs, and those most aggressive promoters of the new triumphant globalised capitalist orthodoxy, the IMF and the World Bank'.[17] Importantly for the future, the style of a Paul Kagame is well suited to dealing with the Chinese diplomats and economic operators who ask no questions about democracy or human rights, but want only to talk business.

The pretence that the official organs of government actually function in reality as they do on paper has become institutionalised in Africa over decades and it can easily be integrated into wider circuits of deception used by international operators who wish to hide their activities behind a screen of formality and law. These include secret services, money-launderers, offshore bankers, corporate lawyers, sanctions-busters, drug-traffickers, arms-smugglers and many others. Some years ago, I published an article showing in detail how international systems-breakers could cooperate with an indigenous political elite in the case of one small country, Seychelles, the tourist paradise of the western Indian Ocean.[18] There, in the 1980s, Italian money-launderers with connections to organised crime and to Italian political parties made common cause with drug-traders, US covert warriors, South African sanctions-busters and Middle Eastern political fixers, all under cover of a sovereign state, in fact one with a relatively high reputation for what is nowadays called 'good governance'. In the process the Seychelles became one of the few African states to become literally criminal in the sense of drafting legislation designed to evade laws both domestic and international. A bill introduced in the islands' national assembly provided immunity from prosecution to any foreign businessman investing at least $10 million in the country, 'the perfect present for drug barons, fraudsters and money launderers' according to the director of the UK's Serious Fraud Office.[19]

In order to explore not only the texture of business and government in Africa, but above all its integration into global circuits that usually remain out of sight, it is useful first to consider dependency and the rule of law, or rather the absence thereof, in slightly more detail, since both are conventionally seen as holding back Africa's development. We will then be in a better position to investigate corruption, often seen as Africa's biggest home-grown problem.

Dependency: Political Ju-jitsu

The lopsided shape of Africa's relationships with the world's powerhouse economies was noted decades ago by writers who interpreted it in terms of dependency.[20] Dependency theory, originally formulated in regard to Latin America, is based on the perception that Africa is subservient to the rich world, especially the wealthy countries that border the North Atlantic, and that this relationship is so unbalanced as to be unhealthy and even immoral. The theory posits that the developed core of the capitalist world, situated in Europe and North America, strives to maintain its privileged position by keeping peripheral countries of what was formerly known as the third world in a subservient position. These poorer countries are encouraged to produce raw materials that can be consumed in the metropoles of development or transformed in the rich countries into manufactured items that may then be sold worldwide with high mark-ups on their price, handsome payment for the work that goes into transforming basic commodities into consumer goods.

Most African politicians and thinkers of the era of Kwame Nkrumah and Julius Nyerere, two icons of liberation who heartily loathed each other, were persuaded by these insights. African nationalist leaders sought allies from Asian and Latin American countries in a situation similar to their own and looked to sympathisers overseas for support. A few became close allies of the Soviet Union, but this was generally not a preferred option since it brought with it other constraints, not to mention the hostility of the USA and Europe.

The development industry has popularised the view that a properly implemented policy will wean Africa off this dependency, and that all people of goodwill should support such an endeavour. If this does not come about, it is often assumed to be because it suits rich Western countries to keep things the way they are. Many African intellectuals and politicians as well as significant numbers of people in the West hold opinions roughly along these lines, although for the last quarter-century dependency theory or anything resembling it has been deeply unfashionable in Western universities.

'Nobody has attained political maturity', wrote the great economist Joseph Schumpeter, 'who does not understand that policy is politics'.[21] Applying this dictum, we may note that dependency theory was embraced most warmly by those power-holders and power-brokers who found it consistent with their interests. Dependency theory in various guises continues to have intellectual and political support in Africa to this day not least because it provides a reading of the world in which little agency is attributed to Africans themselves, who are represented as the victims of powerful, ruthless and even sinister metropolitan lobbies. If it is traditionally popular with development enthusiasts, no doubt this is largely because it accentuates their role in the front line of a fight for justice. However, two generations after the end of colonial rule in most of Africa, it has become easier to see just how much key groups there have actually worked to maintain or create patterns of dependency. They include not only politicians and top businesspeople but large parts of the population that have adopted a strategy of extraversion, sometimes over very long periods of time.[22] Of course, relations of dependency can also be made to work for specific groups or bodies in the rich world, including multinational companies that source their supplies in Africa and governments that use financial aid to further their strategic or commercial interests. An example comes from Mozambique. In 1995, its government was looking for investment to develop an offshore gas field. The best two bids came from South Africa and Argentina, but US diplomats reportedly threatened to withhold development aid if the tender was not given to a US company. Since two-thirds of the country's budget came from development funds, this was a threat that could not be ignored. The US company that got the contract went by the name of Enron.[23]

It is not just by providing the muscle to favour their national companies that the aid relationship is useful for donor countries. Making donations of development aid, which in theory has the long-term goal of ending dependency, can serve governments in rich countries by enabling them to leverage their standing in the world more generally. Giving speeches about development and signing cheques for projects intended to help the world's poor enables politicians to satisfy certain domestic political demands at relatively low financial cost. The leader of a centrist European government can show that his heart is in the proper place (on the left-hand side) by pleading for help for Africa and getting photographed with Bono.[24] It is easier and cheaper for a rich country to find the money for an international peacekeeping mission in Darfur with personnel drawn mostly from Africa and to give money to humanitarian organisations than to undertake the difficult diplomatic and military steps that would be necessary actually to stop the fighting there.

The Nigerian academic Claude Ake was one of the earliest and most persuasive of African intellectuals to state clearly that it was not only Western neo-colonialists and their lackeys who might have vested interests in keeping Africa underdeveloped, and therefore dependent, as had already been repeated ad nauseam, but also certain groups in Africa that amounted to more than a handful of mercenaries and cynics. He realised that the last thing many African governments really wanted was development, since it was the development *effort* that kept them in power; actual progress on this front would be counter to their interests. 'The assumption so readily made that there has been a failure of development is misleading', Ake wrote in a small book published in 1996. 'The problem is not so much that development has failed as that it was never really on the agenda in the first place'.[25]

For decades, the domination of all political discourse by the notion of development allowed African politicians simply to dismiss any matter they found inconvenient or any information that was embarrassing by arguing that it did not serve the cause of development, whatever that might mean. More prosaically, the flow of development aid gave African governments access to resources beyond the limits of any tax contract with their own citizens.[26] Skilled operators can actually turn dependence on a powerful foreign patron or institution to their own advantage. It is the political equivalent of ju-jitsu, the martial art in which a relatively weak fighter uses an opponent's superior weight and strength to his own advantage.

This is another situation that has deep historical roots, perhaps going back even as far as the era of the Atlantic slave trade, when African entrepreneurs could offer slaves in exchange for imported goods that they could not otherwise afford to buy,[27] distributing the imports in such a way as to increase their domestic political standing like any good constituency politician. The colonial governments that are the forebears of today's African states set themselves up as gatekeepers or *rentiers*,[28] encouraging imports and exports as the best available means of bringing entire African populations within the purview of a monetary economy and simultaneously raising income for the government by levying duties on trade. While this strategy was generally successful in encouraging a rapid growth in exports, notably of agricultural products and minerals, the growth of imports was even more impressive. Even though they were generally only lightly manned, colonial administrations earmarked an exceptionally high percentage of their budget for the salaries of their own employees.

African nationalism took shape in this environment. However, the nationalist politicians who began to occupy senior positions in government in most parts of Africa in the 1950s, even before the end of colonial rule, had to deal with a variety of pressures from which colonial bureaucrats were relatively immune, especially to provide benefits for their voters, family and friends. Since quite a few experts at that time believed that development could be achieved quite quickly by radical programmes of modernisation, in the form of infrastructure projects and through the provision of mass education in particular, the recommendations of technical committees were often agreeable to African politicians. Modernisation demanded a massive expansion of civil service establishments, creating salaried jobs for a generation of school and college graduates. With state-run programmes of development, politicians could pursue progress and create a political clientele in one swoop. In the early years after their new flags had been raised many governments also attempted to develop import-substitution industries in line with the then fashionable theory of modernisation through industry. State officials therefore generally favoured the maintenance of tariffs, ostensibly to defend fledgling industries, but also because this was a formidable instrument of political management. Meanwhile, the availability of foreign aid and, especially, after the massive increase in world oil prices in 1973, the possibility of borrowing large sums from foreign banks or development agencies placed at the disposal of Africa's political leaders funding that was independent of domestic constituencies.

While Africa's politicians generally tried to reward their supporters by handing out jobs and access to education or other benefits that were seen as flowing from the grace and favour of those in control of the state, they often took the exact opposite approach when it came to issuing import licences or using other official instruments of economic policy. People who could make money independently, whether in production or trade, were liable to be viewed with suspicion since they could potentially use their wealth to finance an opposition political party or a rival faction in a ruling party. When ministers and officials did hand out import licences they therefore often favoured foreigners or groups that, for one reason or another, were not regarded as full members of the national political community. Even governments that fulminated against neo-colonialism were often happy to give trade privileges to companies from the former colonial metropole and various other expatriate groups such as the Lebanese in West Africa and Indians and Pakistanis in East Africa, together with specialist traders such as the Malinke and Mandingo of West Africa, many of whom in effect received commercial privileges in exchange for supporting incumbent political regimes and otherwise staying out of politics. Dependency thus acquired distinctive political patterns at home.

All of this means that if we are to understand Africa's relationship to the rich world, it is quite instructive simply to turn dependency theory upside down. If African countries have continued to supply the developed world with raw materials and to import much of what they consume rather than to build up their own capacity to produce, it is in part because powerful interest groups in Africa find this to be in their interest.

The Rule of Law

One of the most important debates on development in recent years has been that between writers who insist it is largely a matter of cash (in retreat intellectually, but enjoying support from the development industry and from many African governments) and those who claim that development involves broader questions including the quality of institutions and the rule of law.

A mystique surrounds the notion of the rule of law in societies with long traditions of literacy and, revealingly, with sacred texts of long standing.[29] In Africa, by contrast, the rule of law was established only in colonial times. This is a factual statement, not a euphemism for saying that colonial government was just. It is neither more nor less than the observation that colonial government was based on the idea that a formal state apparatus should be responsible for promulgating a code of laws and associated rules, usually in written form, that have a binding force on society and even on the state itself. The fact that the rule of law was established by colonial governments does not mean that public life has been effectively regulated ever since then by the consistent application of written laws. The point is that from colonial times up until today, African countries have *in principle* been governed by the consistent application of written laws. This is a condition for mem-

43

bership of the international family of states. In reality, as we have seen, African politicians and power-brokers and their foreign partners or collaborators may manipulate the gap between principle and practice to their advantage.

This observation about the colonial origin of the rule of law does not imply that African societies before colonial times were chaotic. Any functioning society has norms. However, these do not always take the form of a body of rules, written or even unwritten, that is consistently applied, including to those who implement the code. In many African communities before colonial times, justice was the prerogative of a ruler acting in accordance with whatever could be represented as tradition rather than being the application of a code of laws. Law devolved upon the person of a leader, a king or a chief, often sitting in council, and not upon a fixed code. In almost every case, justice was inseparable from spiritual knowledge, articulated by ritual experts or priests, who in effect articulated a series of constitutional checks and balances on a ruler. Laws were indistinguishable from rituals. 'Tradition' in societies without writing consisted not so much in an unchanging corpus of rules of behaviour as in a way of thinking about change.

It is precisely because African societies generally were governed by such a pragmatic style of decision-making that the business environment there eventually became unsuitable for European purposes. Something that may properly be called a 'world economy' took shape in the third quarter of the nineteenth century,[30] of a denser texture than the intercontinental trade that had existed earlier, powered by technological innovations and facilitated by new forms of diplomacy, law and finance. Lobbies emerged in the world's leading industrial and military powers that took an interest in the internal affairs of distant areas on humanitarian or religious grounds, such as missionary societies and the anti-slavery movement, or that pressed for market access for their manufactured goods, and these groups were able to put pressure on their home governments. European and US governments increasingly took formal responsibility for the welfare of their citizens worldwide and were prepared to hold others to account in terms of an emerging body of rules and conventions that constituted the growing field of international relations and international law. The political economist Walter Bagehot, writing in 1867, thought that correct commercial and financial dealings now required 'a continuous polity; a fixed political morality; and a constant possession of money',[31] qualities that earlier traders had not required so urgently, if at all.

The globalisation of the *belle époque*—the period that ended in a world war in 1914—produced a new breed of bankers and businessmen prepared to loan or invest money anywhere. They needed a world governed by rules that could be enforced by institutions of a type they understood. They wanted to see Western-style jurisdictions everywhere. Since Africa generally lacked these, the establishment of colonial rule became a serious option. Colonial rule brought with it regimes based on written agreements and laws, enabling bankers to lend money to governments that, unlike the transient authority of African kings and Big Men, would guarantee the security of a loan over long periods. Investors could seriously contemplate putting money into mines and railways, safe in the knowledge that these assets were located in a specific territory that was party to international legal conventions. Humanitarians could ensure that laws against the slave trade were enforced. Colonialism endowed Africa with legal-bureaucratic government in the many places where there was nothing fitting this description already, and it strengthened the legal and bureaucratic elements in the few cases where these already existed in some degree, mostly in areas ruled by Muslim potentates.

That Africa today is, in theory, governed through the consistent application of written laws is a legacy of colonial rule. But in many countries, this nominal form of governance does not correspond to the reality. Formal sovereignty has ceased to be accompanied by many of the substantive attributes it is deemed or presumed to possess, such as a monopoly of violence within a designated territory, control of a bureaucracy with a countrywide reach, and even, in extreme cases, the capacity to conceive or administer anything that really deserves the name of a policy at all. In Liberia in the 1990s and in Somalia up to this day, state law courts hardly existed or had no real authority, public bodies did not maintain archives and therefore lacked a bureaucratic memory, and fewer children than before learned to read and write and assimilate the disciplines associated with modern statehood.

In many other countries less afflicted than these, the institutions of legal-bureaucratic government, introduced in most of Africa by colonial rule, have been hollowed out. This process, often labelled 'state failure', offers political entrepreneurs the opportunity to exploit to the full the gap between two measures of reality. One is described in legal terms, based on national and international law and its related norms, the ground on which formal diplomatic relations are conducted and formal commercial contracts are signed. The other measure is the reality of political bargains made between an African leader and those whom he or she seeks to represent, include, or assuage, paying particular attention to sectors where capital is produced and reproduced. This state of affairs offers opportunities not only to African political entrepreneurs but also to their foreign partners or collaborators. Both may contrive to arrange matters to their mutual satisfaction outside the framework of formal rules.[32]

This 'reality gap' is an area in which corruption is likely to occur. Although there is no watertight definition of corruption, it is generally understood to entail the use of a formal position for private purposes deemed illegitimate or illegal.[33] Corruption is not only hard to define but also notoriously hard to measure, and therefore it is impossible to determine scientifically whether it is increasing or decreasing in any given country or whether it is more prevalent in one place than another. The best-known international authority on relative corruption is the annual index published by Transparency International but this is hardly an exact instrument, being based only on the perceptions of those persons or institutions consulted by this anti-corruption body.[34]

In the fairly recent past, in what quite a few Africans think of as happier times, there were many politicians who, while being massively corrupt in amassing personal fortunes in contravention of the law, were nevertheless widely admired. Some of their achievements seemed impressive at the time. Félix Houphouët-Boigny, president of Côte d'Ivoire from 1960 to 1993, oversaw two decades of spectacular economic growth and development often known as 'the Ivorian miracle'. Yet Houphouët-Boigny also commandeered state resources on a huge scale, using them to build an imitation of Rome's St Peter's basilica in his home village. He boasted openly about his Swiss bank accounts. René Amany, a former head of the national cocoa marketing board from which Houphouët-Boigny took so much money over the years, has tried to explain how a corrupt president could nevertheless govern with conspicuous success. Amany recalled nostalgically in a newspaper interview how Houphouët-Boigny 'used money as a means of advancing his political project, not politics as a way of making money'.[35] The use of an official position to divert public funds that are then invested in political activities has also been noted in regard to Nigeria. Ike Okonta describes how politics in Nigeria is 'itself a struggle for control of the country's oil largesse, which, once secured in the form of loot, is used to further and consolidate political ends. In this struggle, the state and the means of violence at its disposal are the ultimate spoils'.[36]

It is therefore interesting to speculate why corruption in Côte d'Ivoire during the 1960s and 1970s could be part of a system internationally acclaimed for its political and economic success, whereas twenty-first century Nigeria is widely regarded as a potential giant tragically handicapped by corruption. The essential difference between the two cases seems to lie not so much in the existence of corruption—massive in both cases—as in the political uses to which it is put.

To be successful, any political project has to inspire its supporters with hope and confidence. These qualities have been in short supply in Africa since the late 1970s, when the bright vision of progress offered by postcolonial governments turned dim in so many countries. When corruption is disconnected from any serious political project, it encourages a get-rich-quick-and-enjoy-while-you-can mentality that can spread throughout society. People come to perceive time in a short-term perspective that discourages investment or long-term planning.[37] Mortgage-payments and pension premiums may seem unfeasible. The loss of hope and confidence tends to drive assets away. In 2006, around 30 per cent of sub-Saharan Africa's GDP was estimated to move offshore, making Africa probably a net provider of finance to the rest of the world at that time.[38] Money has flowed outwards, even as the continent has also attracted comparatively heavy investment in more recent years, as we shall shortly discuss.

The fact that many Africans have become poorer in recent decades is no doubt an incentive to corruption. But it is probably more important that they have lost faith in the various projects of modernisation and development that promised them a better life in the mid-twentieth century. In retrospect, it seems that many mistook the outward signs of material progress for the substance of development. This was at a time when Cold War rivalries could be manipulated by politicians in need of funds, which meant that the consequences of this mistaken perception were not immediately apparent.

Mulling over this analysis, it becomes apparent that what happens in South Africa is particularly important. I vividly recall a conversation with a leading Western ambassador in South Africa whom I interviewed in his office in Pretoria in 1990. He told me that the transition from apartheid was Africa's last chance to join the real world. This was not a very rigorous formulation, since the world is what it is and not what a particular person thinks it ought to be, but it is not difficult to see what the ambassador meant. He was referring to the widespread perception that the countries south of the Sahara had made a hash of their politics and their economies since acquiring sovereign status in the 1950s and 1960s. Perhaps South Africa, the economic powerhouse of Africa, could lead the rest of the continent on a better path if it could succeed in its transition to democracy. The magnificent Nelson Mandela symbolised this new hope. His deputy and eventual successor, Thabo Mbeki (president, 1999–2008) spoke of an African renaissance led by South Africa. When Zaïre's President Mobutu, the notorious henchman of imperialism who had dominated central Africa for thirty-two years, fell from power in 1997, it seemed to Mbeki and his entourage that the moment had really come for Africa to seize its own destiny, with South Africa as its natural leader.

A sense of proportion is in order. Although South Africa has the continent's biggest economy, its Gross Domestic Product of $276 billion in 2008[39] is less than that of Washington State and slightly more than that of Maryland. Its industrial sector faces threats from several quarters, including competition from cheap Chinese manufactures. Most worrying, though, is the threat to South Africa's economic efficiency and to its prestige and the quality of its governance posed by corruption within the state apparatus and the ruling party, which has become rampant. Mbeki's successor as president, Kgalema Motlanthe, once described corruption as 'across the board' in South Africa. He continued: 'It's not confined to any level or any area of the country. Almost every project is conceived because it offers opportunities for certain people to make money'.[40] A major arms purchase in the late 1990s involved bribes to many leading officials of the ANC government, and insiders suggest that some of this money was used to fund the ANC's successful 1999 election campaign.[41]

For the time being, international diplomats and businesspeople continue to see South Africa as one of Africa's few 'normal' states, and the successful hosting of the FIFA World Cup in 2010 strengthens this perception. South Africa has a functioning government, a central bank and financial institutions that are able to offer a conducive business environment, and a legal system that, although creaky, is capable of producing satisfactory and enforceable judgements in commercial disputes. However, recent events cause concern. South Africa's former national police chief, who is also a former president of Interpol, has been found guilty of maintaining a corrupt relationship with a leading drug dealer. The staff of the public prosecution service, so vital in a country plagued by crime, has become demoralised. The country's most mediagenic politician, Julius Malema, head of the African National Congress Youth League, provokes the bourgeoisie both white and black with his outrageous statements, posing as a champion of the dispossessed while enjoying an extravagant lifestyle.

It would be rash to conclude that South Africa is failing, since it remains a resilient society with pockets of economic dynamism. It is positioned to be China's chief economic partner as it advances into Africa. Nevertheless, one of the country's leading black businessmen confided in October 2009 that he fears the country is going the way of Nigeria, a country where he has done business.[42]

But what, historically, is this particular road to ruin?

Corruption and Decolonisation

Some sordid bargains were made during Africa's decolonisation. The mid-twentieth century generation of African nationalist politicians, sensing that independence was in the air but generally lacking a domestic power-base wealthy enough to finance their ambitions, realised that control of the state apparatus could be used to generate funds for their own political movements. Since many African political parties were to a large extent patronage systems dominated by Big Men, the lines between personal and party patronage were blurred. The easiest way to raise money for political activity was simply to demand payment from companies who wanted state contracts. For this, it was necessary to be in power. Getting into government became all-important. Foreign companies soon found that they could secure contracts by bribing the right person or people. In Nigeria, later to be one of the most glaringly corrupt countries, this system was already taking clear shape before independence.[43] By 1966, kickbacks paid to Nigerian politicians were usually 3–6 per cent of the gross value of a contract, although some foreign contractors would pay up to 10 per cent, as a Swedish businessman told a US consul inquiring into business corruption. The Swede added that his company headquarters treated bribes as 'a normal transaction in the firm's accounting system'.[44] In other African countries, too, high-level corruption involving officials and ministers and their foreign business contacts was routine by the mid-1960s although the amount of money involved in those days was small compared to the colossal sums that would later be paid, particularly in oil-producing countries. Leaders who benefited personally were liable to blackmail by their foreign partners-in-crime, and 'as a result, corruption, foreign influence, and domestic politics became hopelessly entangled'.[45] Furthermore, foreign-owned firms, lacking confidence in new governments, often resorted to false invoicing in order to repatriate their profits, despite the fact that this was a criminal offence.[46] If we apply this model to South Africa, it is clear that there are discomforting similarities between the situation in post-apartheid South Africa and that in the rest of Africa in the period of decolonisation. But there are also differences, notably in that, in the 1960s, political corruption overseen by grasping politicians occurred in a situation where there was little indigenous private sector business, where traditional political structures were still powerful and the press was weak. South Africa, in contrast, has a strong private sector, sophisticated media and a bureaucracy that is well established—perhaps too well, in some respects. Crucially, South Africa has an efficient tax bureaucracy that is able to fund the state from domestic resources, enabling a tax contract between ruler and ruled.

The fact that the corruption of African governments became fully internationalised at the same time as Africa was decolonising was more than a coincidence, as the two processes were intimately related. The biggest empire the world has ever seen, belonging to the United Kingdom of Great Britain and Northern Ireland, even as it was disappearing from the political map was able to perpetuate its existence in the financial world, notably by establishing the City of London as an offshore banking centre and inventing the Eurodollar market. City bankers and lawyers discovered the legal possibilities offered by Crown dependencies with archaic jurisdictions, such as the Channel Islands and the Isle of Man, and by colonies such as the Cayman Islands and Hong Kong. US business interests were already making similar use of the Republic of Liberia, whose sovereign status could be used to avoid various laws and regulations notably through the flag of convenience system for shipping, but also in the field of finance. The world's biggest companies reorganised themselves and revised their operating techniques in order to adjust to a world of sovereign states. They took to lobbying governments all over the world with a view to shaping legal structures that would allow them the protection they required.[47] Economic transactions occur in a specific place and at a specific time, but they also take place in a legal sphere that may be separated from these.[48] By exploiting the disconnection between the physical location of a transaction and the legal space where it is recorded, companies exploit the gap between law and reality just as African politicians do.

The offshore system has become a crucial factor in grand corruption in which Africa and the rest of the world collaborate. Early this century, it was estimated that 80 per cent of international transactions (by value) took place offshore and 20 per cent of private wealth was kept in tax havens.[49] The World Bank is reported to have estimated the size of corruption worldwide at some 1.5 trillion dollars.[50] Grand corruption tends to occur in particular sectors, most notably energy, the arms trade, telecommunications and civil engineering. There is every sign that some major firms in these fields participate routinely in corrupt transactions to win tenders for state contracts. Over the last fifty years they have learned to be more subtle about these transactions, setting up elaborate screens by way of transnational transfers booked in tax havens and hiring specialist lawyers as intermediaries.

Legislation enacted first in the USA, and later in most European countries, means that bribes can these days no longer simply be processed through a firm's central accounting system. In reaction, it appears that many major companies have responded simply by keeping funds for bribery off their books, like the electronics giant Siemens, found by a German court in 2007 to have maintained a secret fund with which to bribe officials. Of over one billion euros paid out worldwide, more than ten million went to Nigerian officials in the period 2001–4.[51] The US oil services company Halliburton and its former subsidiary KBR were indicted for allegedly conspiring with other multinationals to pay more than $100 million into a giant slush fund for bribing officials in Nigeria between 1994 and 2002, when Halliburton's chief executive was one Dick Cheney.[52] In 2008, KBR's former chief executive was sentenced to seven years' imprisonment, and a year later KBR and Halliburton paid a penalty of $579 million, the biggest ever imposed on US companies for bribery.[53]

As for the African beneficiaries of grand corruption, the money generated by their activities has usually been deposited in European and US banks, at least until very recently, when Singapore and Hong Kong have emerged as competitors. Nigerians for example have been consistently estimated to hold over $100 billion abroad, much of it derived from the $400 billion in oil revenues that the former head of the Nigerian Economic and Financial Crimes Commission, Nuhu Ribadu, in August 2006 claimed Nigerian governments had stolen or wasted since 1960.[54] During his tenure as Nigeria's head of state from 1993 to 1998, General Sani Abacha presided over the looting of no less than $55 billion of Nigerian public funds. Half of Abacha's personal share of this total was laundered through the City of London (itself a major offshore centre) and went from there to accounts in Jersey, Switzerland, Liechtenstein and elsewhere.[55]

A field of illicit activity of rapidly growing importance in Africa concerns drugs. In late 2007, the United Nations Office on Drugs and Crime (UNODC) drew attention to the growing role of West Africa as an intermediary in cocaine-trafficking from South America to Europe,[56] although the transport of very large quantities of cocaine from South America to Africa had occasionally been recorded in previous years.[57] The UNODC estimated that about 15–20 per cent of Europe's annual consumption of about 250 tonnes of cocaine—up to 50 tonnes per year—transited through West Africa,[58] although some authoritative sources put the volume much higher than that, such as an official of the US Drug Enforcement Administration who estimated in testimony to the US Senate that some 180–240 tonnes of cocaine were transiting West Africa en route to Europe in 2007, in addition to smaller quantities of heroin.[59] A conservative estimate is that Africa's share in the cocaine trade is worth some $1.8 billion at street values.[60] Large cargoes of cocaine are transported from Colombia and Venezuela in ships or light aircraft to West Africa, where Latin American traffickers can benefit from political protection in many countries. The Revolutionary Armed Forces of Colombia (FARC) has installed permanent representatives in some West African countries. In late 2009, the Malian army found a Boeing cargo jet that had apparently been used for trafficking cocaine from Venezuela to West Africa. This was the first evidence that Al Qaeda in the Islamic Maghreb might have a direct interest in the cocaine trade since the plane was found at an airstrip in an area frequented by AQIM.[61]

There is a vast grey zone in which the laundering of profits from drug-trafficking and other branches of organised crime becomes indistinguishable from the processing of money generated by corruption, tax evasion or tax avoidance, and the practice of multinational companies of transferring assets from one national branch to another at whatever price best suits them, since they are in effect buying and selling to themselves. Hence, the financial flows emanating from some of Africa's most corrupt governments use channels that are also important for global finance generally, particularly via offshore transactions. Leading researchers on illicit financial flows estimate that of the total $1.8 trillion moved offshore from Africa between 1970 and 2008, commercial tax evasion accounted for 60–65 per cent, proceeds of crime 30–35 per cent, and corruption only about 3 per cent.[62]

There are many situations where professional criminals, financiers of terrorist groups and secret service operatives rub shoulders with the managers of major corporations and with bagmen working for major political parties. They may frequent the same lawyers' and accountants' offices and, people being what they are, strike up friendships. The proximity of such groups is not to be taken lightly. Militant groups, no longer able to count on funds from great powers as they did in the Cold War period, have to raise revenues and manage budgets, not unlike conventional businesses or state agencies.[63] As one veteran journalist commented in regard to the privatisation of Islamic militancy in the late twentieth century, 'not rogue governments, but rogue private financiers are responsible for much of the post-war political terrorism in the west'.[64] In a world of free trade and financial globalisation, illicit financing can easily become political. The history of the unlamented Bank of Credit and Commerce International (BCCI), which was shut down by regulators in 1991 in the biggest-ever bank collapse at that time, is a specific example of how offshore facilities may be used not only by corrupt politicians and criminals to launder their money, but also by business corporations and even governments carrying out licit transactions. BCCI actually had more branches in Africa than in any other continent.

The lion's share of the money involved in grey or illegal transactions is handled at some stage of its journey by leading banks, and indeed the ultimate aim of money-laundering is to deposit money in a top-class bank in one of the world's financial capitals. That many leading banks in the developed world in fact encourage capital flight was demonstrated years ago by hearings of the permanent subcommittee on investigations of the committee on governmental affairs of the US Senate, which seriously embarrassed the mighty Citibank.[65] The fact that some capital flight takes place legally, notably in order to avoid tax, is precisely the point: criminal money, the proceeds of corruption, and legally generated funds seeking to avoid tax all follow the same routes. During the free-market euphoria of the 1990s and 2000s all sorts of liberties were taken by company lawyers and accountants working on the margins of legality. There was no longer a Soviet Union to scare Western financiers who, being only lightly regulated, had little or no incentive to wonder whether there might be negative consequences attached to their frenetic money-making. The free market doctrines that were so influential for three decades allowed government ministers to absolve themselves from formal responsibility for policies that they favoured.

The offshore financial system and money laundering are closely connected to the phenomenon of so-called 'fragile' states, of which Africa has many. A failing state can rent out its sovereign rights for quite small amounts of cash and can offer important facilities for professional law-breakers of every sort, whether motivated chiefly by money or by politics. Hence, the role of West Africa in the international trade in narcotics may be explained by the exceptionally favourable political context offered by the region's many weak states, ineffective policing and governments that have a reputation for venality. A pliable sovereign state is the ideal cover for a drug trafficker. As the Colombian economist Francisco Thoumi writes:

[p]rofitable illegal economic activity requires not only profitability, but also weak social and state controls on individual behaviour, that is, a society where government laws are easily evaded and social norms tolerate such evasion....Illegality generates competitive advantages in the countries or regions that have the weakest rule of law.[66]

Before the end of the last century, major international crime syndicates had discovered the potential of small states in Africa whose authorities could be bought or manipulated without attracting much international attention. In the mid-1980s Sierra Leone witnessed the arrival of a number of major Russian and Ukrainian gangsters, some of them with connections to Israeli intelligence. The most notorious was Marat Balagula, a mobster who later migrated to the USA, where he served time in prison before being murdered in March 2008. Balagula and his Soviet colleagues used Sierra Leone as a freeport, smuggling in diamonds from Russia and swapping them for heroin from Thailand.[67] The man who brought Balagula to Sierra Leone was one Shabtai Kalmanowitch, a colourful figure who, in his glory days, drove a Rolls Royce that had once belonged to Rumania's last dictator, Nicolae Ceausescu. After leaving Sierra Leone Kalmanowitch gained the dubious distinction of being convicted in Israel of spying on behalf of the KGB, the old Soviet intelligence service. It is said that while he was in prison, the irrepressible Kalmanowitch managed to have an affair with the wife of one of the prison officials. Kalmanowitch was gunned down in Moscow in 2009.

Global Corruption and African States

The Bible tells us that the poor are always with us. The same is probably true of corruption. Nevertheless, the nature of corruption has changed enormously in recent decades.

Some writers argue that the key change came with the end of the Cold War, when the collapse of the Soviet block encouraged professional criminals to make alliances with thuggish political entrepreneurs with no ingrained respect for law.[68] The groups resulting from these fusions are often referred to by the media rather vaguely as 'mafias'. They deal in a toxic mixture of politics and crime.

However, there is persuasive evidence that today's distinctive style of global corruption, in which the criminal underworld, underground economies, the seamy side of government and the legitimate business world merge into one, has rather older roots. One of the best qualified witnesses is Eva Joly, a Norwegian woman who married a Frenchman and for many years worked as a magistrate before returning to her native Norway to work as an anticorruption official and development advisor, eventually going into politics herself. In August 1994, while she was still living in France, she was assigned what at first appeared to be a routine financial case. The lines of inquiry led her to uncover the existence of dubious contracts for African oil that had been obtained by bribing heads of state. She discovered that the parastatal Elf Aquitaine oil company had for years operated a network of slush funds on behalf of French politicians and their parties. She also learned that most top companies in France actually had an off-budget treasury that could be used for illicit purposes.[69] Many of the techniques involved in using French state or semi-state businesses to funnel money to politicians were similar to those used for decades in Italy, revealed by Italy's own wave of corruption trials some years previously.

There is every reason to suppose that these techniques are also used by major companies in other industrialised countries, which make similar use of off-book treasuries. If the relationship between France and African oil-producers was found to be grubby when exposed to public view, one wonders how the British[70] or US[71] relationship with Saudi Arabia might appear if it were ever investigated with the rigour that Eva Joly applied to her own work.

Joly argues convincingly that the scale and scope of international corruption have changed enormously since the 1970s. The financial globalisation that began with the dollar's delinking from gold, the collapse of the Bretton Woods currency system and the flood of petro-dollars after 1973, followed by financial deregulation, resulted in huge politico-financial pay-offs.[72] Although there had been previous bribery scandals in French politics, these were puny by comparison with the Elf affair, in which three-quarters of the corrupt payments—two and a half billion francs, or about half a billion dollars—were shared by just three people.[73] Eva Joly concluded on the basis of her investigations that the global market in corruption that grew in the final quarter of the last century poses a threat not only to democracy, but even to the system of state sovereignty that has developed in Europe since the seventeenth century and that is the basis for international relations.[74] After the banking collapses since 2008, and the threat of default by sovereign borrowers that emerged in 2010 following revelations about the true levels of Greek debt, her analysis becomes all the more compelling.

The scale and scope of contemporary corruption are unprecedented as a result of a fundamental shift in the way the world works. In that respect, the problem of corruption today is comparable to the social question of the late nineteenth century. Both are an integral part of a wider process. A hundred and fifty years ago, the process in question was that of industrialisation and the growth of cities.[75] Today, it is the type of financial globalisation that is made possible by instant electronic communication. The introduction of the internet has created worldwide markets that enable leaders in every conceivable field of endeavour to become rich. In the entertainment business Vanessa Mae, the world's most popular violinist, sells ten million copies of her album. The celebrity chef

Gordon Ramsay was said in 2007 to be worth £70 million and the footballer David Beckham and his wife, former Spice Girl Victoria, £120 million. English Premier League football has an audience of half a billion worldwide.[76] These are all examples of how new global markets have been created and how individuals may exploit them to become fabulously rich.

The process is true not only for legitimate products and services and the individuals who know how to profit from them but also for illicit ones, such as drugs. In the case of Africa, a handful of African heads of state have gone beyond demanding kickbacks for awarding state contracts, which is probably the most common form of official corruption, to become actual organisers of syndicates that smuggle drugs, guns or other illicit goods on a large scale. Being heads of state, they can bring to this business all the advantages of state sovereignty: diplomatic bags and passports, access to central banks for laundering money, exemption from prosecution, and much more. In situations like this, observers need to ask themselves what it is, precisely, that they are dealing with. Is it a problem of corruption among public officials that has got out of hand? Or is it a case of professional criminals having taken control of a state, and using it simply as a tool of their trade? In any case, what really is the difference between politics and crime?[77]

Pursuing this last line of thought may lead to reflection on what the difference is between a state and a criminal conspiracy. This is not a flippant question. A leading sociologist, the late Charles Tilly,[78] is well known for pointing out that the states that emerged in Europe three or four centuries ago did so largely because of their single-mindedness in organising armies. To do this, they required finance, which in turn involved raising money from their people, who needed protection from marauding armies. In effect, Europe's early modern states proposed to their subjects a deal no different from a mobster's demand for payment, since those who refused protection agreements were liable to be regarded as rebels or criminals. Fortunately, associated in European history with the rise of strong states with formidable powers of coercion were countervailing struggles for democracy, freedom of speech and human rights. Subjects in the process of becoming citizens were able to obtain the protection offered by the law of habeas corpus and to establish the principle of no taxation without representation. Civil liberties were not granted by benign rulers out of the goodness of their hearts but negotiated in bruising contests. States became both leviathans that could crush dissent and the guarantors of contracts between rulers and ruled.

It is pertinent to wonder whether the use of violence by states and other organisations and the concentration of wealth in Africa might not, in time, lead to the emergence of powerful bureaucratic states along the same lines as happened in Europe. But the historical cases are dissimilar, as Africa's states have quite different origins from their counterparts in Europe or Asia, having been in most cases created from scratch by the diplomatic action of European powers acting in concert. In most cases, Africa's states as such are not very powerful, but they provide the means for favoured individuals and families to flourish, often by indirect means. Ordinary Africans regularly give bribes to obtain the services they should in theory receive from the state for free. Junior officials in many countries routinely take bribes to compensate themselves for ludicrously small salaries. Police officers shake down travellers as a matter of course. Politicians fund their campaigns with bribe money given by businessmen, domestic or foreign, in search of contracts. Corruption becomes a way of life, a mode of business and politics, that actually dissipates the power of the state as an institution.[79] When certain types of illicit transaction become normal to the point that people hardly bother hiding them, it becomes almost inadequate to describe them as 'corruption' since this word implies deviation from a norm, a falling-away from accepted standards. It was for this reason that the brilliant sociologist Stanislav Andreski invented the word 'kleptocracy' to designate the system of government he observed in Africa in the 1960s.[80]

To be sure, corrupt practices exist elsewhere. The biggest scams in Africa are tiny by comparison with Enron or the crimes of Bernie Madoff in the US. India, often hailed as both the world's biggest democracy and an economic success story, has also witnessed a certain merging of crime and politics: in the parliament that was dissolved in 2009, 128 out of 543 members had faced criminal charges or investigation, including in eighty-three cases of murder.[81] The analysis of corruption is not just a matter of scale, but above all of context. In each case, it is necessary to investigate how corruption works in its individual context and what is its relationship to politics.

We may take Kenya as an example. Evidence[82] suggests that outrageously corrupt practices have become routine at the very heart of government in one of Africa's most important countries. A government elected on a promise to combat corruption used a bogus company, Anglo Leasing, through which it channelled money for non-existent or greatly inflated contracts. The money involved was kicked back to government ministers and ruling party officials. Most importantly, this state of affairs was tolerated by leading international institutions despite their constant denunciation of corruption.[83] Corruption, as we have seen, is so highly internationalised as actually to be, like aid and the rhetoric of development, a central element of Africa's mode of insertion in the world as it has evolved over the last half-century or so.

Situating corruption within a specific historical context suggests that certain illicit practices, even if they are formally outlawed, may be considered morally permissible by large numbers of people in certain circumstances. Since the law does not always coincide with popular perceptions of morality, understanding the real political economy of corruption requires an appreciation of moral repertoires. This inevitably requires making historical inquiries because attitudes to corruption are connected to the longer-term formation of people's views about their own society and about the world in general. Countries that can be considered to have a problem of corruption got into their present situation along paths that need to be investigated historically.[84]

Let this argument not be misunderstood. This line of reasoning is not a plea for tolerating corruption on the spurious grounds that each country has its own norms and values. It is clear that corruption is generally both economically inefficient and politically inequitable. In many cases Africans appear to be as keen as anyone else to see corrupt officials exposed and punished. But perceptions of what is corrupt in any given society change over time and may differ at any given moment between one society and another. Measures aimed at eliminating corruption may also have quite different effects in one situation than in another.

The Asians are Here!

On 8 July 2004, China's ministries of commerce and foreign affairs jointly issued a circular containing guidelines pertaining to investment overseas. This was pursuant to a call by the uninspiringly-named Sixteenth Congress and the Third Plenary Session of the Sixteenth Central Committee meeting of the Chinese Communist Party 'to encourage and support overseas investment by enterprises of all kinds of ownership which have comparative advantages' and to 'improve the service regime for overseas investment'.[85] More colloquially, the Chinese government's promotion of overseas investment is known as the 'going abroad' strategy. It is a logical phase in China's opening to world markets, which dates from 1978.

Appended to the guidelines was a list of countries where the Chinese government proposed to do business, along with the various business sectors involved. Several of the countries listed were in Africa. In fact, Chinese companies and individual entrepreneurs have become active in almost every country in Africa, including many that were not earmarked for special attention in the guidelines published in 2004. As China has industrialised, it has developed its relations with Africa at bewildering speed, to the point that it currently receives some 30 per cent of its oil imports from there, as well as iron ore, copper, wood and a host of other commodities.[86] In November 2009 China's premier, Wen Jiabao, was able to tell African heads of state gathered in Egypt for the fourth Forum on China-Africa Cooperation that his government would provide $10 billion in concessional loans to African countries and a special loan of $1 billion to small and medium enterprises.[87]

Chinese entrepreneurs are as sensitive to prices as their counterparts elsewhere. At the end of 2008 in Katanga, home to the richest copper reserves in the Democratic Republic of Congo, staff at some forty copper smelters, about nine-tenths of the Chinese employed in that sector, faced with falling copper prices, simply packed their bags and went home. According to the governor of Katanga province, Moïse Katumbi, the Chinese had clearly planned their move, neglecting to settle their taxes or even to pay off their local staff. Governor Katumbi swore that he would not allow the Chinese fugitives back as long as he remained in office.[88] But this seems no more than bravado, as China's hunger for raw materials has already resumed. China's industrialisation is unstoppable. Africa is one of the few relatively untapped storehouses of the raw materials that a mighty manufacturing country needs.

China's ruling party is really a corporate technocracy, communist in little other than name. The only thing that is red about the country's rulers is the colour of their silk ties. They think long-term and are highly pragmatic. Not being democrats, they do not have to satisfy the immediate demands of voters and, unlike their Western counterparts, nor do they have to observe the impossibly short deadlines imposed on democratic governments by media time. Having no perception of a civilising mission the Chinese government is under no domestic pressure to take action on human rights issues in Africa. It is interesting to hear Chinese officials explain that they are proud of their relationship with Sudan, pointing out that they have in a few years helped it not only to build its oil industry, but also to develop oil-based manufacturing industries far in advance of what has been achieved in over fifty years of oil production in Nigeria.[89] They are aware of the horrors perpetrated in Darfur but regard this as a political problem rather than a moral one, which, they maintain, concerns the sovereign state of Sudan in the first instance.

Growing in confidence, China shows every sign of playing a greater role in some of the numerous multilateral arrangements by which Africa is bound into global systems of governance. This is an important shift in strategic direction. During the earliest phase of its going-abroad strategy, the Chinese government made a point of developing bilateral links precisely with those African countries that were having the greatest difficulties with the international financial institutions that are so important in mediating Africa's relationship with the rest of the world, namely Sudan, Angola and Zimbabwe. But it is notable how quickly the Chinese government has changed its approach. Not only has China committed troops to United Nations missions in Africa, but it has actually become the most important contributor to UN peacekeeping missions of any Security Council member, as Chinese officials politely point out to anyone who questions their support for the global commitment to peace and prosperity in Africa. China has also greatly increased its contributions to the IMF. In fact, in just a few years, China has gone from actively siding with those African regimes most at odds with the multilateral institutions that have traditionally been dominated by Western donors to becoming a major support of that same multilateral architecture. Chinese policymakers have learned fast, realising that they can make existing arrangements work for them, especially as Europe shows signs of fatigue after its long history of ventures and adventures in Africa.

There are also other emerging players in Africa. India has shown a lively interest particularly in Ghana and in countries along Africa's east coast where communities of Indian origin are well established,[90] although the Indian government is reported now to regard its decision to use the existing Indian diaspora as a way into African markets as a strategic error.[91] Research by South Africa's Standard Bank is reported to reveal that India has some 130 foreign direct investment ventures in Africa compared to 86 from China and 25 from Brazil.[92] As for the US, its interest in Africa's oil has increased to the extent that the country now receives some 20 per cent of its oil imports from Africa, and Nigeria has overtaken Saudi Arabia as an oil exporter to its shores. The US government sees access to oil from the Gulf of Guinea—broadly defined as the swathe from Mauritania to Angola—as a major strategic concern. The neo-conservatives who wielded such influence under President Bush believed that their national interest was best served in this regard by the projection of military power, and they reasoned that the US should therefore plan to deploy its armed forces in such a way that it could secure Africa's oil for the next generation. This was part of the thinking behind the creation of an autonomous Africa Command, Africom, in the final months of President Bush's second term. Africom, now in charge of US military affairs in all of Africa except for Egypt, is in search of a new mission since the war on terror was rebranded in Washington. Promising to deliver development as well as security, it is the only US military command that proposes to work extensively with and through non-governmental organisations. This is an interesting historical continuity in a continent that has been marked by the propensity of colonial powers to rule indirectly.

Many Africans are unsurprised by the new interest in their continent. They are accustomed to thinking of Africa as a victim, permanently at the mercy of more powerful predators intent on exploiting their natural resources. The US National Intelligence Council notes that 'many African leaders believe that the international economy is still rigged so that Africans will never prosper'.[93] The Cameroonian writer Achille Mbembe, observing the propensity of so many people to see the history of their continent as a process in which an external agent over and over again assumes power by force, shrewdly concludes that 'in the last instance, history is seen as part of a massive economy of witchcraft'.[94] The view that Africa is the object of a never-ending imperialist conspiracy is forcefully expressed and adroitly used by demagogues like Robert Mugabe, president of Zimbabwe, and Côte d'Ivoire's president Laurent Gbagbo, who contrive to stay in power by encouraging this paranoia. Playing the card of anti-Western resentment, anxious to court Chinese support in place of the old colonial links, leaders often pay little heed to whether Chinese investment will bring anything much beyond new roads and sports stadiums and, crucially, money in their own pockets. It is often easier for a president intent on survival to praise the extraordinary speed of Chinese construction companies rather than to think hard about the long-term interest of an entire nation. A leading specialist on international relations points out that the historical tendency of Africa to accept a relationship of dependency may well be repeated with regard to China and its other Asian partners as African rulers accept rents that may advance their personal or factional interest only.[95] Or, as Ghana's former finance minister puts it, 'if we go on like this, African resources will be used for Chinese development like they were for European development before'.[96]

Broadly speaking, there is a possibility that, in conformity with its history of perverse integration into world affairs, Africa could increasingly function as the dark place of the global system, a continent where international codes function more in the breach than in the observance. Africa is already flooded with counterfeit products, the most damaging of which are fake pharmaceuticals. As the China-Africa connection develops, it is quite possible to imagine Africa becoming an important platform for the distribution on world markets of the counterfeit and pirated goods that China produces in such abundance: 80 per cent of counterfeit goods seized in the US originate in China.[97] According to a European Union estimate some 20–25 per cent of Chinese exports are fake goods, worth $250–500 billion per year.[98] Chinese capitalism is embedded within an unsavoury political-criminal nexus.[99]

As always, both optimistic and pessimistic scenarios remain imaginable. Some analysts[100] see Africa as having a rosier future than that of Europe, in terms of economic growth, in the medium term. After all, Europe has an ageing population, a diminishing share of world manufacturing, and seems generally set in the decline of its once formidable energies. Africa, on the other hand, for all its problems, has a young population and a growing relationship with Asia's trading giants. It also has more money than is generally realised, which is the next point to consider.

3

MONEY AND LAND

Africa south of the Sahara is experiencing the greatest capital investment in its history. In spite of the turmoil on world financial markets, foreign direct investment (FDI) inflows in 2008 rose to a new record level of $88 billion, resulting in an increase of FDI stock in the region to $511 billion. Cross-border mergers and acquisitions were an important contributory factor in the increased inflows, more than doubling their level of 2007.[1] This wave of foreign money comes after years of high economic growth in many African countries, that dipped only slightly during the years of financial crisis and is now expected to continue at an average of around 5 per cent.[2] Much of this record foreign direct investment goes to South Africa or to countries rich in oil or gas deposits, as the discovery of vast oil reserves along the Atlantic coast is now matched by the development of technology that makes deepwater drilling possible.

From Dakar's northern suburbs, where Africa points its elbow into the Atlantic Ocean, to Dar Es Salaam on the Indian Ocean, recent years have seen a frenzy of construction. Shopping-malls and hotels are built with the proceeds from high commodity prices. New houses are financed with remittances from people living abroad, reckoned by the World Bank at $21 billion in 2009,[3] although this is certainly an underestimate as so much cash is sent home through unofficial bankers or simply by Africans abroad entrusting their savings to friends travelling home, for eventual transmission to their families. Economic growth has been high in many countries not only thanks to high commodity prices but also because of the improved quality of macroeconomic management. 'This may sound like motherhood and apple pie stuff', claims Roelof Horne of the South Africa company Investec Asset Management, commenting on improved management, 'but it is actually true'.[4]

Heads of state and government and their aides and military planners, even in countries that historically have shown little interest in Africa, nowadays pay closer attention to developments there than at any time since the early years of independence, when the Cold War superpowers vied for influence in the dozens of new states born in the 1950s and '60s. Russia, aiming to strengthen its role as a world energy power, has its eyes on Nigeria's gas reserves, for which reason President Dmitry Medvedev was motivated to visit Africa in June 2009. The European Union, fearing that the Kremlin's Africa strategy forms part of a wider Russian design to tighten its grip on energy supplies to Europe, has offered Nigeria backing for a €15 billion trans-Saharan pipeline to pump gas directly to Europe.[5] Some Asian and Middle Eastern policy-makers and strategists see Africa as a producer of food for export, which they will need as their economies industrialise and their workforces become more urban, as well as of bio-fuel.

The spectacle of diplomats, officials and business executives studying maps of Africa and soaking up information from their representatives on the spot suggests to many journalists the image of a new scramble for Africa, a reference to the European rivalry of the late nineteenth century that led to the Berlin conference of 1884–5 and Africa's division into spheres of influence, the prelude to the formal colonisation of the continent. In truth, this is a lazy comparison. When Africa was carved up by foreign powers in the nineteenth-century scramble for colonies, no Africans were consulted. Now, by contrast, African elites are key players in the agreements being made in regard to exploitation of their raw materials, and they are often in a strong bargaining position.[6] If anyone is being cheated out of their fair share of oil and gas money, it is not the people who run Nigeria or Angola, Africa's leading oil producers. Even such a weak state as Chad has been able to defy the World Bank and humiliate leading oil companies with impunity by unilaterally cancelling arrangements made for banking its oil revenues.

The lingering image of African leaders being bullied and bamboozled by mighty oil companies, which contained some truth four decades ago, has long ceased to correspond to reality.[7] African political elites are well entrenched and have decades of experience of international business and diplomacy. The rise of Asian industrial powers has given them a new form of diplomatic leverage. Rich Angolans still like to own property in Lisbon, and Nigerians in London, but the exclusive relationship with western European countries imposed in colonial times has gone forever.

A New Financial Elite

The image of the vastly wealthy African president with a foreign bank account is a familiar one, to the extent that it can be considered another of the tired clichés that abound in discussion of Africa. The most notorious example is Mobutu Sese Seko, the president of the Democratic Republic of Congo, renamed by him Zaïre, from 1965 until 1997. Famous for his extravagance, Mobutu built in his home town a palace that is the epitome of kitsch. Scattered around the grounds are Chinese-style pavilions that were a gift from Chairman Mao when China was still in its pre-capitalist age.[8] Mobutu liked to hire the Concorde for his epic shopping expeditions to Paris and New York, so the grounds at Gbadolite had to contain an airstrip long enough to accommodate the supersonic airliner.

When it comes to serious money, a Swiss banker remarks that he has never seen so many wealthy Africans coming to his country to open bank accounts, even as he laments the rise of competition from Hong Kong and Singapore as the new financial centres where Africa's plutocrats like to keep their cash.[9] In 2008 alone, the illicit outflow of money from all of Africa was estimated at close to $100 billion,[10] although most of this came from big business rather than being deposited by individuals.

In Mobutu's heyday, the wealth of Africa's richest people was almost invariably generated by tenure of public office or at least by close association with state power. In the last decade, however, a number of African countries have seen the emergence of a substantial number of wealthy people whose money is associated with the private sector rather than being derived directly from the political process. The continent's new professionals are particularly notable in service industries. Reasonably well-to-do Africans are likely to have bank accounts and to use conventional forms of saving or loans. The middle classes buy consumer goods, generally imported, in appreciable quantities. They travel. They read newspapers and watch television. Relatively free to enjoy their wealth, they display many of the same tastes as their counterparts elsewhere.

Calculating the size of this social stratum depends on what precisely is meant by 'the middle class' or 'middle classes'. One way of estimating numbers is by reference to formal sector employment. In Zambia, in spite of growth of over 5 per cent per annum in recent years, there are only about 500,000 formal jobs and 80 per cent of the workforce is in the informal sector.[11] Tanzania is also reported to have only about half a million people in formal employment, while 650,000 new school-leavers arrive on the job market every year facing little option other than to join the informal sector.[12] If, instead, membership of the middle class is measured by income, we may note that in Nigeria the number of households earning more than $25,000 is expected to increase fivefold by 2015.[13] Increasing numbers of people feel a need for banks to transfer or save money. An official of the South African asset management company Investec remarks that 'even the person who is now earning $50 or $100 a month can save some of this money in a way they could not have done in the past when they earned next to nothing. This means there is a huge demand for banks...across the continent'.[14] Advertising industry executives have noted the impact on local commerce made by mobile phones, a technology that has been adopted by Africans with enormous enthusiasm. Mobile phone companies spend heavily on local advertising, as do new-generation banks offering car loans, mortgages and other financial facilities for the continent's new middle classes. Rwanda has become the first country in East Africa to manufacture mobile phones, in a joint venture between the Rwanda Information Technology Authority and Chinalink Digital and Technology.[15]

Some of the emerging middle classes come from old trading families that have adapted to new conditions. Over two centuries ago, a French trader who wrote an account of his travels in northern Madagascar described how Arabs and Swahilis from East

Africa did business throughout the region and sold their export products to Banyan traders from Surat and Mumbai, with access to credit networks covering the whole western Indian Ocean.[16] A Zanzibari who lives in Dubai told me that many of the most prominent traders and investors working between East Africa, the Gulf and south Asia are from families that have worked these same trade routes for centuries, 'but now they have more money'.[17] Modern businesses have actually existed in Africa in small numbers for longer than is often realised. In Madagascar, an indigenous joint-stock company was created over a hundred years ago. In West Africa banks existed as early as the 1920s. Nigeria had some two dozen indigenous banks by 1952, although within two years most of these had failed in the face of an array of problems including poor management and under-capitalisation.[18] Today, Africa's top forty companies range in value from $350 million to $80 billion.[19]

Crucial in the rise of the middle class is the spread of financial institutions. The early years after independence rarely saw much improvement in the quality of banks, as the political conditions associated with one-party states, plus lack of competition and the recurrent problem of under-capitalisation, made local banks unable to compete outside a handful of countries, of which South Africa was by far the most important. Now, a new generation of financial institutions has been made possible by the economic and financial reforms enacted by many governments after the old one-party regimes were swept away in the early 1990s. Some financiers argue[20] that the opening of political systems in most countries has led to greater security of property rights and greater possibilities for business operators to make their views known in government circles. Debt relief has also been important in reducing the cost of borrowing on local markets, ending a situation in which it was more advantageous to lend to the state at a very high rate of return than to lend to other businesses or to consumers.

A further factor in the emergence of African financial institutions of an unprecedented size and sophistication is the return to Africa of people with experience of working in leading banks and finance houses in New York, London or elsewhere, who bring home with them practical experience and global connections. Such individuals are to be found in Kampala, Nairobi, Lagos, Accra and a string of other cities that are emerging as hubs of Africa's new financial activity, in English-speaking Africa more often than in French-speaking countries. They cooperate easily with their colleagues in the established centre of financial power in Johannesburg, which is the main conduit for Chinese finance in Africa. These well-heeled returnees, often rather dismissive of the hidebound politics of African nationalism, tend to think regionally. It is quite common for them to radiate a confidence and optimism that are in refreshing contrast to the institutionalised paranoia generated by decades of talk about underdevelopment and neo-colonialism. Nevertheless, a study of Ghana some years ago reported that many entrepreneurs returning from abroad found it difficult to compete with businesses that had better connections to the government or ruling party.[21] This suggests that patronage networks dominated by politicians and state officials remain more influential than business lobbies organised along sectoral lines.

Examples of new financial power are not hard to find. Ecobank, with its headquarters in Togo, describes itself[22] as the leading pan-African bank, providing a range of wholesale and retail banking services. Established in 1988, it has over 500 branches with offices in twenty-five countries. In mid-2008 it succeeded in raising some $554 million on stock exchanges in Accra, Abidjan and Lagos in the form of a rights issue and a subscription for new shares. This was an impressive achievement at a time of acute credit difficulties worldwide. In Nigeria, local banks have shown that they are now able to syndicate major deals and raise finance for construction and business projects. The government of President Olusegun Obasanjo (1999–2007) insisted that its sovereign wealth funds be handled by indigenous institutions, at least in part, rather than going straight to the Wall Street investment banks as used to happen in the past. Nigeria's total market capitalisation in August 2008 was reckoned at some $70 billion, before a precipitous decline as the world financial crisis hit, exacerbated by revelations of fraud that undermined confidence in the Lagos stock market. Two-thirds of the market at its height was accounted for by a banking sector that has grown fast since the government enacted laws obliging banks to operate with a higher degree of capitalisation than in the past, eliminating one of the historic causes of banking weakness. The current governor of Nigeria's central bank, Lamido Sanusi, has been ruthless in acting against badly managed banks.

There are now several African capital cities where substantial domestic funds can be mobilised for investment by making use of local institutions, local expertise and local capital markets. In Ghana, the government is making private-sector pension and provident funds tax-deductible and social security funds are appointing private fund managers.[23] There is also better access to global financial markets. In October 2007, Ghana became the fourth African country to issue a bond on the international market, following Egypt, Morocco and South Africa, when it issued a sovereign bond in London, raising $750 million. Some 40 per cent of the bond was placed with US investors and 36 per cent with UK investors, with the remainder going to the rest of Europe.[24] Private companies, such as Ghana Telecommunications Company, have also raised funds by issuing bonds, indicating that it is possible for large Ghanaian companies to diversify their source of funds and their investor base by accessing overseas markets without any government guarantee.[25] One of Africa's most sophisticated companies, the Angolan oil company, Sonangol, has itself become a significant investor overseas, operating much in the manner of a sovereign wealth fund by buying stakes in foreign companies. By mid-2008 it had acquired some 10 per cent of Millennium bcp, Portugal's largest publicly listed bank,[26] and was particularly active in Portugal and the US. The chief executive of Sonangol announced his intention to list the company on the New York or Johannesurg stock exchanges. At home, Sonangol formed joint ventures in such fields as banking, aviation, catering, telecommunications, and shipping.[27]

Importantly, Africa's emerging middle class is now showing signs of wanting to invest at least some of its money at home rather than to deposit it in bank accounts overseas. When shares in the Safaricom mobile phone company, valued at more than $4.5 billion, were offered to the public in June 2008 in East Africa's biggest-ever initial public offer, the Nairobi Stock Exchange was mobbed by enthusiastic investors. Safaricom acquired more than 860,000 shareholders, quite a few of them Kenyans.[28] The Nairobi Stock Exchange, which began in 1954 as an overseas branch of the London Stock Exchange, is now the fourth or fifth biggest on the

African continent, depending on how its size is measured, and has a system of cross-listings with its sister-exchanges in Kampala and Dar es Salaam.

Prior to the crisis that began in 2007, the international financial press was increasingly inclined to see Africa as a promising 'frontier' market, a new adaptation of the idea of 'emerging markets' popularised by the International Finance Corporation some thirty years ago. These expressions are applied to developing countries with stock markets that are beginning to demonstrate the features of mature stock markets, offering investors the opportunity to participate through financial instruments in economies offering high rates of growth and high potential profits. According to a senior advisor in the IMF's African Department, there are eight sub-Saharan African countries that qualify as frontier markets, as defined by indices managed by Standard and Poor's. They include Botswana, Ghana, Kenya, Mozambique, Nigeria, Tanzania and Zambia, which together account for about 40 per cent of the sub-Saharan population outside South Africa, and half of its GDP.[29] Some 30 to 40 per cent of share purchases in Africa are made by buyers from outside the continent, particularly via the Johannesburg Stock Exchange, which is by far the oldest and most venerable in Africa. Before 1990 there were eight stock exchanges in the whole of Africa, of which five were south of the Sahara. Today, there are nineteen.[30] Unlike investors in the first generation of emerging markets, today's investors are able to access not only equity markets but also domestic bond and foreign exchange market instruments.

Crucial to the future shape of African business will be the strategies of Asian investors, especially from China. For Chinese institutions, many of them state-controlled but operating increasingly as quasi-autonomous entities, buying into existing banks is an ideal method for investing in Africa since it makes the best use of local expertise. South Africa offers the best perspectives. Thus, in 2007, the Industrial and Commercial Bank of China paid some $5.5 billion for a 20 per cent stake in Standard Bank, a veteran of the British empire, founded in 1862, with over 746 branches in South Africa and approximately 240 in the rest of Africa. From its base in South Africa, Standard Bank, the largest in Africa with a market cap of $18 billion, aimed to acquire footholds in other African markets via

local mergers.[31] Indian and other Asian businesses participate ener-
getically in mergers and acquisitions, for example in Africa's
booming mobile phone market, where they compete with South
African and European operators especially. South Africa is crucial
to the future shape of Chinese influence in Africa generally. The
rising star of South African politics, ANC Youth League leader
Julius Malema, counters criticism of his radical anti-white invective
by asserting that if investors were to leave, 'the Chinese would
come in', and by pointing out that 'the Chinese will work with
anybody'.[32] The fact that Malema is also an outspoken supporter of
China's long-term ally President Robert Mugabe of Zimbabwe
gives some idea of the size of the strategic contest being played out
in southern Africa, the outcome of which will have profound consequences for the style of governance in the whole region and for
the white population in particular.[33]

Where local financial institutions are less sound than in South
Africa, Chinese firms are developing other techniques to access the
raw materials that their national economy craves. In the Democratic Republic of Congo, the Socomin company has been created
as a joint venture between Congolese and Chinese state-owned
enterprises. An initial Chinese investment of $3 billion in mining
will be repaid from profits generated as minerals are exported to
China. In effect, loans made by China's state-owned Eximbank will
be paid directly to the Chinese state-owned enterprises China Rail-
way Engineering Company and Sinohydro, by-passing Congo's
dysfunctional bureaucracy. Part of the eventual profits will be used
to fund major infrastructure projects that will be necessary to
export minerals but that will also serve Congo's people.[34] The Congolese and Chinese backers of the scheme claim that it benefits all
concerned, since China gets the minerals it wants and Congo the
infrastructure it so sorely lacks. International financial institutions
and Western donors, however, have been mightily upset by China's blunt intervention in the DRC and by its offer of new money
at a time when some sort of order was at last being imposed on the
DRC's chaotic public debt. They see China's Congo initiative as
irresponsible since it threatens to undo years of debt renegotiation.
Some African commentators consider these quarrels as the reflection of a strategic game whereby Western countries, using lending

and debt relief as an instrument of policy, aim to wrest control of Congo's vast mineral reserves and are annoyed by China's success in intruding on what they had previously regarded as their turf.[35]

While Africa is now financially connected to an unprecedented degree, questions need to be asked about the quality and durability of Africa's new financial institutions. In April 2008, Nigeria's United Bank of Africa, one of the most prestigious new names, was fined $15 million in New York for banking violations. With several other banks, it was said to have laundered money on behalf of some corrupt state governors who played a prominent role in successive administrations led by President Obasanjo. According to the US Financial Crimes Enforcement Network, the United Bank for Africa 'recklessly disregards its obligations under the Bank Secrecy Act and continues to operate without an effective anti-money laundering program, despite repeated warnings'.[36] The United Bank of Africa is not only one of Nigeria's top four banks, but it is also one that has worked particularly closely with China, having a cooperation agreement with the Industrial and Commercial Bank of China.[37] More recently, Arunma Oteh, head of Nigeria's Securities and Exchange Commission, has promised to bring charges against up to 200 brokers suspected of the fraud that contributed to the $50 billion collapse of the Lagos stock market.[38]

Investing in Society

An acid test of whether capitalist institutions permeate entire societies in Africa will be the degree to which its banks expand from their traditional role of servicing state deposits into the more difficult business of assessing private sector risk.

Some development institutions are making specific efforts to encourage the spread of new financial opportunities to those sectors of the population that have historically been excluded. The South African investment group GroFin, established in 2004, has launched a $160 million fund that will provide loans of between $50,000 and $1 million to African entrepreneurs in the manufacturing, service and trading sectors. GroFin's capital comes from groups with roots in development finance, including the International Finance Corporation, and one of its co-founders is a senior official of the Shell Foundation.[39] Ghana Home Loans, a non-bank financial institution that offers mortgages for home ownership, has also received support from development institutions. Its shareholders include Standard Bank of South Africa and the Netherlands' Development Finance Company, FMO.[40] As with many of Africa's emerging financial institutions, it is notable that many of the Ghana Home Loans staff have experience working in Europe and North America.

Some investment analysts go as far as to speculate that an improved financial system, able to provide credit to industrial entrepreneurs, could contribute to a revival of manufacturing. A former chief economist at the World Bank points out that China's industries are already moving up the value chain and suggests that Africa has a realistic chance of becoming a major source of low-cost manufacturing.[41] On the face of it, this seems unlikely. In the first two decades of Africa's independence, the creation of a domestic manufacturing industry was generally seen as essential to development, but rarely was it a success. The import-substitution schemes that were tried in those years fell victim to political interference, restrictively small markets, and an inability to compete internationally. National manufacturers were often dependent on inputs of imported materials that put them at the mercy of currency exchange rates. Moreover, those footholds of manufacturing industry that were established in the earlier twentieth century in Zimbabwe and South Africa are today being destroyed by domestic turmoil in the first case and by Chinese competition in the second. Other obstacles to industrial investment include poor infrastructure, which makes transportation expensive and raises the cost of marketing, poor regional market integration, and political uncertainty. Yet there are also examples of industrialisation taking place in Africa, for example in Madagascar's export processing zone. Nigeria's largest private-sector employer, Aliko Dangote, has successfully built flour mills, a pasta factory and a sugar factory, and is now investing in cement factories in various parts of the continent.[42] The sheer increase in Africa's population is creating larger markets for consumer goods, making it more interesting for foreign suppliers to consider establishing production plants in Africa itself.

Currently, the benchmark wage for textile manufacture is no longer China, but Bangladesh (and Vietnam for footwear).[43] In principle, there is no reason why low-cost production could not in future be established on the East African coast, integrated into the 2,000 year-old Indian Ocean trading and financial complex. Just as Bangladesh combines a low-wage economy with a long tradition of textile manufacture (not to mention an appalling reputation for corruption), so too do southern and eastern Africa have traditions of weaving, notably among women. In Africa more generally, the connection with Asian countries with funds to invest could prove crucial. Taiwanese firms have collaborated with Nigerian manufacturers in the past, and mainland Chinese entrepreneurs are now doing the same. Dubai Ports World, the world's fourth-biggest port operator, has made a long-term investment in Africa's commercial future, taking control of strategically located ports in Dakar, Djibouti and Maputo, complemented by its acquisition of the venerable old colonial shipping line P&O.[44]

Asian investors seem more confident in Africa than their European and American counterparts not least because they have not inherited the same set of prejudices about African markets. Asian investors have an outlook, associated with the trust characteristic of family firms and with the nature of their relations with their home governments, that makes them more confident in African environments than their less nimble European and North American rivals. In the Western tradition, capitalism is dependent on the sanctity of private property, ownership of which has to be firmly established in law. In China, the spectacular rise of a capitalist economy has been overseen by an authoritarian government and has not been associated with the rule of law or the emergence of individual rights in the same way as in the European experience that has shaped the views of economists and sociologists. As the philosopher John Gray points out, 'like other branches of the study of society, economics remains culturally parochial, and its underlying concepts based on a few centuries of Western experience'.[45]

An orthodox view is that the single main obstacle to successful investment in Africa has been its lack of institutions that can generate capital and use it effectively. The economist and ex-finance minister Hernando de Soto maintains that it is to a large extent the lack of a secure and accessible legal framework that stymies the spread of capital in poor countries, since it prevents people from offering collateral for loans, notably in the form of their own homes. Capital is a social construction that can exist only when it is supported by a network of institutions. Capital, De Soto writes, 'consists of the productive economic aspects of the things people own, which are ordinarily invisible to the naked eye. The process that allows us to make the invisible visible is hidden deep in the property systems of developed nations'.[46] Capital is more than just money; a capitalist society and economy consist of more than banks and insurance companies. For capitalism to flourish, it requires a system of property ownership in a context where people are confident they will not be arbitrarily dispossessed and where they have access to institutions that will provide them with credit.

Nearly fifty years ago, an American economist working for a Nigerian development bank pointed out that it was not so much the shortage of capital that was holding back the country's development at that time as the lack of effective demand in the absence of the reliable institutions and a secure property regime that can create capital or allow imported capital to do its work. He described the situation as one of *capital vainly seeking viable private projects*.[47] The lack of an effective demand for capital is the main reason for the flight of capital that has been such a striking feature of many African countries, as holders of capital in Africa, both indigenous and expatriate, have sought to transfer their assets to jurisdictions that are safer and to locations where capital can be invested with a reasonable expectation of profitability.[48]

The latter condition now exists in some urban contexts. A major question, however, concerns rural property, where the interest of Asian investors is intense.

Land and Property

Africa has large areas of cultivable land that are at present unused, especially in just three countries: Angola, Congo and Sudan.[49] These wide-open spaces are attractive to investors from Asian and Middle Eastern countries who foresee a future in which they will be unable to produce food from their own resources and who have only limited confidence in world markets. Since the coming decades may well see permanent worldwide shortages of food and oil and local shortages of water,[50] generating political and even military pressures, the geopolitical importance of African farmland is not hard to see.

Few African countries outside South Africa have an effective land market. In some of them, foreign nationals are in theory forbidden to own land at all. Where provision for the purchase and sale of land does exist, the registration of ownership is cumbersome to complete and difficult to enforce. Buying building-land in a city is generally easier than acquiring land in any other area of the country, and many Africans over the years have invested their savings in building a house that they can occupy themselves or rent out for a cash income.

Every country south of the Sahara is to greater or lesser extent still wrestling with the legacy of attempts made in colonial times to provide a new legal basis for land tenure. This was most radical in the colonies of settlement in the south and east of the continent, where high-quality land was made available to European immigrants and the previous African inhabitants were driven off the land or turned into wage-labourers or squatters. One of the strategic aims of nationalist movements in those parts of the continent where foreign settlers took up agriculture in colonial times was to repossess the land. Consequently, in most of these former settler-colonies, families of European origin have abandoned farming, although a few remain in Kenya and Zambia. Zimbabwe has witnessed since 2000 the largest redistribution of land in the recent history of southern Africa, under chaotic conditions. Only in Namibia and South Africa do large tracts remain in the hands of owners of settler descent. In all these cases, systems of landholding are divided between designated areas where land is made available for purchase or for long lease on a market basis, and other areas where land is held under a traditional system of tenure.

Until the mid twentieth century, Africa was a largely agrarian continent. Colonial governments tried, quite successfully, to stimulate farmers to produce export products for metropolitan markets and to earn revenue for the government through taxes and duties. As a result, fifty years ago Africa was the source of some 10 per cent of the world's tradeable food; today its share is less than 1 per cent.[51] Comparisons between Africa and southeast Asia show how important was the decision made after independence by many Asian governments to aid peasant agriculture, whereas many African countries at that time preferred to go for rapid industrialisation.[52] So many African governments chose the urban option in the 1960s largely because of political pressure to give more attention to town-dwellers than to their village cousins.[53] Town-dwellers, living in concentrated clusters, and being highly dependent on the state or on politically sensitive markets for their well-being, are more closely connected to the state than are rural populations. African ruling classes have generally received financial support from interests linked to cities, import trade and the state itself, always the principal channel of capital accumulation. The consequence of African government policies has been to encourage populations to live in dense settlements where surveillance is easier and where services may more readily be provided. In an earlier generation, some governments made ambitious attempts to reorganise rural populations through policies of collectivisation or villagisation, like Tanzania's famous/infamous *ujamaa*. These generally did nothing for productivity, and in the worst cases they led to chaos.[54] If African agriculture has been neglected, it is also because the European Union and the US have preferred to subsidise their own farmers rather than to invest in Africa. At the same time they have encouraged the provision of food to Africa on humanitarian grounds, which may help feed the starving, but at the risk of undercutting Africa's farmers by the provision of free food.

Despite the abysmal record of African agriculture, the continent's farmers do not lack initiative. Urbanisation and the purchasing power of a new middle class that has largely severed its personal links with the agrarian world may, at least in theory, encourage agricultural development.[55] The remarkable spread of mobile phones has brought rural Africans into proximity with city markets. There are numerous examples of farmers developing new product lines to satisfy growing market demand, and even of highly-educated professionals investing money and skills in modest production for urban markets or for export to European supermarkets. The export of vegetables, fruit and flowers from Africa is now worth about $2 billion per year.[56]

The present juncture, then, could conceivably open the way to significant investment in African agriculture from both inside and outside the continent. With world food prices seemingly destined to stay high, greater agricultural production would be of benefit to Africa on several counts. Depending on how it was done, investment in agriculture could create employment, ease the debt burden and relieve some of the pressures that are leading to the growth of cities to unmanageable proportions.

High-level policy debate is framed between those who advocate the creation or strengthening of individual property rights, said to promote economic growth, against those who call for protection of the livelihoods and subsistence rights of small farmers, often couched in terms of traditional claims. In fact, in the absence of land markets, major investors in African land often deal directly with heads of state, who may neglect to inform their own agriculture ministers about the agreements they reach. In the many countries where all farmland is legally deemed to be owned by the state, it is easy for a president to allot land to foreign companies at the expense of the farmers who are living there. The occupants may be required to produce crops for the new companies investing there, or, in the worst cases, simply be expelled from their ancestral land. Governments have a tendency to favour such arrangements in regard to land in marginal areas or places regarded as nests of support for the political opposition. Jacques Diouf, the director of the Food and Agriculture Organisation, himself an African, has consistently warned of the risks posed by foreign investment in agricultural produce for export.[57] There is a real danger that food and bio-fuel crops will be exported to foreign markets while hunger grips local populations,[58] as seems already to be happening in Ethiopia.

This is indeed political dynamite. The massive investment in 1.3 million hectares of agricultural land in Madagascar announced by the South Korean firm Daewoo Logistics in November 2008 is a telling example.[59] Daewoo wanted this land, about half the size of Belgium, for growing food and bio-fuel crops.[60] The disquiet caused in Madagascar when information about the negotiations was leaked to the press was one of the factors behind anti-government protests that resulted in the overthrow of President Marc Ravalomanana in March 2009.

Several African governments are known to have welcomed expressions of interest by foreign countries or companies in investing in food-for-export schemes. By coincidence, in the same month that the Malagasy government was overthrown, King Abdullah of Saudi Arabia was reported to have received a formal gift of rice harvested in Ethiopia by Saudi investors.[61] In Sudan, a US businessman, Philippe Heilberg, has gained leasehold rights to 400,000 hectares of land by taking a majority stake in a company controlled by the son of a local Southern strongman.[62] Analysts are reduced to accumulating evidence piece by piece. The highly personalised nature of many land deals makes it difficult to find reliable data on exactly who is buying or renting out land to whom. According to one calculation, Sudan heads the list of sub-Saharan countries that have sold or leased large tracts of land to foreign interests, mostly in North Africa, the Middle East and Asia, totalling some 1.1 million hectares. Uganda comes second with 844,000 hectares rented or sold, and Senegal third.[63]

Much of the sensitivity surrounding the issue of land purchase and leasing by foreigners arises from the relation between land occupancy and politics in the deepest sense—not just elite manoeuvres but a profound sense of belonging that is reflected in culture and religion. In rural areas especially, land ownership is governed, sometimes in law but more often in practice, by the principle of group tenure. Even vacant land is widely held to be the property of one or other social group, usually held in trust by a chief or other traditional authority who is deemed to act on behalf of the group as a whole. Land is often associated with ancestral spirits. Hence, land in rural areas is connected not only to agrarian livelihoods, but also to the possession of political rights. This is why town-dwellers and African expatriates who have enough money often build a house in their home village, as it provides proof of membership in an ethnic community.[64]

The prospect of land law reform, which has been on the international agenda since the donors, the World Bank and the IMF led the move to liberalise markets late in the last century, therefore raises issues relating to fundamental political rights. For this reason, legal debates that might otherwise be dry and technical become transformed into referenda on the nature of citizenship, political authority, and the future of the liberal nation-state itself.[65] There are many cases of political and land issues combining in struggles that are complex and bloody. In Kenya, a disputed national election in 2007 generated deadly violence that was often connected to conflicts, taking on an ethnic form, concerning the occupation of land by people perceived as outsiders. Hundreds of people were killed in the early weeks of 2008, and hundreds of thousands made homeless. In Côte d'Ivoire, the deadliest violence in years of low-intensity war has been in the west of the country, where land used for valuable cocoa-farms has been the subject of dispute between people claiming descent from the earliest settlers of the area, on the one hand, and the descendants of more recent immigrants from elsewhere in the country or from abroad, on the other hand. The most notorious case in recent years has been Zimbabwe, where many of the white farmers whose land has been confiscated are actually Zimbabwean passport-holders, in principle enjoying full rights of citizenship. Conversely, many farm labourers in Zimbabwe who have lost their jobs in recent years were immigrants from neighbouring countries, whom the government could dispossess without too many political repercussions. South Africans, too, increasingly acknowledge the sensitivity of current land tenure arrangements in their own country, where agricultural land is still overwhelmingly in the hands of whites, especially Afrikaners, for whom it is a potent symbol of belonging; not for nothing are Afrikaners also known as *boere* ('farmers'). Nervously contemplating what has happened in Zimbabwe, they point out the dangers if land reform were to become politicised in their own country.

As a fairly typical example of how land claims can be linked to political and social tensions, we may take the case of Ghana. A team of researchers at the University of Legon has done research[66] into land disputes in a country that has undergone extensive political and economic reform since the early 1980s and that is often seen as one of a handful of African countries poised to make a breakthrough into sustained development. The researchers describe how property acquisitions even in the suburbs of Accra are often subject to dispute, particularly when the putative owner of a piece of land begins to invest in building. The beginning of construction work is often the signal for another person or party to claim the land as his own possession, with or without justification. Prudent landowners may therefore pay unemployed youths to act as 'land guards' on their property, with instructions to use force if necessary to discourage trespassers. Clearly, this practice carries a risk of property disputes turning into violent conflicts. In several rural areas surveyed by the same team of researchers, tracts of unused land were claimed by different ethnic groups. In rural areas of Ghana, investment in an agricultural production scheme can become the catalyst for dormant claims to be articulated, which take on complex political overtones as rival families vie for a position of chieftaincy or as local politicians espouse the claims of one or other party. Although the Ghanaian state has various legal and administrative mechanisms and institutions for adjudicating such claims, and in theory individual tenure can be recorded in a land register, in practice the formal mechanisms of state control are often ineffective in ensuring security of tenure. 'Politics in northern Ghana are often fuelled by a lethal cocktail of simmering land disputes, ethnic and chieftaincy disputes and a gun culture', observes the newsletter *Africa Confidential*.[67] It is such a hot political issue that direct involvement in seemingly intractable land disputes is a complication that successive governments avoid if possible. Politicians regularly promise in the pre-election period that they will encourage agricultural investment, especially in the wide open spaces of northern Ghana, and they just as often shy away from taking the measures that might cause such investment to materialise once they are in office. In this context, it may be appreciated just how sensitive is the news that a Norwegian company has acquired a lease on 400,000 hectares for the production of bio-fuel in Ghana. ScanFuel is the biggest of some fifteen similar investors in bio-fuel in Ghana, including firms from the US, Italy and Brazil.[68]

Although much research remains to be done on foreign investment in agriculture, a common model appears to be for investors to acquire a long lease in the name of a company in which overseas directors sit with a national partner, often someone politically well-connected, who in effect draws an income from lending his or her name to a venture. This is a textbook case of rent-seeking. Some sources report success with contract farming, whereby a buyer guarantees to buy a farmer's entire output, freeing the farmer from the burden of marketing his crop and from fear of his crops rotting for want of a purchaser. If, however, some of the new import-hungry consumers in Asia were to implement contract farming on a massive scale, it could discourage local food markets by instituting a system of tied production for export. Of all the available ways of investing in agriculture, the most promising from a development point of view appears to be the encouragement of relatively small-scale production.

In some countries with substantial tracts of fertile land that are largely unused, the influence of the central government is so diminished that the state is almost incapable of implementing any agricultural policy at all. An example is the Democratic Republic of Congo, where in the fertile far east of the country, the writ of the Congolese state hardly runs. This is the main zone of murderous conflicts, closely associated with claims to exceptionally rich farmland, that have caused perhaps millions of deaths from a mix of violence, disease and hunger in the last ten years. The government of Angola, in contrast, has both the ambition to formulate major plans and, as one of Africa's largest oil producers, the resources to back them up. In late 2008, the government said that it planned to invest $6 billion in agricultural projects over five years.[69] As a consequence of some forty years of war, large areas of agricultural land in Angola are virtually empty, meaning that the government has a relatively free hand in deciding what sort of enterprises it wishes to establish in the country's main farming areas. At present, only 10 per cent of the country's productive land is actually cultivated, and it imports more than half its food. The government has been in negotiation with private-sector farming companies from Brazil, Spain, Canada, the US, Argentina and Portugal. Chinese interests are also reportedly interested in the possibilities of major agricultural investment there.[70]

Some African countries have effected improvements to their agricultural production by less radical means. Perhaps the best known example is Malawi, where impressive improvements in farm production have been widely attributed to the government's successful implementation of a scheme to provide subsidised fertiliser to farmers through the provision of vouchers. The government estimates that the 2007 maize crop was 73 per cent higher than the average for the preceding five years. Malawi has also profited from the collapse of Zimbabwean agriculture to increase its exports, including the 286,589 tonnes of maize officially exported from Malawi to Zimbabwe in 2007. Based on this case it is possible to speculate whether cotton cultivation in neighbouring Zambia, sometimes cited as a success story, would not be far more productive if the supply of inputs were improved. At present, Zambia's cotton is ginned at a small number of ginneries mostly run by foreign firms, which do not invest in inputs. A leading Zambian agriculturalist estimates that with the right inputs, current production of 600 kilos per hectare could improve to as much as 2,000 kilos per hectare.[71]

However, as is very often the case when agriculture is overwhelmingly rain-fed rather than irrigated, a question remains concerning the extent to which a rise in production is due to government policy and the extent to which it is due simply to favourable weather. Productivity can also be related to other issues such as inheritance practices, which can result in the subdivision of a single farm into tiny holdings among several children.[72] There are also still other factors that make it difficult to conclude that Malawi's success could be reproduced elsewhere. Malawi's exceptional population density makes the distribution of fertiliser and other inputs relatively easy in comparison with a country such as neighbouring Zambia, where the rural population is far more dispersed.

In regard to the risks of foreign investment in African land, the Chinese government is prudent. China's deputy minister for agriculture, Niu Dun, has said that Beijing prefers to depend on its own land to investing in African arable land.[73] This announcement is less clear than it may appear, however, since it is not the Chinese government but private-sector companies that are leading the drive to invest in African farmland, overwhelmingly in joint ventures. One Chinese company has announced plans to invest some $3 billion in a bio-fuel project on 700,000 hectares in Zambia's Northern Province, to be run jointly with a local firm.[74] There are similar examples from many parts of the continent.

The stakes surrounding Africa's agriculture are extraordinarily high. The Food and Agriculture Organisation has warned that unless the nearly seventy million smallholder families in sub-Saharan Africa apply fertilisers and start practising sustainable land and water management on their farms within the next decade, they 'will seriously jeopardise their long-term food security, productivity and incomes, while environmental degradation will accelerate'.[75] Many parts of Africa are particularly vulnerable to climate change.[76]

The relationship between population, technology and resources worldwide has changed many calculations that were taken for granted even a few years ago. Political leaders, according to the Organisation for Economic Cooperation and Development, 'must abandon the view that agriculture is a transient phase on the linear road to the post-industrial age. A focus on agriculture as the foundation for new prosperity is not a return to the past, but a new step forward in our socio-economic evolution. The demands of the new agriculture require executive leadership'.[77]

In almost every African country, providing such leadership would break the habit of decades, based on rent-seeking from urban interests, accessed through the state itself. How African politicians use their power in regard to the most precious of all productive resources, land, will have enormous consequences for the continent's future.

4

HOW TO BE A HEGEMON

On 7 May 2009, the government of Gabon announced that President Omar Bongo, head of state for forty-two years, had suspended his official duties and gone to Spain. His stated purpose was to mourn the recent death of his wife,[1] herself the daughter of another head of state, Denis Sassou-Nguesso, president of Congo-Brazzaville.

It was not clear why Bongo should go to Europe to mourn rather than stay at home. International media announced that the president was in fact undergoing treatment for cancer in a Barcelona hospital. The Gabonese government conceded that he was 'undergoing a medical check up'.

The media then reported that Bongo's cancer had reached 'an advanced stage'. On 7 June, French media announced that President Bongo was in fact dead.

The government of Gabon denied the report. An hour later, however, the prime minister of Gabon released a very odd statement. 'This morning I visited the president', he revealed, 'accompanied by the president of the national assembly, the foreign minister, the head of the president's cabinet and senior members of the presidential family and after a meeting with the medical team we can confirm that the president is alive'. Normally, one would expect senior ministers and officials to be able to judge whether or not their president is alive without recourse to medical advice.

The next day, the Spanish foreign ministry confirmed that President Bongo was alive. But the Spanish media reported that he was dead. The Gabonese government affirmed that the president was 'not dead'. He was, an official communiqué maintained, 'continuing his holiday in Spain'.

Shortly afterwards, the prime minister confirmed in a written statement that President Omar Bongo was indeed dead. Two months later, Ali Bongo succeeded his father as Gabon's head of state after an election notably lacking in transparency.

Omar Bongo's demise is a graphic illustration of how power has been monopolised by certain families in many African countries in spite of constitutions that provide for free electoral competition. Only Lesotho, Morocco and Swaziland are formal monarchies, but a number of African presidencies have acquired many of the hallmarks of personal rule, extending even to successful attempts to transmit power from father to son. North Korea has a communist hereditary monarchy. The US has seen a son succeed his father as president. So why should Africa not have republican hereditary monarchies?

Republican Monarchies

It has been quite common in Africa's modern history for young men of obscure origin to acquire immense power at a single stroke, notably by means of military coups. Modern Africa's first military seizure of power, in Togo in 1963, three years after independence, was led by Gnassingbe Eyadema. He was just twenty-five. Eyadema had served as a sergeant in the French army in Algeria under a young officer named Jacques Chirac, later to become president of France (1995–2007). After killing his country's first president, Eyadema went on to become head of state himself four years later, running Togo for thirty-seven years and renewing his acquaintance with his old comrade-in-arms, the former Lieutenant Chirac.[2] When Eyadema died in 2005, one of his sons replaced him as head of state, with other family members occupying strategic positions in the new government.

The Democratic Republic of Congo, too, has gained the status of a republican hereditary monarchy since Joseph Kabila replaced his father, a former bandit-chief and smuggler, as head of state after the assassination of Kabila Senior in 2001. In Botswana, another presidential son, Ian Khama, has taken over the reins of government, with conspicuous success, although in this case after an inter-regnum. In other countries—Egypt, Kenya, Libya, Mozambique, Namibia, Senegal and others—presidential sons have embarked on political careers without yet managing to get the top job.

Many other political dynasties have shown their staying-power since the early years of independence. Kenya's President Mwai Kibaki was a minister as far back as the 1960s, while his current prime minister, Raila Odinga, is the son of the leader of the opposition from that period. In Zimbabwe, not only President Robert Mugabe but also many senior ministers have been in office since independence in 1980. In some other countries, though, members of the elite who gained money and power in an earlier generation have calculated that the best long-term strategy for their advancement is to stay out of the political firing-line and to influence governments more discreetly. In Nigeria, for decades prominent Northern leaders, forming a network nicknamed 'the Kaduna mafia', have preferred to work from behind the scenes rather than to contend for the presidency themselves. Since Nigeria's return to democracy in 1999, elected heads of state have continued to be beholden to powerful kingmakers. There are many other countries where powerful lobbies prefer to exercise back-room influence rather than to occupy the most senior positions of the state in person.[3]

Even in South Africa, where majority rule was established only in 1994, many senior politicians come from families with a political pedigree. The Mbekis, the Sisulus and others have provided leaders to the ANC over two generations. South Africa's cabinet has been particularly notable for containing a large number of married couples, reflecting the degree to which political families seek alliances with one another. The current president, Jacob Zuma, was married to former foreign minister Nkosazana Dlamini-Zuma until their divorce in 1999, and one of his daughters is married to a government minister in Zimbabwe. Other ANC ministers have been similarly linked by marital or family ties. Former deputy president Phumzile Mlambo-Ngcuka was married to Bulelani Ngcuka when he was still director of public prosecutions. Geraldine Fraser-Moleketi and Jabu Moleketi are another recent ministerial couple. Two brothers, Aziz and Essop Pahad, were mainstays of President Thabo Mbeki's government.

A good place to observe South Africa's elite in full display is a formal occasion at Johannesburg's Rand Club, founded in 1887 by the mining tycoon and arch-imperialist Cecil John Rhodes. At a Hollywood-style business award ceremony in October 2009, the men wore dinner jackets and the women sported glamorous designer gowns.[4] Among those present were government ministers, the governor of the central bank and many of the country's top businesspeople including the billionaire mining magnate Patrice Motsepe, brother-in-law of a government minister. A white businessman who received a lifetime achievement award, Stephen Koseff, chief executive officer of Investec, shed a few tears as he thanked his family like a film star receiving an Oscar. His son had flown in specially from London and his daughter had come with her husband from Australia. This last detail says something about South Africa's old white business elite, many members of which have spread their options by encouraging their children to study abroad and to acquire foreign passports. However, it is not so much departing whites that are the cause of the skills shortage that is threatening South Africa's business prowess, but the collapsing system of school education that makes the country unable to produce qualified people in the numbers it needs.

Political dynasties can be found in many parts of the world, but Africa's are often marked by their association with colonial institutions and the continuing importance of their foreign connections. Behind the façade of immobility presented by presidents who have been in power for decades, like the late Omar Bongo of Gabon, whose ministers had such difficulty in coming to terms with his demise, lies a dynamic set in motion in the 1940s. For decades, foreign donors encouraged the domination of African politics by individuals whom they thought they could trust. During the Cold War, foreign powers often supported such dominant figures as Félix Houphouët-Boigny in Côte d'Ivoire or Mobutu Sese Seko in Zaïre, the present-day Democratic Republic of Congo. It was thought that a strong leader could keep a country stable and deliver on international deals and strategic alignments. This attitude both contributed to and reflected the personality cults of political leaders who were deemed to be the fathers of their nations, personally responsible for the liberation of millions and the well-being of entire countries.

Although the more elaborate personality cults have disappeared since then, aid donors sometimes continue to attribute exceptional importance to dominant personalities. The development industry tends to pursue an almost messianic quest for a head of state who will make all things good. Previous donor favourites have included Julius Nyerere (Tanzania), Yoweri Museveni (Uganda) and Paul Kagame (Rwanda), the latter two being among the group of so-called New Leaders who, until they started fighting each other, were heavily promoted by President Clinton's team of Africanists, which was top-heavy with political appointees rather than relying on career diplomats. African intellectuals, too, often attribute their continent's ills to the personal failings of this or that ruler. Each time a favourite president turns out to be unable to meet all the expectations placed upon him, or is seen to be enmeshed in the corruption that is inherent in Africa's politics, the development industry and all the seekers for a new messiah look for a replacement. It puts one in mind of the search for a new Dalai Lama, thought to be a reincarnation of the previous one.

Until 2005, 'donor darlings' were always men. Now, however, Africa has a female version, the first woman to be elected as a head of state in any African country. Ellen Johnson Sirleaf, president of Liberia, is celebrated worldwide not so much for her undoubted talents but above all for what she is deemed to represent. In Western countries with strong feminist movements she is seen as proof that a woman can succeed where men have failed, in her case in restoring a country wrecked by war.[5] She is a favourite with the US state department, itself headed by a strong-minded woman who is known to admire Liberia's president. Johnson Sirleaf is actually a veteran of Liberia's political establishment, her first ministerial appointment having been as long ago as the 1970s. As she admits, for some time she helped to bankroll the warlord Charles Taylor, now on trial for war crimes. To many Liberians, Johnson Sirleaf represents not so much a new type of ruler as the return of the old Americo-Liberian class that ran the country like a vast private estate for over a century before the military coup in 1980 that plunged the country into violence. Some of the ministers and officials in Johnson Sirleaf's government are massively corrupt. There is a case to be made that, on balance, she is the best person to lead Liberia in present circumstances. Nevertheless, the distance between the Liberian reality and the international image is vast. Foreign cheerleading for progress in Africa often amounts to little more than the projection of personal ideologies onto a space on the map sufficiently little-known as to accommodate fantasies of every type.

The emergence of an Ellen Johnson Sirleaf provides matter for reflection as to where Africa's political dynasties actually come from. Johnson Sirleaf has herself written about her ancestry with a view not least to refuting the perception that she is an Americo-Liberian.[6] Her maternal grandfather was a German trader. On her paternal side, her grandfather was a chief who received patronage from a powerful Americo-Liberian family. On both sides it was the success of an ancestor two generations back that made the family fortune. Many other upper- or middle-class Africans are similarly beneficiaries of the decision taken by a parent, a grandparent or another not very distant ancestor to send their children to good schools. This is no doubt true in many parts of the world, but in the case of Africa it was often in the days when most countries could boast a smattering of good schools, quite often run by churches. For the last thirty years, as national systems of education in many African countries have declined in quality, giving children a top-grade education has frequently meant sending them to Europe or the USA. As a consequence, many of Africa's most successful families are today headed by men and women who were educated abroad before coming home to run their family affairs. This distinguishes them not only from the great majority of their compatriots who have not benefited from an expensive education, but also from the generation of mid-twentieth century nationalists who had often grown up in rural areas, living among or in close proximity to the peasantry of that time. Early generations of nationalist leaders often had a deep understanding of rural life stemming from their own experience. Today, power is often in the hands of people who have not spent extensive periods in rural areas or in poor households and who, by comparison with their forebears, have little experience of how the poor live.

Nowhere is the gulf between relatively well entrenched elites and newcomers more important than in South Africa. The business sector is still dominated by whites, in the case of Afrikaners quite often descendants of families raised out of poverty only a couple of generations ago. One of the reasons for the relatively smooth transfer of political power in the early 1990s was the calculation by leading white businesspeople that they were well enough ensconced in the private sector to survive the loss of state power. The country's first black president, Nelson Mandela, was a descendant of an aristocratic family and one of the first black South Africans to practise as a lawyer. His successor, Thabo Mbeki, was from a leading ANC family and was also highly educated. However, the current rising star of the ANC, Julius Malema, is a barely educated man from a very modest family, as is the current head of state, Jacob Zuma, who worked as a cowherd in his youth and owes his scant education to his enforced leisure during his years as a political prisoner on Robben Island.

An elite, according to a Nigerian newspaper editor writing in sardonic mode, is 'a predatory, carnivorous, clannish specie of mammals that hunt in small groups called families'.[7] It is difficult to decide which is more desirable or, perhaps better expressed, which is more threatening to stability: an elite that has pretensions to hereditary status, and that risks losing touch with popular feeling, or the leadership of demagogues.

The Search for Hegemony

'Hegemony' is the word used by one of the twentieth century's most influential political theorists, Antonio Gramsci, to designate the situation in which a ruling elite is so widely accepted as to be uncontested. When a ruling group has hegemony, its political superiority appears to most people to be simply a matter of common sense, a reflection of the natural order. But even a ruling group confident of its legitimacy has to work to maintain its hegemony in a world in constant change. The quest for hegemony is a continuous process inseparable from politics itself.

The political scientist Jean-François Bayart maintains that there are two basic ways of studying how quests for hegemony take shape, both of which may be used in conjunction. One approach is to consider hegemony in terms of the strategies adopted by dominant actors over time, such as the historic achievement of the English ruling class that arose after the political revolution of 1688 (later incorporating the dominant classes in other regions of what was to become Great Britain and eventually the United Kingdom of Great Britain and Northern Ireland) in pursuing a strategy of respectability founded on financial power. As we have seen,[8] the staying power of this financial elite, whose style is sometimes dubbed 'gentlemanly capitalism', is not to be underestimated, as it has continued to exercise global influence through the City of London even after the demise of the British empire. A second possibility is to study the imaginative repertoires associated with politics in any given society over a lengthy period with a view to understanding how a ruling stratum emerges.[9]

Bearing these approaches in mind, it is notable not only that many African elite families can trace their prosperity to an ancestor who flourished during the late colonial period, but also that the terms in which struggles for hegemony take place are often derived from techniques or instruments introduced by colonial governments. These include the use of bureaucratic methods of administration, the culture of statistics, an appeal to national consciousness, the ideology of progress and monotheism.[10] The discourse of national unity, favoured by politicians in the last period of colonial rule, continues to be a major buttress of power. The notion of a colonial 'civilising mission', or in other words the proposition that a key justification of the state is its role in educating the mass of the African population in just about everything from matters of personal hygiene to the nature of the cosmos, remains current even fifty years after independence.[11]

Since the 1960s, when most African states gained their political independence, there have been two generalised attempts to change the manner in which power is administered. The first of these consisted of the programmes of economic liberalisation that were introduced to Africa by the international financial institutions, supported by national aid donors, in the 1980s, after many African countries had experienced acute foreign currency shortages and some had reached the verge of bankruptcy. The second was the political democratisation that many members of what were then quite small middle classes were calling for, and that was encouraged by donor governments in the 1990s. By and large, the political elites that arose in Africa in the mid-twentieth century in the struggles surrounding decolonisation were successful in surviving these and other challenges to their dominance, and even in turning them to advantage. More recently, in those countries that have been favoured by high levels of investment and economic growth over the last five to ten years, elites have continued to entrench themselves, still by using the density of their international connections but also by associating their power with the interests of a middle class that has expanded visibly. Generally speaking, then, African elites have managed to retain their status in spite of the upheavals that have been a feature of African societies since the mid-twentieth century by drawing directly or indirectly on the resources of the state, showing impressive political staying-power. Their achievement has been at a certain cost, however, as some of the institutions established in colonial times have become mere shadows of their former selves, and some practices and conventions that were regarded in colonial times as being of major importance have more or less ceased to exist, causing observers to talk of failing, fragile, or collapsing states even as Africa has become financially better integrated than ever before.

Even the most formidable president can work only with the material constituted by societies, deriving power from the fact that large numbers of people subscribe to common ideas and activities, whether in the guise of formal institutions or simply in informal networks. This is an observation that runs contrary to the idea, so often advanced by analysts both African and foreign, of a continent ruined by poor leaders. Whether leaders are seen as wise (Mandela, Nyerere) or as the corruptors of entire nations (Mobutu, Mugabe), it is unsatisfactory to attribute everything to the characteristics of just one person. The Great Man/Really Awful Man theory of history can continue in use only as long as we are unable to reconcile individual and society.[12] It is therefore important to connect the deeds of Great/Really Awful heads of state to the popular currents flowing through their societies. It is useful to consider some of these.

Any woman or man of advanced age living in Africa today—someone eighty years old, say—has seen massive changes take place within their own lifetime. First and foremost, the population of their continent has increased by several hundred per cent over that time. This increase is, in the opinion of a leading historian, 'of a scale and speed unique in human history'.[13] Many families have moved from the country to the city, with the result that about 40 per cent of Africa's billion people[14] today live in towns. This compares with probably less than ten per cent of its population of some 130 million in the early twentieth century. During the golden age of development, in the 1950s and 1960s, education gave substantial numbers of young people the opportunity to adopt a style of living beyond the imagination of their ancestors, opening up dazzling perspectives. Millions of people entered salaried employment. Hundreds of millions of people attended schools, with a relatively small number completing a course of education up to university level. These were all things pretty much undreamed of a century ago. A much smaller number, including the parents or grandparents of many of today's elites, were able to acquire substantial wealth. This they did almost invariably through access to the resources of the state, as decolonisation created positions for those skillful or lucky enough to benefit.

New ways of living produce new forms of sociability. In a continent where most of the population is under the age of eighteen, the ways in which the young struggle to make their mark in life and the novelty of their lifestyles are often shocking to older people who, in Africa, are steeped in respect for age. Ways of thinking and behaving that evolved over centuries in the supposition that land was plentiful and people were scarce have had to make space for new realities. These huge changes bring new intellectual and mental perspectives, some more edifying than others. 'Wild music, wild language, wild attitudes' was how the Liberian writer Moses Nagbe summed up the youngsters he was forced to live with during the weeks he endured on a rusty old ship taking refugees from the war in his home country in 1996.[15] The extreme youth of the population creates a political dynamic all of its own, as it means that most people have short memories—for them, the colonial period belongs to the realm of myth. The sheer vitality they incarnate can be channelled for both positive and negative outcomes. It is small wonder that warlords recruit child soldiers for their armies. They are uniquely malleable, and they are available in large numbers.

Africa's high population growth is now finding its way back onto the policy agenda after a period when experts believed that birth rates would diminish as countries developed. In general it has become apparent that the connection between economic growth and the birth rate is not straightforward. In any event, countries that remain poor may have such high fertility rates that family planning begins to look like a necessity if disaster is to be averted. In Mali, for example, the average woman has more than five children, but agricultural production cannot keep pace with the growing numbers of mouths to feed, especially as agricultural land is being lost to the Sahara desert.[16] The fertility of land, cattle and people has always been of paramount importance to Africans and the traditional concern with fertility remains central to popular worldviews even as the continent becomes more urban.

The mental revolutions that accompany radical changes in ways of living are difficult to capture in figures even on the rare occasions when reliable statistics are available. Novelists have often been more successful than social scientists in describing the rags-to-riches stories that have been a feature of modern life. The tale of the country boy who receives an education and lands a job in the government, and the moral problems he faces, was for years a classic theme of African writers.[17] The same idea recurs in dozens of autobiographies.

Some of Africa's social revolutions have remained relatively opaque to outside observers, such as in West Africa's Sahel region, where societies have traditionally been divided into class-conscious strata, with aristocratic families at the top, specialist blacksmiths and artisans at mid-level, and domestic slaves at the bottom. In the colonial period, quite a few proud Muslim families refused to send their children to schools that were run by secular governments or by Christian missionaries. They sent their slaves to attend school in their place, and hence it was often people from the lower social grades who benefited from education and were best placed to occupy senior positions in new state bureaucracies at independence.[18] Today, fifty years later, there are aristocratic families that live in penury while their former slaves have become generals and heads of state.

Some of the major social transformations that have occurred have been associated with single people who have taken whole families or even wider groups with them in their ascent. In some countries, the first rulers after independence went beyond creating opportunities for their immediate family and friends and had a grander ambition of creating a quasi-aristocracy, like Kenya's Jomo Kenyatta, who encouraged his fellow-Kikuyu to occupy farmland abandoned by departing British settlers. As Kikuyu businessmen and farmers acquired land outside their traditional home area, they risked being seen as interlopers by other people, all the more so because the quality of Kenya's land varies between the well-watered highlands and Rift Valley and areas of extreme dryness. Ever since Kenyatta's time, Kikuyus living in the Rift Valley have looked to Kikuyu politicians to protect them, creating dangerous tensions as ethnic labels have become associated with intense political animosities and economic discrepancies. A high rate of population growth adds a further ingredient to this noxious brew.

Kenya is an example of how the use of state positions and state resources to promote the interests of particular families or entire ethnic groups can create murderous conflicts. When news of an ethnic clash appears on television or in the newspaper, it is common for Western viewers and readers to suppose that the ultimate cause is the age-old existence of 'tribes' whose territories were disrupted by colonial partition, forcing unnatural partners to live together in countries with oddly shaped borders. It is sometimes inferred that peace would be encouraged by allotting each group its own territory once more. But this is a false reading of history, from which fallacious conclusions risk being drawn. The social divisions of a century and a quarter ago bore little resemblance to those of today, and the social groups of those days had little in common with today's ethnic groups beyond their ethnonym. The colonisers used the social divisions they found in Africa at that time as an instrument of political management. The form of ethnicity on view now is actually the outcome of what has happened subsequently, a historical engagement with bureaucratic government under both colonial and nationalist rule.[19] A general rearrangement of borders would therefore not solve ethnic conflicts, as is sometimes suggested. Nor would re-dividing current states in such a way as to ensure that each 'tribe' has its own sovereign territory stop competition for power from taking an ethnic form as 'tribes' would simply sub-divide into smaller components.

Ethnography—identifying and classifying specific ethnic groups and studying their languages and customs—was just one of a range of bureaucratic techniques introduced in colonial times whose ultimate purpose was to make Africa legible to outsiders. The bureaucratic forms with which African states have historically been endowed by colonial rule—government departments, codes of law, armed forces, parliaments, volumes of statistics—exist because the international system continues to require these institutional forms for purposes of legibility and that is the main reason that African politicians continue to have recourse to these techniques. When they do not exist, the outside world finds it difficult to understand how things work. Outsiders may not even know who to talk to if they wish to get things done.

Shadow States

Several writers have resorted to images of shadows to evoke the ways in which Africa is governed and how it is integrated into world affairs.[20] The state, they imply, is like a solid object that casts a shadow. They deploy this image in an attempt to explain why concentrating on the official institutions of the state and of commerce deflects attention from some important relationships and institutions that from an official point of view have only an insubstantial existence. Actually, the metaphor of a shadow is slightly misleading, as the shadow cast by official institutions often has more real substance than the formal structures of the state. One could better describe the state as a hologram discernible amid the complex of relationships by which African societies are actually governed. Whatever solidity official institutions have often derives only from the fact that they enjoy legal recognition.

No one foresaw this fifty years ago, when the act of independence endowed Africa with states committed to developing the means to implement policies in conventional bureaucratic mode. They had constitutions endowing citizens with civic and legal rights. In the years following, most states grew in their degree of social penetration, acquiring vast numbers of civil servants in the process. This was consistent with expert advice concerning development, which in those days was usually conceived in terms of specific policies that would be implemented by the state through its functionaries.

Beginning in the early 1980s, most African states were obliged to reformulate their ambitions to greater or lesser degree. In some cases, rulers who lacked the money to pay civil servants regularly lost whatever interest they had in developing an efficient bureaucracy. As states withered from lack of cash, political power was increasingly located in the gap between the official structures of the state and the law on the one hand, and everyday reality on the other. In these circumstances, some canny operators ceased to attach much importance to formal institutions of governance at all. An effective civil service no longer served their political interest beyond the minimum necessary to maintain international credibility. Dismantling large parts of the bureaucratic apparatus inherited from colonial times and the formal economic activity that went with it—in many cases, urged on by aid donors in the name of privatisation—rulers in many countries re-founded their power on those elements of society most closely associated with the production and reproduction of capital,[21] whether formal or informal, legal or illicit. The declared aim of governing entire nations, as proclaimed by nationalist political parties, tended to be replaced by an aspiration 'to control markets and their material rewards'.[22] In this way, the formal structures and official declarations of states became less significant than the shadows that they cast. These 'shadow states', although relatively new creations, draw on much older traditions that evolved during the indirect rule of the colonial era.[23] To put it simply, two systems of government have come to exist simultaneously: the official one, and the unofficial one. These two cannot be detached from each other. They are like two sides of a single sheet of paper with different writing on each side.

Although Africa's states differ in their power and reach, there are still some that, like South Africa, aim to provide some form of welfare for the entire population. The South African state directly sustains a large percentage of the population, including not only those directly employed as civil servants, but also the more than thirteen million people who receive a state handout, out of a population of forty-nine million. Whole families survive on the old-age pension that in 2008 was less than $100 per month at the prevailing exchange rate.[24] Such a high level of welfare dependency is hardly something to strive for, but it is a sign that the governing ANC, much criticised for its corruption, does still aspire to do something for the population at large, in the classical manner of a nationalist movement. At the same time, some of South Africa's provincial administrations are actually unable to spend their annual budget because the lower levels of bureaucracy are staffed by people who are incompetent or even illiterate, appointed solely on account of their political connections. The country is also experiencing an informalisation of employment practices as there is a growing tendency for companies to employ casual labour that is cheap and non-unionised.[25] The fact that the powerful trade union federation COSATU wields strong influence inside the government and acts to protect its members in the first instance is creating a relatively privileged group of workers in regular jobs amid a growing number of people with informal jobs only, who may easily be persuaded to support local strongmen. South Africa is coming to resemble other countries within the continent more closely even as those other places cast off ever more of their colonial heritage.

The key to ruling a shadow state is to concentrate on those elements of society that are politically or economically useful and to ignore the others unless they constitute a security threat. As a consequence, power takes a new topographical form. Locally-based armed groups flourish in the absence of proper policing. At their most benign, these may have the ability to maintain order vigilante-style, but in other circumstances they constitute criminal gangs or private armies that operate protection rackets on businesses and demand money from people travelling through the areas that they dominate. Under certain conditions the leaders of private militias may become warlords competing for national power, as happened in Liberia, Sierra Leone, Congo-Brazzaville and many other places during the 1990s. When some sort of peace is re-established after major bouts of national violence, the warlords and the private armies do not actually disappear but simply revert to a less violent mode, quite often occupying niches of the shadow economy,[26] like the Tuareg ex-rebels who have become truck-drivers transporting migrants across the Sahara, or the ex-fighters in Sierra Leone who operate motorbike taxis.

As a result of changes like these, many African states are now suffused with a political logic in which the classic approach to development, which starts by identifying a need and a service-deliverer, has little relevance. In countries where the state bureaucracy has become arthritic or gangrenous, it is difficult to know how or by whom policies can be implemented. Yet, time after time, development experts propose to solve a problem by devising a policy that is to be implemented by a bureaucracy, usually an African government. Two authors describe this as 'skipping straight to Weber', by which they mean 'seeking to quickly reach service delivery performance goals in developing countries by simply mimicking (and/or adopting through colonial inheritance) the organisational forms' of a European country.[27] There is growing recognition among those with long experience of the development industry that such methods rarely lead to success or have even 'in fact been a root cause of the deep problems encountered by developing countries seeking to deliver key public services to their citizens'.[28]

Throughout sub-Saharan Africa, people who no longer have access to properly equipped clinics or hospitals have recourse to traditional healers, who at their best may provide herbal remedies and psycho-spiritual healing but who in the worst cases do more harm than good by plying people with purgatives that are sometimes made from industrial cleaning agents. Where state courts and tribunals have ceased to exist or are too expensive for most pockets, people may have recourse to oracles, trial by ordeal or other quasi-traditional methods. These are cases where the informal or 'shadow' aspects of governance are actually more real than the formal ones. The emergence of shadow states even finds an echo in Botswana, normally regarded as Africa's star performer, classified by the World Bank in the first division for economic growth, with an average of over 7 per cent growth per year for twenty-five years and a continuous history of multiparty elections. Botswana has one of the highest income inequalities in the world, with 47 per cent of the population living below the poverty line.[29]

Hundreds of millions of Africans, making a living in circuits that have little or no existence in terms of the formal texts and conventions of a bureaucratic state, are described by social scientists as living in the informal sector, but to many people it hardly appears to be informal at all. It is just the only possible way of doing things. It is notoriously difficult to gather any reliable statistics on the informal sector, but its existence is the only explanation for the fact that hundreds of millions of Africans manage to survive despite earning less than a dollar per day according to statisticians. The official figures are nothing less than 'mad' in the opinion of the president of a mobile phone company in Niger. 'People have more money than the UN says', he asserts,[30] and he is surely correct. In similar vein, it is worth noting, since there are so many misperceptions on the point, that while the poor generally fall outside the ambit of the formal economy almost entirely (whereas the rich and powerful maintain their position by working at the nodes of formal and informal networks), this does not mean they are untouched by international influences. The poor, too, buy imported consumer goods, although in their case this often means second-hand clothes cast off by people in North America and Europe. Even Africa's poorest people usually have access to radio, and sometimes to television and even mobile phones. All except those living in very remote areas are directly and immediately affected by changes in international economic conditions, such as by way of food prices. An attachment to the global economy through markets rather than through direct rule was one of the most profound effects of colonial government. At the high point of colonial rule, the great political economist Karl Polanyi noted how it was above all the spread of minted currencies that was binding the rest of the world to Europe. 'This effect of the establishment of a labour market is conspicuously apparent in colonial regions today', he noted. 'The natives are to be forced to make a living by selling their labour'.[31]

The emergence of shadow states is one reason why attempts by aid donors to identify 'drivers of change', defined in terms of policies or structures that are expected to produce particular outcomes, are often misplaced. Quite a few African governments are more or less incapable of implementing any policy at all in the conventional sense because power has ceased to be primarily bureaucratic in nature. The US National Intelligence Council actually defines a 'failed state' as one 'where basic government institutions have decayed to the point where they cannot make governance decisions'.[32]

The existence of a shadow state alongside its official double is perhaps most stark in oil-producing countries. Sated by wealth that is channelled through the state itself in the form of the taxes and royalties paid by oil companies, political elites have the means to satisfy those networks within society that are important for the maintenance of power and key organisations like the army and the police. They can more or less ignore the bulk of the population, living on a pittance, for as long as the masses do not threaten to support some sort of insurrection. For a government flush with oil money, it is not even worth the effort of taxing the general population, since that would necessitate establishing an efficient bureaucracy that may become the power-base for a rival.[33] Recent analyses of Africa's leading oil producers, Nigeria and Angola, suggest that they have many of the hallmarks of so-called 'failed states', yet they are dominated by entrenched elites that show every sign of being able to reproduce their system of rule for as long as there is oil to sell, in other words for decades. The Angolan government, in particular, has a healthy income and presides over a fast-growing economy. It has ambitious plans for the development of infrastructure, financial services and agriculture. It has some of the most effective armed forces in Africa, which have in recent years intervened in the Democratic Republic of Congo, in Congo-Brazzaville, and as far away as Côte d'Ivoire. Yet, with perhaps the sole exception of the oil company Sonangol, most civilian arms of state administration are massively inefficient and ineffective.[34] Angola is a prime example of a 'failed state' that is, in effect, remarkably successful.[35]

Signs of the emergence of shadow states could be seen already in the 1980s. At that time, commentators often described the period they were living through as a lost decade for African development. This description was not inaccurate, but it was profoundly misleading. By drawing attention only to the chimera of development, its use at that time diverted attention from the fact that what was happening in or to Africa was an early indicator of enduring changes for the world as a whole. The travails of African states were too often regarded as an anomaly or a special case, reflecting

Africa's place in the Western imagination in a time-zone all of its own. It would have been more perceptive to see Africa's problems thirty years ago as an early sign of a challenge to the global system of government. Only with the current worldwide financial crisis, with its epicentre in the US, have many observers begun to wonder whether the system of world governance established after 1945, cast in the American image and reflecting America's dominant role in the world, may be heading into serious difficulties. From an African point of view, there have been signs for years already that the post-World War Two international system has been fraying at the edges.

Prior to the 2007 financial crisis some Western writers with long experience of high-level policy-making were detecting the emergence of 'market-states' or post-modern states in some of the world's richest countries. They meant by this that the purpose of the state is no longer the old nationalist aim of representing an entire nation, but rather of ensuring that the rules of a market society are respected.[36] It remains to be seen whether this analysis will survive the current financial crisis, since Western governments have had to pump such huge amounts of money into markets in order to protect them from their own excesses. While the state bureaucracies of Angola or Nigeria are far less efficient than those of the world's richest countries, all have been subject to the same pressure to allow market forces to do their work. Even in the rich world, states wield a power that is increasingly discontinuous, and African states are thus not altogether peculiar in this regard. African countries are perhaps not so unusual as they often appear.

So, we are all part of the same world. But it is one in which people hold very different views about how exactly reality is constituted. For African leaders to be accepted as legitimate, they must be conscious of the ways their people think about the world, and the leaders themselves may share these worldviews to greater or lesser extent.

Religious Worldviews

Everyone knows that the world consists not only of tangible objects and visible actions but also of invisible entities. It is commonly accepted, for example, that social structures exist although they are invisible to the naked eye. Equally invisible are trust, confidence and legitimacy, all of them intangible forces or qualities that are of great importance in shaping societies and economies.

Capital is another invisible entity. Capital 'consists of the productive economic aspects of the things people own, which are ordinarily invisible to the naked eye'.[37] It is not to be confused with money, one of several forms in which capital can become manifest. Money is tangible when it takes the form of coins and banknotes, although these days most of the money supply of a rich country does not consist even of banknotes, but of electronic credit. Whatever form it takes, money derives value from the great mass of habits, ideas and laws—enforced by institutions—that societies need if they are to turn the human and physical resources they contain into capital. According to a leading anthropologist, money is 'only an extreme and specialised type of ritual'.[38]

Even today, when Africa is receiving the highest levels of investment in its history, it lacks capital. More than anything else, capital finds it difficult to gather in Africa because of the weakness of its legal and financial systems. This is more than a technical failure, but a reflection of a distinctive worldview that shapes Africa's economic and political environment. Throughout most of Africa's history, its people's ideas about a wide range of transactions have been conceived less often as an invisible world framed in terms of capital and other entities recognised by economists than in terms of one inhabited by beings or forces of a spiritual nature. In some respects the difference between these two modes is not great. Spirits, where they are perceived to exist, are actually rather similar to capital. Both spirits and capital are abstract concepts that can be made active, and used for material purposes, through a dense network of human activities, conventions and institutions that have evolved in conformity with people's worldviews.

So central are spirits to Africa's various religious traditions that religion in Africa may be provisionally defined as 'a belief in the existence of an invisible world, distinct but not separate from the visible one, that is home to spiritual beings with effective powers over the material world'.[39] At the same time, Africa's religious traditions show a striking lack of dogma, which is related to the fact that they had no written texts until very recently, with only a few exceptions like the ancient Christian kingdom of Ethiopia and the Islamic tradition borne by traders along the Nile valley, the maritime trade routes of East Africa and the caravan routes of the Sahel.

It would be hard to emphasise too strongly the importance of Africa's oral heritage in matters reflecting society. The lack of writing in most African communities before the twentieth century has had a formative effect on how people have governed themselves and how they have thought of themselves in regard to the natural world. In the past, knowledge was transmitted in most areas exclusively by word and gesture rather than by writing. Government was mediated by similar means, to the extent that, as the historian John Lonsdale puts it, 'the most distinctively African contribution to human history could be said to have been precisely the civilised art of living fairly peaceably together *not* in states'.[40]

States and written records have been so central to Western traditions of communal life and religious practice over centuries that it is hard to conceive of societies that could cohere without them. Yet it is perhaps the most important aspect of Africa's history. It is when we investigate how African societies succeeded in reproducing themselves for so many centuries, often without entities that a modern European would recognise as states, and without written law, that the importance of religion becomes clear. The idea that the boundary between the visible and invisible worlds is fluid and permeable is fundamentally different from the highly systematised religion that evolved in the West over centuries, regulated by professional priests and clerics by reference to written texts. In most African societies before colonial times, legal authority did not stem from scripture. It was not independent of the people, but was discerned by them through interaction with the spirit world via prayer, divination and other ritual techniques. In this tradition, the invisible world is extraordinarily intimate, since it is perceived as inseparable from the visible one. It is widely thought to be possible even for non-specialists to enter the invisible world temporarily, for example in the form of spirit possession or religious trance. Until the establishment of bureaucratic rule in colonial times it was normal for Africans to regulate matters of government, law and justice by reference to the spirit world.

'Prior to colonialism', a Nigerian criminologist has observed, 'Africans primarily saw crime as a threat to religious morality and responded with rituals for the purification of the community for the benefit of all'.[41] In terms of a modern sensibility, legal regimes of this sort were not always benign, since a threat to religiously based morality could arise from the breaking of a taboo, and the punishment for an offence of an essentially ritual nature could be enslavement or death, penalties whose severity reflected the gravity of breaking rules that were considered to reflect the cosmic order.

Constantly subject to reinterpretation, free of dogma because unwritten, African religious ideologies have been remarkably flexible and absorptive throughout their history. Africans have maintained this open-minded approach in their encounters with religions of the book, with the result that Islam has spread widely in the form of Sufi mysticism and Christianity has been interpreted by thousands of Independent Churches. Even nowadays, when the Qur'an and the Bible are widely read, Africans generally continue to emphasise personal experience and the personal interpretation of these texts rather than submitting to the authority of professional clerics and theologians. It is for this reason that African cultural interpretations of the world religions have often been described by intellectuals in terms of syncretism and by theologians in terms of heterodoxy. It has often been assumed that personal communication with the invisible world will gradually recede with development, as writing supplants religious communication as the main form of organising society. But there is no reason to believe that this is an inevitable process.

Pursuing this line of inquiry, we may perceive some of the effect of Africa's incorporation since the late nineteenth century into a world community that is formally regulated by written texts in the form of laws and treaties and into a world of religion that is based on the interpretation of scripture. To appreciate the enormity of this innovation, it is helpful to place matters in a deep chronological context. The French philosopher Rémi Brague has drawn attention to the historical significance of the ancient Middle Eastern practice of setting down the law in writing as an example of a cultural choice made millennia ago that has been of decisive importance for the world today.[42] Associated from an early period with religious scripture, writing created an authority that is independent of the people.[43] Accordingly, in European traditions of both church and state, a law has force because it emanates from an authority. This does not sit easily with the view generally held throughout many centuries of Africa's history during which, as one theologian expresses it, 'the African believe[s] that, ontologically, every being has its own natural law, as well as its own essence. This law…is the normality [of] its functioning which is grounded in the essence of that being'.[44] In this reading, every being in our world, animal, mineral or spiritual, is what it is. Wisdom consists in discerning the true properties of each thing. The morally right course of action is the one that proceeds from a correct identification of the natural law in a specific context; the context in which morality is discerned is invariably a social one. Hence, according to the Ghanaian philosopher Kwasi Wiredu, 'one of the safest generalisations about African ways of thought is that morality is founded therein purely upon the necessity for the reciprocal adjustment of the interests of the individual to the interests of the community'. Moral rightness or wrongness is understood 'in terms of human interests'.[45] Most other philosophers who have written on African concepts of morality agree on the importance of their relationship to collective well-being.[46]

In short, in African societies, shaped over many generations by orality, the moral value of given acts—their essential legitimacy—is judged less by reference to written texts emanating from an external authority than by reference to spiritual powers. This contrasts with the history of the Western world where, since the eighteenth century, law has come to be seen as a set of rules no longer revealed by God through scripture, but produced by a society that organises itself.[47] It is in this last sense that development experts exhort African governments to institute the rule of law. African politicians have contrived to govern in two modes at once, by reference to the written law of the state and the situational requirements of societies steeped in oral tradition and spirit belief.

Ever since the imposition of colonial administration, the authority of written law has faced a problem of legitimacy or credibility. Nationalist politicians assumed that this was only because colonial rule was itself illegitimate, but the problem goes deeper. In many

African societies people have not been brought up to believe that the law created by legislators and enforced by states has overwhelming moral force, particularly in cases where the elites running those states are regarded as avaricious and self-serving. Many people may continue to seek justice in other locations, such as through consultation of oracles or by divination.

The effect of having rival sources of law, one based on the authority of a bureaucratic state, the other based on the many varieties of religion on offer, has been to produce 'a cacophony of chaotic existence', in the words of a Nigerian scholar,[48] the consequences of which extend throughout religion and government. In some circumstances, people may come to think that untamed or even malign spiritual forces have taken a temporary grip on society, since communities have lost control of the techniques by which they have traditionally regulated the invisible forces that pervade them. The feeling is similar to the panic induced in a capitalist society by a collapse in credit, which has the effect not only of destroying jobs but also of undermining people's confidence that they control or even understand what is happening. The feeling that people have lost control of the invisible forces that shape their lives can be easier to perceive than to describe. 'Within the local experiential frame', notes an anthropologist with particular knowledge of Kinshasa, the capital city of Congo, 'the double that lurks underneath the surface of the visible world somehow seems to have taken the upper hand'.[49]

'No condition is permanent' is a phrase commonly written on lorries and taxis in West Africa. Societies formed by centuries of orality are indeed extraordinarily flexible. Their sense of transience can be a source of great strength and adaptability, as it equips people with the ability 'to face life with patience, endurance, and perseverance'.[50] On the other hand, the absence of a socially and politically validated means of taming the invisible forces that society unleashes on itself may also fill people with a sense that their universe has lost its points of reference. People who are unconfident of their control of the invisible world become inclined to fulfilment in forms rapid and fleeting.[51]

In reaction to the weakness of positive law and its failure to deliver order in so many African countries, some people seek a solution in the restoration of what they see as a pure tradition. In Muslim areas this takes the form of a demand for sharia law. Christians may opt for styles of Pentecostal religion in which the Bible is the only point of reference.[52] Others seek to revive traditional community religions. In any event, people continue to judge the moral value of human action by reference to the spirit world far more readily than they do by referring to a legal system that is remote and often deficient when it is not downright corrupt. Social and political developments are also interpreted in this way, by reference to scripture or by ritual means.

The prevalence of religious thought in Africa is often described by Western academics in terms of a religious revival caused by globalisation and uneven development.[53] However it is not strictly accurate to talk of a religious revival since this implies that there was a period in which religion was dormant. It is true that religion played little formal role in African public life during the period from the 1940s to the late twentieth century when colonial and postcolonial governments were making a determined attempt to remodel public life on secular, bureaucratic lines, but religious activity within society itself does not seem to have declined during that period. Religion has never ceased to be present in African societies. It has simply gained in public importance as political life has assumed the characteristics of the shadow states described earlier and as the colonial way of making society legible recedes into the past. Since religious practice takes the audible and visual forms of words and actions, it is no surprise that it has adapted to circumstances in which states have been reconfigured, economies have been deregulated and international migration has gained in importance.

People do not think religiously because they are unable or untrained to interpret the world in any other way. They do it because it is a mode of understanding the world and oneself within a single frame of reference, with deep historical roots, connecting people to their society and their environment. There is no reason to suppose that education and development will produce secular societies in which religion fades away or becomes an entirely personal affair.

If the financial crisis that descended on the world in 2007–8 had any positive aspects at all, then perhaps it was to cause at least some people in the developed world to reflect about money, prosperity and wealth more deeply than usual. 'Finance is about the unknowable future', the banker's newspaper, the *Financial Times* informs us. 'This makes it vulnerable to the human frailties: greed, fear, ignorance and fraud'.[54] Finance is not something inherent in human beings, like speech. It is a technique that has developed historically, and it is possible to identify in detail how this has occurred in particular societies. In the history of Western Europe, starting about four centuries ago, finance came to occupy some of the functions previously taken by religion as faith in credit gained in importance and eventually supplanted faith in the deity. Theologians and clerics ceased to be the key interpreters of the future, to be replaced ultimately by economists. Money was applied to time in the form of weekly salaries and hourly rates. In modern economies it is applied to 'that redemptive eternity that economists call "the long run".'[55] In other parts of the world, religion and finance have had different historical relationships. In these countries, people think about the future, and try to keep greed and other vices under control, by techniques other than money, credit and statistics alone. Africans poor and rich live in such societies, and power and authority are regulated accordingly.

There is a wealth of literature on the relationship of money and society even in the classical springs of Western learning, among the ancient Greeks. The Greek *polis* of the sixth century BCE is said to have been one of the first societies in history to be pervaded by money, and the effects of this financial revolution preoccupied the philosophers and tragedians of antiquity.[56] Like Africans to this day, the Greeks had a vibrant oral culture in which the invisible world was represented as the home of identifiable beings with which humans could enter into dialogue. Religious communication was a means for people to shape their own destiny, by means of divination and oracles.

The Greeks had several myths concerning the corrosive effects that a monetary economy can have on society. The best known is that of King Midas, who had the power to turn everything he touched into gold, and who became utterly frustrated as a result. Less known, but perhaps more appropriate to the twenty-first century, is the myth of Erysichthon, a man who cut down a sacred woodland grove in order to build a banqueting hall. Erysichthon was punished by the gods for his insolence by being made insatiable. Labouring under the curse that he had brought upon himself, Erysichthon could not be satisfied by any amount of food. He gave his daughter in marriage to one suitor after another but she always returned home childless, making him unable to ensure the future through the fertility of his offspring. Permanently hungry and unable to provide for the future, in the end, Erysichthon eats himself.

As Richard Seaford notes, like many Greek myths, this one can be applied to modern times. Some 2,500 years after Greek thinkers came to appreciate some of the characteristic effects of money, advanced capitalist societies find themselves trapped in a sequence resembling Erysichthon's self-destruction. They are unable to abstain from seeking constant economic growth, yet they know that this will stimulate the very effects that will cause destruction in the foreseeable future. The most advanced capitalist economies have progressively lost the ability to regulate their own consumption other than by a self-negation that they find it difficult to exercise because they have abandoned the idea that there are external constraints on mankind's ability to shape the world. The myth of Erysichthon is one that is particularly suited to reflection on global warming and environmental destruction, since the moral of the story is that the exploitation of nature produces a pathological insatiability that sacrifices the future and in the end destroys itself.[57]

If we include Africa in this context, then the religious-philosophical mode of thinking about the world that is so widespread there can no longer be taken, as it habitually was during the mid-twentieth century golden age of modernisation and development, as just another habit that Africans must lose if they are to proceed into the future. The technocracy promoted by the development industry stems from a conviction that human societies must control themselves and their environment by the application of technology and reason. Convinced that the invisible world of capital and debt can be regulated by reason and mathematical calculation alone, development policy-makers and experts have had little patience with cosmologies that suppose a dialogue between mankind and the invisible forces of the world, and between individuals and society, in any other form. But there is now irrefutable evidence that think-ing about the world in a religious mode is not in itself an obstacle to technical progress. Asia shows many examples of sophisticated academics and activists who are able to act on the basis of ideas embedded in indigenous philosophy and religion.[58] Religion may even be a source of new instruments for the management of society and its relationship to nature that are of increasing relevance in an age of shortages and environmental challenges. For, while Africa has little responsibility for the accumulation of greenhouse gases in the atmosphere, it is threatened by climate change. With the Sahara desert expanding southwards, water shortages in some regions, and a growing population to support, this is a matter requiring attention not only in the technical forms that dominate current debates.[59] Proposals for dealing with climate change on a market basis, such as by creating carbon credits that may be traded, probably will add more grist to the mill of political corruption. Activists national and international are most likely to achieve more durable results in Africa by engaging with religious networks.

5

MATTERS OF STATE

The sovereign status acquired by most African countries in the 1960s was not a milestone in a process of becoming less dependent on the rich world. On the contrary, as measured by debt, imports and a number of other yardsticks, Africa's economic and financial dependence was established in the second quarter of the twentieth century and has grown steadily ever since. The much-vaunted independence of African states is an ideology rather than a description of a political or economic mode of existence.

If the combination of sovereign status plus dependence has nevertheless lasted for half a century, it is for a reason. It creates advantages for some Africans and their foreign partners. But it also comes at a cost. Not least, it is demeaning to the point that hundreds of millions of people have become convinced that under the current dispensation they cannot take control of their own destiny in the ways most familiar to them.

It is useful to bear this observation in mind in considering the wider effects of the financial crisis that began in 2007. Every commentator has noted China's arrival as a superpower, although the US will surely remain the world's foremost military power for the foreseeable future, vulnerable to irregular warfare but not to conventional operations. The dollar is currently irreplaceable as the world's key marker of value, used for pricing international commodities. Whatever else happens to the US's debt-burdened economy, the country is likely to remain a powerhouse of knowledge and innovation. China is a country without democracy or freedom of speech. It is unclear whether it is capable of inventing and developing a new Google.

Since the onset of the crisis, media pundits and television-friendly academics have been offering practical suggestions for changes in the institutional arrangements that govern international affairs. Most of these go in the general direction of loosening the grip on international institutions maintained since 1945 by the USA and the Europeans and increasing the representation of emerging powers, notably in Asia. In regard to the UN Security Council, for years there has been pressure to expand its permanent membership, 'deep-frozen in time',[1] from the present five countries, the victors of a world war that ended over sixty years ago. But every specific proposal for reform of the Security Council encounters formidable obstacles. Meanwhile, some commentators call for the US and China to form a Group of Two to meet regularly with a view to managing the world's finances. Going in the opposite direction as far as size is concerned, the Group of Eight major economies has expanded into a Group of Twenty (G-20) whose meetings in fact are attended by more than twenty countries, including China, India, Brazil and South Africa.

In practice, the most seemingly monolithic institutions are constantly changing even when their formal rules and external appearance remain untouched. After all, institutions consist of people. Each new generation brings fresh ideas about the right and proper way to do things even as the old guard transmits some of its knowledge and working practices to the newcomers, providing continuity. In the case of the international financial institutions that were established at a conference held in Bretton Woods, New Hampshire, in 1944, the gradual change in their global role has been a matter of comment for a long time already. Conceived with a mission to restore Europe after the devastation of the Second World War, originally operating within a system of fixed currency exchange rates based on the price of gold, they have assumed other functions as time has gone by. In Africa during the last years of the Cold War, the Bretton Woods institutions, dominated by the US and Europe, became enforcers of capitalist orthodoxy. So rigid did their thinking become that one analyst dubbed it 'scientific capitalism'[2] in a parody of the old Soviet concept of scientific socialism.

Actually, this barb is closer to the mark than may appear: Strobe Talbott, a senior official of the Clinton administration, recalls Larry Summers, at that time an under secretary at the US Treasury and later a top aide to President Obama, telling Russia's prime minister that the rules governing IMF lending reflected the 'immutable principles of economics, which operated in a way similar to the rules of physics'.[3]

Asian leaders have not forgotten how a regional financial problem in 1997 was mismanaged by an IMF then dominated by the West, with massive capital outflows leading to the downfall of the president of Indonesia. For Africans, the overwhelming experience of the international financial institutions over the last thirty years has been of Western-dominated institutions that oblige client-countries to adopt their allegedly scientific policies, leaving little room for manoeuvre. Little room, that is, other than dissembling, a tactic often used by African governments as they strive to present to institutional diplomats and bankers a correct array of formal institutions and policies that in fact screens a set of political practices better adapted to their domestic requirements.

The International Community

The vestigial links between Africa and its former colonial masters, none of them any more than middle-ranking powers these days, are fast being eroded by the new Sino-African relationship. Recalling its own past as a victim of imperialist aggression, the Chinese government proclaims its respect for the sovereignty of small states and its lack of imperialist designs in Africa. This should not blind onlookers to the fact that China, too, exercises power beyond its borders and that even within its frontiers it has some of the characteristics of an empire, as Tibetans may affirm.

The words 'imperial' and 'empire' are generally regarded as pejorative since they are at odds with the criteria of democracy and self-government that have been officially paramount since 1945. In reality, empire (in the loosest out of a very broad range of meanings attached to the word) can quite easily be seen as neither more nor less than the default condition of the world.[4] It is not very useful, therefore, to suggest that one form of empire—dominated by the West, in cahoots with the international financial institutions—is retreating in Africa, only to be replaced by another, this time under Chinese domination. Equally, it would be naïve to suppose that China, simply because it has a nice line in rhetoric, is not committed to securing its own interests in Africa. If we are contemplating the likely future, it is more to the point to wonder how China might indeed pursue its interests, and in what emerging international context.

It is helpful to consider this matter in historical perspective. For centuries, African relationships with an international order originally conceived by Europeans, ever growing in its reach, have been shaped by certain realities of which perhaps the most important has been the arrangements that Africans have made to govern themselves. Over the long term, governance in Africa has been notable for the relative absence of states, as we have seen, and for many centuries, foreigners wanting to transact commercial or diplomatic business had to adapt to the fact that there were no literate, record-keeping bureaucracies in most parts of the sub-continent to the south of the Sahara.

In the mercantilist age, European navies fought each other for possession of trading-posts on Africa's coasts, sometimes swapping them with each other when hostilities were over. Fort Jesus at Mombasa on the Kenya coast, Elmina castle in Ghana and Gorée island in Senegal, favourites of Western tourists, are all visible reminders of the slave trade. Histories of slavery and anti-slavery binding Africa, Europe and North America produced settlements in Freetown and Monrovia that were at the beginning of the national histories of Sierra Leone and Liberia. The history of the slave trade and of humanitarian intervention became embedded in the national DNA of several other African countries as well. The Scottish missionary David Livingstone remains a national hero in Malawi. The Italian-French explorer Savorgnan de Brazza is a cult figure in Brazzaville, the city that bears his name. There is a direct line of descent from the European humanitarians of the past, through generations of missionaries, geographers, adventurers and ethnographers, to the aid and development workers of today.

Already in the mercantilist age, Europeans tended to prefer doing business in Africa with centralised authorities. 'I find that the terms and prices of trade are scarce to be settled, but where there is a king, who has a settled authority to back and maintain what is concluded on with him', noted a British slave trader as long ago as 1738.[5] Over time, the interaction between Europeans, carrying with them notions of political order connected to a state, and Africans, with different ideas, became inextricable from the self-image of the ensemble nowadays called the international community, influencing its various techniques of action. When Africa was partitioned into spheres of influence, at Berlin in 1884–5, it was by decision of the Concert of Powers, as it was then called, a collective with Europe at its core. During the twentieth century, some African territories were placed under the formal authority of the international community in the form of mandates held by the League of Nations and the United Nations. More recently, many African states have had key aspects of their policy determined by the international financial institutions and quite a few of them are dependent on international aid for half their budgets. The Republic of Liberia, founded by American émigrés, has been put in various forms of receivership or under international tutelage no fewer than two dozen times since 1870 and its rulers have, over generations, become adept at circumventing international controls and turning various forms of external intervention to their financial and factional advantage. At least twelve African countries in recent years have hosted international peacekeeping forces. While a great deal of political rhetoric concerning Africa refers to an ideal of autonomy, the reality has been thoroughly infused with a practice of dependence that is actually at the core of how many of the continent's states and political systems work. Dependence has often been not on an individual foreign patron, but on the international community as a whole. Before colonial rule, there was a concert of powers; after colonialism, there was an international community.

At the heart of this relationship between Africa and a putative collective of world states is the problem foreigners have had dealing with societies that have historically had few of the hallmarks of European-type states. Victorian intellectuals conceived of the state as 'the ultimate, most civilised form of organising social and political life',[6] the necessary vector for all historical change. Since Europeans by the late nineteenth century could hardly imagine their interests being safeguarded or their aspirations realised without a

121

state organised on lines they understood, they increasingly 'had no respect for a community which neither was a nation nor a colony of a nation', the pan-Africanist intellectual Edward Blyden wrote at the start of the colonial period.[7] The European urge to create states in Africa was related to an increasingly specific European notion of utility and propriety in matters of society and politics generally. In regard to war, for example, in the age of European nationalism before 1914, this was considered proper when it was conducted between nation-states accepted as members of an international community that respected formal rules, such as declarations of the commencement of hostilities, peace treaties and the respect of non-combatants. As far as populations outside the community of states were concerned, however, European powers believed they were justified in annexing and conquering these at will. They simply 'never thought of Africans as sovereign peoples',[8] since Africans were deemed not yet to have advanced to a historical phase commensurate with sovereignty. In warfare against irregular forces, Europeans permitted themselves to commit atrocities that would be beyond the pale in wars against the national armies of recognised states. Rights, like history itself, were thought to be transmitted only by states.

Contrary to popular belief, the Berlin conference that partitioned Africa in 1884–5 did not actually mark 'the beginning of a full-blooded drive for African territory' by drawing precise borders on the map of Africa.[9] Rather, it reached an agreement as to which regions of Africa were within the sphere of influence of various European powers. It was only in the two or three decades following Berlin that the new masters endeavoured to institute effective government over their vast new territories and to mark their exact borders. Those indigenous states whose sovereignty the Europeans grudgingly recognised, namely Ethiopia and Liberia, were obliged to do the same. It is a matter of historical fact, then, that most African states were not consolidated in their present form until the early twentieth century. It was just a couple of generations later, after the end of the Second World War, that they were being incorporated into the emerging worldwide ensemble of sovereign states.

The recognition of sovereignty in most European colonial territories in the years after 1945 may have seemed to some as the simple extension of an existing principle, but it actually marked a major change in the system that European powers had developed to govern their relations over a period of centuries. The modern state system is generally reckoned to begin with the Treaty of Westphalia of 1648, which brought an end to the devastating wars that had ravaged Germany for thirty years by establishing the principle that one ruler should not interfere in the internal affairs of another. The Westphalia system was thus based on the legal recognition of existing states. The test was empirical: where a state-like entity clearly existed, it should be recognised. Thereafter, during the evolution of the international community that emerged in Europe three and a half centuries ago and expanded to global level, such exotic political growths as the empire of Japan and the kingdom of Madagascar were somewhat reluctantly recognised by Europeans as members of the family of states. Rulers of state-like entities learned that their existence could be formally recognised if they subscribed to the main requirements of the club they aspired to join. At the same time, the Asian and African experience of contact with the West produced its own internal dynamic, as new generations assimilated Western ideas, translated them into local cultural terms and sought to apply them in their own countries, as in Japan after the Meiji restoration of 1868.

After 1945, by contrast, the empirical test of statehood became far less important. The operative principle enshrined in international law was now the right of nations to sovereign status. This was a subtle but distinct shift, since it meant that if nationalists could demonstrate the existence of a nation, with a political will of its own, the United Nations was in theory bound to recognise the existence of a new state.[10]

The realisation that their African territories were heading towards a new status as sovereign states within a short time came as a powerful incentive to colonial regimes after 1945 to create the institutions of state appropriate for modern systems of government. Whereas the ambition to improve Africa was inherent in the self-proclaimed civilising mission that European powers invoked to justify their rule over Africa, this aspiration now took a narrowly defined technocratic form as a process of social and financial engineering conceived by policy-makers, informed by social scientists and implemented by bureaucrats. As governments throughout Africa adopted policies of economic expansion, it became increasingly clear that the continent's emerging states would need to be endowed with the technical capacities commensurate with the juridical sovereignty they were set to acquire. This was the headlong rush to independence that swept Africa along in the 1950s and early 1960s.

The leading actor in the system that emerged in the post-war world, the US, was itself born out of a struggle for independence from a colonial power. To many American policy-makers, dismantling the European colonial empires not only represented a just principle, but was also calculated to open up vast new territories to their country's economic influence. The Soviet Union enthusiastically endorsed this approach as long as its own official myth—to the effect that it was a post-nationalist union of emancipated peoples rather than a Russian empire—was not questioned. The archives of the old Soviet intelligence and security service, the KGB, reveal that the Soviet government came to see the third world as the key to a global victory in the cold war.[11]

Before the late nineteenth century, great powers had been able to regard with relative equanimity a world where the vast basin of the Congo river and many other inland areas of Africa were blank spaces on a map. Although the cartography was vague, these were in reality inhabited areas, with histories and political dynamics of their own. Through the act of colonisation, they became the charges of the various colonial powers. Decolonisation turned them into elements of the world community of states. One of the effects of colonisation, therefore, was to turn the politics of Africa into a formal concern of the major powers inasmuch as the latter stood at the apex of an international system of governance.

Fragile States

In the last quarter of the twentieth century, many of Africa's new states lost a number of the attributes that they had so recently acquired during the frenzied period of state-making after 1945. Nowadays, international diplomats and businesspeople generally regard only a handful of states south of the Sahara as functioning normally. Botswana, Mauritius and South Africa are the foremost in this category. Other states are conventionally seen as on the road to development: Ghana is a current favourite, with Zambia, Mali and a few others receiving honourable mentions. Others go in and out of favour, like Côte d'Ivoire (once a French donor darling) and Uganda (ditto for the US and the UK). The rest are considered more or less dysfunctional because they are unable to provide the public goods expected of them under international law. In development-speak, it is customary to regard deficient states as suffering a temporary setback on their road to progress, but this is an unsatisfactory point of view for anyone who does not accept that there is a single path to prosperity and that history moves through predictable phases.

For some time, many observers found it difficult to appreciate the true nature of what was happening to African states because their thinking had been conditioned by the particular circumstances of the Cold War. As long as the Cold War lasted, imploding states were cushioned from the full consequences of their condition by superpower support. In Liberia for example, a leading US client in West Africa, the old Americo-Liberian political order associated with the True Whig Party was overthrown in 1980, but the ramshackle and murderous government of Samuel Doe continued to receive extravagant US support for as long as the Soviet Union was deemed to be a threat, making the implosion of the state appear as a temporary aberration. Then, an invasion by the motley force of dissident soldiers and foreign adventurers led by Charles Taylor in December 1989 became Africa's first full-scale emergency after the fall of the Berlin Wall just a few weeks previously. Immediately it was made brutally clear that the rules of the international game had changed in the interim, as the US government decided that there was no longer any need for it to prop up any Liberian government. In effect, the US decision condemned Liberia to years of war as rival politicians slugged it out for control of the country in the absence of any external power willing and able to impose its will.[12] Conflicts in Ethiopia and Somalia were similarly allowed to unthaw from their Cold War freeze after 1989. Conversely, South Africa's last apartheid government, quick to realise that the whole world had changed with the end of the Cold War, seized the initiative by unbanning the main opposition organisation, the ANC in February 1990.

As the consequences of imploding states and superpower abandonment began to dawn on foreign diplomats, a new vocabulary emerged. Distressed countries with dysfunctional bureaucracies became known to Western policy-makers as 'failed states', a phrase popularised by US secretary of state Madeleine Albright, who used it on 24 January 1997 at her first press conference.[13] A decade later, in diplomatic circles this expression had been replaced by 'fragile states', apparently for no reason other than that it sounds more respectful. Some years ago the UK's department for international development estimated the number of such states, with scientific precision, at forty-six, of which most were in Africa,[14] or about one quarter of the world's total number of sovereign states. 'Fragile' states are now an established feature of the diplomatic world.

For some years, the US government believed that it was not threatened by fragile states in distant parts of the world. It left not only Liberia to its own devices, but also Afghanistan. This illusion was punctured by the attacks of 11 September 2001, which caused policymakers to realise that, whatever name they give to states that do not or can not fulfil their international obligations, violent politics and dysfunctional bureaucracies cannot be ignored with impunity by leading powers even if they are half a world away. Among African countries the best illustration that 'fragile' states matter to just about everyone is Somalia, where the lack of a working state is of concern not only to its neighbours, but to every country in the world that has a merchant fleet or that relies on oil transported through the Suez canal. The US, the European Union, China, India, Japan, Malaysia, Russia and others have all sent warships to Somali waters to protect merchant shipping against piracy organised by Somali military-economic entrepreneurs.

The vocabulary of state failure is dominated by mechanical images derived from engineering, a sure sign that commentators and diplomats who talk this way are thinking about states in a formal, institutional sense that pays little regard to the informal aspects of government that are so important in Africa. International observers and policy-makers intent on developing Africa are often persuaded by their own ideology of progress that traditional forms of governance are destined to wither away. However, not only have many traditional institutions and practices failed to disappear, but they have actually become more important since the liberal economic reforms imposed by the international financial institutions in the 1980s loosened the formal grip of the state. All of today's 'fragile' states, while unable to deliver such public goods as a countrywide control of violence or a truly national policy in almost any field, are nevertheless home to longstanding and pervasive structures and practices through which power is exercised, often in ways that are not immediately obvious to people born and raised in Europe or North America. This is no doubt the main reason why international diplomats and development administrators have tended to misread shadow states, often detecting a political void where power in fact takes consistent forms associated with networks that have real historical roots. For some years leading international officials actually interpreted the shedding of bureaucratic capacity in African states enthusiastically, seeing it as consonant with liberal economic theory and failing to appreciate what it was doing to the social and political fabric.

So much comment on Africa focuses on what the continent does not have, such as efficient state bureaucracies and the rule of law, reflecting what generations of people of European descent have regarded as normal, that it diverts attention from what African societies *do* actually have. Even when an efficient state bureaucracy is absent, power, hierarchy and even institutions may still exist. Somalia's pirates have actually established a rudimentary stock exchange in their stronghold of Haradheere, 250 kilometres northeast of Mogadishu, to fund their offshore raids. Seventy-two syndicates are represented in this organisation, of which ten are reported to have carried out successful hijackings. The syndicates listed on the stock exchange are open to public contributions. 'The shares are open to all and everybody can take part, whether personally at sea or on land by providing cash, weapons or useful materials', claimed a wealthy ex-pirate to a Reuters journalist. 'We've made piracy a community activity'.[15] He alleges that syndicates share out part of the profits made from ransoming captured ships and crews, financing local infrastructure including a hospital and schools. Somali pirates even have their own international networks, including even their own lawyers who may represent them in ransom negotiations.[16]

A process of state formation, then, can continue in the absence of a functioning bureaucracy.[17] But clearly this depends on what is meant by a state. If a state is a legal entity able to carry out the duties required of it by international treaties and by diplomatic convention, then state formation cannot continue in any positive sense when the bureaucracy is decaying. If, however, the state consists simply of 'hegemony covered with the armour of coercion', as Gramsci thought,[18] then the process of state formation may continue even when the apparatus of government is fragile in almost every regard. Most African governments thus take great pains to maintain the outward signs of statehood, since this formality remains vital for continuing international recognition of their sovereignty, even while they may make extensive use of informal methods of governance that have no legal standing or that even involve breaking the law, as in most forms of corruption. The importance of keeping up appearances was well stated by a Nigerian police chief, who said in 2004 that 'Nigeria is a distinguished member of the international community and as such we must, at all times, conform and be seen to conform with all norms, conventions and rules that are *sine qua non* to peaceful living and respectable human co-existence'.[19]

Ironically, shortly after making this pronouncement of exemplary correctness, Nigeria's most senior police officer was found guilty of embezzling a vast sum of money.[20]

Authenticity

The 'state-like' features of African states have been interwoven with traditional forms of governance or with improvised methods for a long time. In every colony, the centralised administration established by European powers depended to greater or lesser extent on the existence of African rulers wielding authority of their own. One of the most prominent of all British colonial administrators, the very Lord Lugard whom we met in Chapter One, called this Indirect Rule, which he regarded as a fundamental principle of sound colonial administration on the grounds that it was proper to keep African governance separate from European administration in order to preserve the integrity of indigenous systems. French colonial theorists and administrators, on the other hand, generally proclaimed the universal and homogenising nature of their republican tradition and appointed traditional rulers to bureaucratic positions only out of expediency. But whether hailed as a virtue or condemned as a failing, in practice all colonial systems made use of African agents, towards the end of the colonial period in senior positions of the central government. Looking back at colonial rule now, it is apparent that indirect rule, far from preserving indigenous traditions of governance intact, as Lugard intended, often had a radical effect that had not been foreseen. It permitted local rulers to dispense with many of the more subtle checks and balances that had traditionally operated.

Some analysts consider this story in terms of the rise and fall of Western-style institutions in Africa. They take the poor performance of many African states, as measured by standard indicators, as evidence that a transplanted state, imposed from outside, never really took root in African soil.[21] In this view, the imported state never did much more than coexist with an authentic African way of doing things. But, however brutal colonial administration was in many cases, strictly speaking it was never an assault on African authenticity, since this does not exist. The concept of an authentic Africa that continues through the ages, outside history and outside time, is a figment of the imagination. Its roots lie in European philosophy of the Romantic period, more specifically in the writings of Hegel.[22]

The notion of an authentic Africa was popularised by intellectuals of the colonial period, both African and foreign, whether they had ever heard of Hegel or not. It was seized upon by African nationalists as evidence of the existence of distinct nations in Africa, since after 1945 this was a prerequisite for making a successful bid for sovereign status. The claims of nationalists that African peoples had a right to govern themselves were often based on a simple inversion of the colonial prejudice that Africans were unfit for self-government on the grounds that their culture made them unsuited to run a modern state and economy. African intellectuals could reply that Africa, like every other continent, has its own genius that should be celebrated rather than regarded as an embarrassment. After the establishment of the United Nations in 1945, ushering in a world order based on a system of sovereign states extending to every continent, they could also riposte that every nation in any case had a right to sovereignty. This argument was henceforth irrefutable as it was enshrined in international law.

The romantic concept of an African authenticity embedded in culture remains a key element of African nationalist thinking to this day. Some accomplished scholars go as far as considering the slave trade, and even Islam, as external impositions on the real Africa.[23] Authenticity combines easily with another common idea, namely that the historical record of foreign intrusions on Africa's sovereignty and dignity has placed Africans in a position of powerlessness and explains their poverty. When a tendency to cultivate victimhood was discussed critically by Achille Mbembe, the former executive secretary of a leading African academic body, his views were greeted with howls of rage by many of his peers, incensed by an attack on such a central tenet of nationalist ideology,[24] although other intellectuals had made the same point before.[25]

It is easy to see why the idea of Africa as a permanent victim may strike people as valid. The continent was a source of slaves for foreign countries for centuries. Everyone has heard of the Atlantic slave trade, but it is less well known that there was also a Sahara slave trade and an Indian Ocean slave trade, both of which continued for much longer and were not much smaller in overall scale. It is also true that Africa has been a source of raw materials up to and including the massive Asian interest of today. However, there is more to this story than exploitation by foreigners. Throughout the long history of the insertion of sub-Saharan Africa into global networks of commerce and diplomacy, the royal way to political power has often been to turn external interest to one's own advantage,[26] not least in the form of whole-hearted participation in the slave trade by rulers who were able to increase their power by exchanging people for guns and consumer goods.

The slave-trader kings of two or three centuries ago were not the last political entrepreneurs with the skill to turn unequal relationships to their advantage. African politicians regularly solicit foreign intervention in their internal affairs when it suits them, including through pleas for funding, in a tradition that continues to the present day. In 2007, when a senior official of the International Criminal Court (ICC), herself an African, was asked why the ICC seemed to be pursuing only African suspects, she pointed out that the first formal investigations by the Court were instigated at the request of African states themselves.[27] Wily presidents may see in international institutions an opportunity to use the strength of an external force as leverage in struggles with domestic enemies. At other times they denounce international justice as an imperialist intrusion on the sovereignty of their countries. This is political jujitsu[28] in operation.

A representation of the relationship between indigenous and foreign traditions of governance that is more accurate than a theory of victims and exploiters, or good Africans and bad foreigners, may proceed by noting that relations between Africa and its external partners have been defined by a series of bargains whose form has changed over time, going back even before the colonial period. Radical changes in the legal dispositions governing relations between Africa and the outside world over the decades—the outlawing of the slave trade, colonial rule, protectorates, independence, UN missions—are the outward signs of these relationships. Very broadly speaking, they form two sets of implicit bargains that belong together like a simultaneous equation in mathematics. On the outward side is the relationship between African elites and the foreigners who are often so vital to their power, and on the internal side is the relationship between the same elites and the bulk of the population of their countries.[29] Whether these two broad clusters of relations are regarded as satisfactory at any particular time depends on the expectations that accompany them and the resources available for their support.

State formation, in the broadest sense, has proceeded throughout the various phases of Africa's insertion in the world, even as specific arrangements have been implemented or have declined in importance. After 1945, the convention was that African elites would maintain institutions of a type required by the international community of states to which their countries henceforth belonged and could rely on outside assistance to do this, in the form of development aid. However, any real likelihood of achieving substantive political and economic sovereignty was possible only for a brief moment in the 1960s and 1970s. The economic malaise that affected so many African countries towards the end of that period caused one government after another to go to the Bretton Woods institutions for help as their finances collapsed. The response of the international financial institutions, fired by the ideology of market fundamentalism in vogue after the election of Ronald Reagan to the US presidency in 1980, was catastrophic. A policy of radical liberalisation imposed on African clients as a condition for receiving financial help laid waste to the state apparatus so recently acquired in many countries. Those that were no longer able or willing to maintain institutions to the satisfaction of their foreign interlocutors became the 'fragile' states of today.[30] While they may look fragile to outsiders, the quality of their relationship with their own population may not be easy to determine, since it may depend largely on informal mechanisms. It is difficult to ascertain the nature of the pact between rulers and ruled when this is not reflected in the formal dispositions of the state. What donors call 'good governance' is a set of practices designed to make markets efficient, although other styles of governance may actually be compatible with economic growth.[31] 'At the heart of talk about state failure', one commentator correctly asserts, 'is the definition of what states should be, in whose interest they should function, and thus *for whom* they fail or succeed'.[32] ·

It is by no means certain that 'fragile' states will acquire or be re-endowed with the characteristics of conventional states within the foreseeable future. The world may have to get used to living with such people as the Somali pirates with their stock exchange. Strange as it may sound, the loss by some states of the effective instruments of sovereignty is not a sign that they are falling off the map of the world, but actually marks a phase in their deeper integration. A Somalia or a Guinea-Bissau does not cause anxiety because of its disconnection from world affairs but, on the contrary, on account of its role in such key concerns as the security of world shipping, the spread of Islamist violence and the drug trade. For foreigners, the main problem posed by these countries is the difficulty they pose to the relationship between African elites and foreigners with specific requirements. How is this relationship to be articulated, if it is not by a functioning state?

Interventions

The founders of the United Nations, recoiling from the shock of the Second World War and awed or appalled by the atomic bombs used in anger for the first and only time in 1945, did their utmost to design a system in which wars between states would be avoided as far as possible. New laws and mechanisms were created to prevent wars or at least keep them within limits. At least formally, African countries generally have a good record of respecting these conventions, since few have officially made war. On the other hand, they have not shied away from using unofficial methods to despoil their neighbours, particularly as the logic that has led to states becoming fragile and developing a shadow has unfolded.

Many African economies depend heavily on commodity exports. State revenues (or the income of senior officials by way of corruption) are derived largely from customs duties or other taxes on trade. This tends to generate a quasi-mercantilist logic that induces governments to secure commercial advantages by force if necessary. In the worst cases, rulers resort simply to plunder.[33] Among the many wars that scarred Africa from the late 1980s onwards (including older conflicts that mutated), hardly a single one was not supported or even instigated by rulers of neighbouring countries intent on seizing control of long-distance trade routes and valuable commodities.

Since the international system in force since 1945 denies the right of conquest, any African government that feels impelled to make war against a neighbour is obliged to do so by subterfuge. It is most likely to succeed if it can secure the diplomatic backing of at least one major power. Rwanda, for example, has manipulated violence in its giant neighbour, Congo, for years, supporting and even initiating large-scale campaigns in what has probably been the world's deadliest war in the last sixty-five years. Notwithstanding its aggression, Rwanda has had the consistent support of the US and the United Kingdom, embarrassed by how little they did to stop the 1994 genocide and intent on purging their guilt by a policy of unconditional support for the current government in Kigali.[34] In the original Westphalia system, Rwanda's right of conquest would most likely have been recognised after it had invaded Congo in

1998. Since states remain formally forbidden to annexe their neighbours' territory, the current international system has an inherent problem of regulating the rise and fall of individual powers.

Sometimes, if hostilities occur in areas that are of little outside interest, political-military challenges to states that have lost effective sovereignty take place to the general indifference of the international community. For years, there was little concern about the suffering in northern Uganda brought about by an inarticulate rebellion and a brutal government counter-insurgency campaign. From time to time humanitarian concerns attract major attention from Western media especially. An index of international concern, whether arising from challenges to strategic interests or from public sensibilities, is the increased activity by the UN Security Council. Between 1946 and 1989 it met 2,903 times and adopted 646 resolutions, or less than fifteen per year on average. In the following decade, it met 1,183 times and adopted 683 resolutions, or 64 per year.[35] A disproportionate number of these resolutions concerned Africa, addressing the problems posed by imploding states.

In principle, if the stability of the international order is threatened as a result of a domestic conflict within one of the sovereign states that are its basic components, then the ideal solution is for leaders of the international community to promote political reconciliation between the warring interest-groups involved. Accordingly, there is a long list of African crises in which outside mediators have brokered peace deals. Some have been highly effective, such as the Mozambican accords of 1992. However, it is often difficult for outside mediators to achieve lasting peace. Numerous peace deals, sometimes negotiated over many months, have collapsed after a longer or shorter period. Most worryingly, some peace accords obtained through external pressure on conflicting parties have actually encouraged even more violence by changing the balance of forces involved. The worst case in this regard was the 1993 Arusha peace accords on Rwanda, which inadvertently hastened the genocide that took place in the following year.[36] The reasons why one peace negotiation results in a durable accord while another does not vary from case to case.

The donor community generally refrains from making a real political analysis, for which it substitutes moral concern and humanitarian action. Nonetheless, there have been occasional cases of an external actor using both political action and military force in an attempt to force a solution to an intractable conflict. The British military intervention in Sierra Leone in 2000 was a striking success, saving a UN mission from disaster and hastening the end of an exceptionally nasty war, even if the political aftermath has proved more difficult. More often, a problem is foisted by the permanent members of the UN Security Council upon the United Nations Organisation itself. Between 1946 and 1990 there were twenty-four Security Council resolutions citing Chapter Seven of the UN charter, which is the most robust form of peacekeeping. Nowadays, there are roughly the same number of Chapter Seven citations every year.[37] The number of troops serving under UN colours rose from some 20,000 in 2000 to 110,000 in 2008, most of them in Africa.[38] The total cost of UN peacekeeping in 2009 may have exceeded $7.75 billion, equivalent to 1 per cent of global military spending. One quarter of this sum was paid by the USA.[39] UN peacekeeping has reached the very limits of its capacity and it is now facing its most serious challenge ever. The biggest UN peacekeeping mission at present is in the Democratic Republic of Congo, which is also where robust peacekeeping was inaugurated in the 1960s.

It is because many UN missions in Africa are required to conjure a solution to a problem that is fundamentally political in nature that they so often risk eventual failure and ignominy. UN peacekeeping missions are most effective when they simply act as a witness to a peace accord between two well-organised parties, such as in Cyprus. Such conditions never apply in the sort of imploded states that attract UN missions in ever-larger numbers. Often, a UN mission is rather cynically created by the UN Security Council as diplomatic cover in circumstances where none of the permanent members wishes to commit its own forces. It is seen as the least bad option in a situation where the breakdown of order creates a humanitarian disaster in a country that is not of the greatest strategic importance. Darfur is a prime example. The violence there was considered in the US during the mid-2000s to be a scandal that should not be tolerated, but no US government has judged the matter important enough to warrant committing its own troops.

A set of more or less standard procedures for UN peacekeeping missions has emerged over time. After the Security Council has made a decision to commit UN troops to an emergency, a call is made for military contributions. The leading Western military powers—the US, the United Kingdom, France—generally refrain from placing their own troops under UN command, although China is increasingly prepared to do so. The top three troop contributors to the UN are in fact all from South Asia, not least because governments there see an opportunity to assert their international presence while also earning hard currency. Ghana, Nigeria, the Ukraine and many other countries are also enthusiastic providers of troops for similar reasons. Soldiers from troop-providing countries, understandably enough, are reluctant to risk taking casualties in conflicts that are often of no strategic interest to their own governments. While soldiers attempt to enforce often inadequate mandates in difficult conditions, UN civilian officials, some of whom have deep humanitarian motives and others of whom do not, generally try to organise democratic elections, after which they aim to leave. If the whole endeavour is accompanied by a sufficient degree of commitment by a major power, plus a dose of good luck, it may produce a satisfactory outcome. But it often leaves the UN courting humiliation and failure, as in Congo, where a major UN mission, squeezed between an incompetent and brutal government army and numerous militias, the most formidable of which have been supported by a neighbouring country, stands no realistic chance of playing midwife to the birth of a new Congolese state. In Darfur, a UN force stands between a cynical government and the embarrassment of Western and African powers that want to halt killings and displacement but lack the will to do so themselves. Obstructed by the Sudanese government, the UN has been unable to mobilise even half of the soldiers it needs for its mission in Darfur. There are persistent calls for the creation of a permanent UN force, an idea mooted from time to time since the 1940s that remains full of difficulties.

Alex de Waal has argued that,[40] if we are to analyse peacekeeping in Africa's fragile states, we must start by considering how they actually function. He describes the matter in terms of a patrimonial marketplace in which political loyalties are up for auction at every level and violence is a routine tool for political bargaining. Because international peace support missions enter such situations in a legal-technocratic frame of mind, they assume that problems are amenable to an institutional solution and that every agreement is legally binding. But this isn't really the case, and so any mission that tries to operate in this way becomes both frustrated and deeply enmeshed in the host country's socio-political fabric. Moreover, because a mission will act, by design or default, as a patron itself, it influences the price of loyalty, raising or lowering the cost according to which groups it supports or opposes. This in turn means that a peacekeeping mission cannot withdraw without a market correction, usually violent. Peacekeepers therefore get sucked into conflicts from which they are unable to disengage since they have become part of the calculus.

Other than the UN, various peacekeeping alternatives are on offer, none of them offering an ideal solution, all of them less or more feasible according to circumstances. In general, internationalists place much hope in African interventions in line with the slogan 'African solutions for African problems'. Plans are being implemented to organise and train stand-by brigades in each of Africa's five constituent regions, but none of these brigades is close to the level of preparation where it could be deployed successfully. During a burst of energy following its creation in 2002 out of the ashes of the unlamented Organisation of African Unity, the African Union (AU), motivated by South Africa's post-liberation dynamism and pan-African ambitions, showed a strong commitment to intervene in continental conflicts. The AU sent a successful military mission to Burundi as part of a larger peacemaking initiative in the Great Lakes region that was championed by South Africa. Little noticed by the rest of the world, the AU even intervened to depose an illegitimate regime in one of its member-states, the Comoros. However, when it comes to Sudan, the AU's military mission has faced similar problems to the UN, being politically constrained in its freedom to take military action. Just as the Security Council hands some of the hardest peacekeeping tasks to the UN, like someone passing on a bad penny they have found in their change, so do leading African powers find it convenient to request the AU to assume the most difficult and least palatable tasks on their continent, in Darfur and Somalia. It is hardly surprising that the AU is gradually losing its initial energy, sapped by lack of political commitment and by the difficulties of peacemaking and peacekeeping. An optimist might argue that in the fullness of time, the AU will grow in stature to the extent that it can take full responsibility for peacemaking through diplomacy and be in a position to back this up with peacekeeping forces. If this is to be achieved, however, the AU will need an infusion of money, resources and energy from some source that is not apparent at present.

The AU is by no means the only multinational grouping that has intervened militarily in African conflicts. So too have some regional organisations, such as the Economic Community of West African States (ECOWAS) and the Southern African Development Community (SADC) in their respective areas. Both these organisations were originally intended primarily for economic purposes. In the case of ECOWAS, its military role has now far outstripped its economic one. Of all Africa's regional organisations, ECOWAS has the most substantial record of military peacekeeping, but it is many years from having the multinational, ever-ready force that is projected. It remains hampered not only by material shortages but by the overbearing role of Nigeria, the founder of ECOWAS, home to its secretariat, and the leading light in earlier military interventions in Liberia and Sierra Leone. SADC has had a similar problem in assimilating the influence of one member that is more powerful than the others, South Africa. Its greatest weakness as a peacemaker has been its inability to deal with the problem of Zimbabwe.

In name at least, the European Union has also intervened in African wars. In 2003, the EU launched a military mission in the Ituri region of Congo that was successful in holding the deadly conflict there in check while the UN prepared to take over. In fact, Operation Artemis was almost entirely a French mission, with French forces being re-branded to benefit from EU legitimacy. The EU has also sent peacekeeping missions to the Central African Republic and Chad, both also French-dominated. France finds it convenient to use the EU as cover for its gradual withdrawal from the very particular form of relations, so closely related to colonial models, that dominated Franco-African relations from the 1960s until the

1990s. Beyond France's commitment to the EU label in Africa, the future of European peacekeeping in the continent is predicated on the perennial problem of reluctance on the part of EU member-states to develop an EU army or even an EU foreign policy.

Finally there is the North Atlantic Treaty Organisation, whose forces have been used outside the European theatre—in Afghanistan—and which has organised anti-piracy patrols in the Indian Ocean. NATO is yet another organisation originally designed in the wake of the Second World War, this time with western Europe in mind, its original brief being neatly summarised as to keep Germany down, the Soviets out, and America in. More than sixty years later, it, too, is struggling to rethink its role. At times, its members seem tempted to follow US exhortations to turn it into a club for the defence of the democratic capitalist world. Those who see its role as the defence of Europe itself may wonder whether that task would not be better served by a European Defence Force.

International peacekeeping missions may offer a more or less effective short-term solution to problems of state implosion, but they always leave a political void. Even the more successful missions, such as in Sierra Leone and Liberia, have not succeeded in creating a political dynamism that can create states able to fulfill their international responsibilities for the foreseeable future, as both countries have reverted to the sort of corruption that caused their breakdown in the first place. The situation cannot accurately be described as a 'crisis', implying a turning-point, a period of short duration. The current state of affairs is better described as intractable, and therefore its long-term consequences need to be considered frankly.

Since the end of the true postcolonial period, in the late 1970s, few African states have managed to evolve the combination of democracy, institutional stability and steady economic growth that Western diplomats and bankers prefer and that are generally the preconditions for the sort of policies recommended by humanitarians. Countries without a government that is able or willing to fulfill its international responsibilities can easily become threats to global systems of governance, most dramatically in the person of the pirates, drug-traffickers and terrorists who are the figures of international nightmares but who often turn out, on closer inspection, to be little more than political-military entrepreneurs whose need for income has gone beyond what their own states can provide. The populations of countries without effective governments may suffer to an extent that poses fundamental questions about the responsibilities of powerful states to intervene in the affairs of less powerful ones. A hardheaded judgement must be that the inability of so many African states to exercise sovereignty in a manner deemed satisfactory by their international partners is long-lasting, has deep historical roots, and is not going to cease any time soon. In the absence of a really successful peacekeeping formula, there is every reason to suppose that some African states will continue to cause problems both to their neighbours and to external powers.

The Sovereignty Issue

The rhetoric of human rights, which has moved since the late 1970s from a concern of libertarian groups to a central element of the Western diplomatic vocabulary, has undercut claims to absolute sovereign immunity, the hallmark of the Westphalia state system. After the end of the Cold War there was a sharp increase in intervention in troubled countries on humanitarian grounds, championed notably by the British prime minister Tony Blair (1997–2007). For a brief period, it seemed that Europe and the US were adopting a style of muscular interventionism that could halt wars and impose new political settlements in their wake, in the Balkans and Sierra Leone and potentially elsewhere too. Since then, the notion of liberal intervention has been discredited by Iraq and Afghanistan.

The number of wars in Africa as well as their cost in lives has gone down in recent years.[41] But this does not mean that the hunger, homelessness and disease that are associated with political insecurity have disappeared, and climate change can only make this problem of human suffering worse. A longer-term vision is sorely needed. And reflecting on the longer term requires giving some attention to the vexed issue of sovereignty. This is made difficult not only by specific principles of international law, but by a habit of thinking that has underpinned the United Nations from its inception. In the euphoria of making a new world from the ruins of the old in 1945, it was somehow supposed that once a country was granted sovereignty, it would never lose it. In light of the ups and downs of history, this is bizarre. The gradual disappearance of real substance from Africa's sovereignty has been reflected to some extent in formal dispositions although, as yet, only rarely is there talk of removing or suspending the sovereign status of a state that is judged to have failed completely.[42]

In the case of Africa especially, views on the issue of sovereignty tend to be polarised between defenders of national sovereignty and enthusiasts for intervention, who increasingly use a language of humanitarianism mixed with security. Positions for and against intervention have hardly changed in the last fifty years in some respects, with African nationalists maintaining a right to self-determination (while often demanding special financial aid and other assistance that will supposedly help them develop) and great power strategists insisting on a right or even a responsibility to intervene (but only when it suits them). In September 2005, the UN General Assembly voted in favour of assuming a responsibility to protect, empowering the Security Council to intervene in the internal affairs of member-states in circumstances where a national government is unable or unwilling to protect its own people. If it were enforced, a responsibility on the UN to intervene in humanitarian disasters could bring some relief to the suffering of victims of state neglect or abuse. However, the responsibility to protect as it has been defined in law entails no obligation on the great powers to intervene in such cases. Rather, it gives the Security Council the authority to intervene on humanitarian grounds if its members are so disposed. If they are not thus inclined, the humanitarian problem remains and the responsibility to protect goes unfulfilled. The responsibility to protect is regarded with scepticism by many African diplomats and intellectuals who suspect it of being a cover for interventions that have ulterior motives. Concern for human rights can be represented simply as a cover for imperialist meddling, a cynical camouflage for economic and strategic interests.[43]

Whatever one's opinion of this argument, it is a fact that the burgeoning number of 'fragile' states can be lethal for large numbers of people. The greatest scandal in Africa remains the war in eastern Congo, which has cost millions of lives[44] over more than ten years without motivating any meaningful intervention by the great powers beyond funding a UN mission that cannot succeed. Darfur and Zimbabwe are other humanitarian disasters in Africa that have provoked calls for intervention but where the strategic issues are not sufficiently important to motivate much action beyond rhetorical appeals and the provision of humanitarian aid when circumstances permit. Both the Sudanese and Zimbabwean governments have made a point about their sovereignty and look to China for support. Both these governments punish their domestic opponents by playing out a kind of national hostage drama with international humanitarians. In effect, they say, support us or we will allow our people to die in front of your eyes, even on your television screens. It is as though the population had been kidnapped, and one person taken out to be executed every few minutes to apply pressure on outsiders. This is a grim business.

The existence of humanitarian and development NGOs is highly dependent on media representations of suffering, which may prompt sympathetic members of the general public to donate money to their causes. This in turn creates a marketing logic, based on an NGO's need to advertise its work in order to attract funding. Some go for shock tactics, presenting pictures of starving babies. Others may opt for more congenial images of those who are benefiting from development. Young people, generally motivated by idealism, may begin a career in development as a salaried employee of one organisation or another.[45] Development and aid organisations have an ability to mobilise public opinion on a significant scale, increasingly making use of music and film celebrities—Sir Bob Geldof, Bono, Angelina Jolie, George Clooney and many others. This has created a constituency that no serious politician can ignore. Some African governments have become adept at appealing to these lobbies directly. Before his retirement, Nelson Mandela spent a lot of time receiving world celebrities, which did wonders for the bank balances of the organisations that he championed.

Perhaps the most instructive case of media-driven politics in recent years has been the controversy surrounding Darfur. In the US especially, a pattern of repression that the State Department has labelled as genocide has mobilised Americans on a scale unparalleled by any African issue since apartheid. At least until recently, a substantial number of Americans believed that Washington should intervene militarily to save lives, to the extent that, after the Iraq expedition had run into serious trouble, it was often said in the US that the armed forces had invaded the wrong country: liberals argued that the US should have been a force for good in Darfur instead of blundering into Iraq. However, for Washington, no overwhelmingly strategic issue is at stake in Darfur. Various parts of the US government have had their own policies on Sudan, with the Central Intelligence Agency in particular being more inclined than the State Department to cooperate with the authorities in Khartoum. US policy on this matter is driven in large part by a public opinion that has been mobilised by the humanitarian lobbies and their celebrity associates.

Interestingly, it is not only Western countries that have in effect delegated much of their Africa policy to the non-governmental sector. The same has occurred throughout the Middle East, where many Islamic NGOs funded by charitable contributions have developed strong interests in Africa. Islamic NGOs vary from purely proselytising organisations such as the Tablighi Jamaat, based in India, through those that specialise in mosque-building and others that undertake a range of health and welfare issues in the name of charity. A few have distinctly political objectives. It is partly through such Islamic networks and the traditions associated with them that in some parts of Africa the population, or sections of it, is reorienting itself away from Europe and towards the Middle East and Asia. The growth in trade and cultural connections to Dubai, Mumbai and points further east is rooted in old historical networks. What may appear to Europeans as the arrival in Africa of new forces in the person of Asian and Middle Eastern diplomats and business operators is better seen as the resumption of older patterns after a rather unusual period in which commercial and political relations were rechannelled towards Europe.

The agreement on neoliberal economic prescriptions for Africa that prevailed in the 1980s and 90s, known as the Washington consensus, was probably the last time that North Atlantic powers could get away with creating an Africa policy only among themselves. Any new consensus on a policy designed to deal with problems caused by the lack of effective sovereignty in parts of Africa will need the support of powers beyond the West. The situation in

Africa poses real problems in a world whose international rules are based on sovereignty, to the extent that Asian countries proud of their anti-imperialist credentials nevertheless feel obliged to send a warship to Somalia in a way that Lord Palmerston, Britain's flamboyant foreign secretary of the mid-Victorian period, might have approved.

Somalia's lack of a state able to control its territorial waters touches a range of global issues more delicate than piracy. Contemporary Somali piracy is sometimes said to have sprung up as members of the Hawiye clan tried to deter illegal dumping of toxic waste and overfishing in their waters,[46] both activities being associated with entrepreneurs from industrialised countries in Europe and Asia. Since the deeper cause of Somali piracy is the absence of a viable state, a lasting solution might begin with discussing with Somali regional authorities the creation of a regional naval task force, modelled along the lines of the anti-piracy patrols by Asian navies in the Malacca straits.[47] This task force could also ensure that Somali territorial waters are not used for dumping toxic waste or for illegal fishing. Similar reflections occur in regard to West African territorial waters, for example another pirate-ridden zone around the Niger Delta, and the waters off Mauritania, scandalously over-fished by foreign fleets. For rich countries to combine in a naval action of this sort would require them in effect to take on some of the duties normally associated with sovereignty.

While the larger African governments especially are highly sensitive to questions concerning sovereignty, there are many Africans who might have an interest in new arrangements, notably in eastern Congo. The territory is now so much under the dominance of Rwanda and Uganda, militarily and economically, and a revival of the power of the Congolese state in the region is so unlikely, that a solution to the suffering of the area must surely in the fullness of time involve an adjustment of sovereignty. In general, however, recognition of secession or a simple border rectification would be unlikely to solve deep-seated problems. Power in Africa is increasingly related to social networks rather than to territory, and legal arrangements may need to take this matter into account. The situation of the Great Lakes, Darfur, the Mano River area of West Africa and many other regions suggests that the international community will need in the future to develop legal regimes that are informed by realities in Africa itself and that take into account the reality of fluid cross-border relations and of social networks.

It is likely that, in future, different approaches will increasingly be taken to different problems. Liberia and Sierra Leone, two countries that have occupied substantial international attention, have histories so intertwined with the North Atlantic since the days of the slave trade that their people are generally well disposed to intervention from the UK and the US respectively. I have argued elsewhere[48] that a new set of measures designed to help these countries beyond the short term may require an international role in the administration of state finances. Both countries are deficient in a variety of technical fields that are of international concern, including surveillance of their territorial waters and control of their air space. In this regard a workable form of cooperation between national and international authorities is not too hard to envisage. Little noticed by the general public, Western countries are actually multiplying the number of law-enforcement units in West Africa, especially in the fields of anti-narcotics and anti-terrorism, where European or US officers work with specialised elements of national law-enforcement agencies.[49]

The more that Europe, and probably the US also, decline relative to Asia, the greater their interest in ensuring that countries live by the rules they have made for themselves. Increasingly, maintenance of these rules depends on what Asians think, and especially the government of China. It seems inevitable that China, despite its proclamations of respect for national sovereignty and its relative indifference to humanitarian issues, will be drawn into intervening in African affairs by the logic generated by pursuit of its own interests. China has clearly moved towards fuller participation in the multilateral institutions designed in earlier times and previously dominated by the West. The chance remains high that African power-brokers will seek to use Chinese power as a form of leverage, as they are accustomed to doing,[50] thereby reproducing the politics of extraversion[51] that have been so formative in their continent's insertion in the world.

6

TWENTY-FIRST CENTURY DEVELOPMENT

'Let freedom reign!' Nelson Mandela proclaimed after being sworn in as state president of South Africa. The ceremony at the Union Buildings in Pretoria is said to have been attended by more heads of state than any gathering since the funeral of John F. Kennedy.

Since that date, 10 May 1994, no significant part of Africa has been ruled by Europeans or people of European descent. In nationalist ideology, this marks the completion of the formal stage of the liberation of an entire continent. Yet nobody believes that sub-Saharan Africa as a whole has fulfilled its promise.

Radical nationalists sometimes refer to the proclamations of sovereignty that were the cause of such pride half a century ago as 'flag independence', shorthand for a situation in which Africans are endowed with the formal authority to govern themselves while having little control over the sinews of financial and economic power. But it is not only radicals who are disappointed at how little has been achieved during the last fifty or so years. Depending on the political sympathies of the observer, Africa's recent history is commonly seen either as a botched decolonisation or as a struggle for liberation that is always incomplete as long as political power is not accompanied by economic power.

Historical Explanations

Rival historical accounts of disappointed expectations differ most obviously in their attribution of blame. Is it Africans themselves

147

who are the main authors of the continent's unfulfilled destiny, or outsiders?

Among African nationalists, the failure to achieve full liberation and to develop is conventionally attributed to the imperialists who colonised the continent in the past, imposing institutions foreign to its genius. Their argument is that colonisation endowed Africa with arbitrary borders and with bureaucracies designed only to extract wealth from the population. At independence, this apparatus was taken over by elites who were too easily cajoled into working with neo-colonialists, perpetuating the arrangements of the colonial past even into the twenty-first century. According to this view, what is most required is a new generation of African leaders with the integrity and the courage to make a definitive break with this burdensome past.[1]

This point of view becomes less convincing with every passing year. In fact, a radical nationalist analysis on these lines has become itself an impediment to Africa's development. It represents history through an ideological lens as the record not of what happened, but of what failed to happen. Regarding the past in terms of a struggle for liberation and true independence that has never been fully consummated, makes it hard to see present-day Africa other than as a place that does not develop properly. Attributing superhuman cleverness to imperialists, neo-colonialists and other devils denies Africans a role as agents in their own history. It makes people unconfident that they can control the forces shaping their lives. In the hands of a Robert Mugabe or a Charles Taylor, the denial of historical agency permits bullies to create chaos while blandly claiming that no blame attaches to them. It is all the fault of the imperialists.

An alternative argument, that Africa suffers from uniquely bad leadership that has caused it to squander its opportunities, makes little sense. There is no compelling evidence that Africa's leaders are on the whole less talented than those in any other part of the world. Two or three generations ago many of them lacked experience of international business and diplomacy and few Africans had been trained in the technical skills necessary to run a modern state and to provide direction to a modern society. This has subsequently ceased to be the case, although whether leaders make the best use of the human resources available to them is a different matter. But the main reason to doubt the contention that Africa's fate can be explained primarily by poor leadership is that, by placing responsibility for Africa's failure to live up to expectations on the heads of its leaders alone, it reposes on a Great Man/Really Awful Man view of history. The current of history can certainly be marked for good or ill by powerful individuals, but it remains necessary to understand the excesses of a Mobutu or an Abacha in relation to the context in which they emerge. Great dictators do not spring from nowhere, and nor do their actions take place in a social vacuum. It is worth noting that kleptocracy literally means rule by theft, which is something more than simple robbery; the kleptocrats who have lasted longest have ploughed money back into the political process in a bid to maintain their power,[2] binding leaders and led in complicity.

In the end, Africans, like other people, get roughly the leaders they deserve. Further inquiry therefore requires us to look beyond the quality of leadership alone and to consider how the texture of African societies has been woven by factors global and local. If the issue is to ascertain why Africa has produced more than its fair share of dictators and life presidents, then nationalists are not wrong to point to the enduring effect of the colonial state. However, they often neglect to place the matter in a wider context, overlooking that it is not just the state as an institution that maintains a studied inattention to some key indigenous traditions of governance. Very many institutions and practices that receive official endorsement and support in Africa tend to ignore, to despise or to run counter to many historically rooted forms of knowledge, including of society and of the natural order. In the academic world the latter is often called indigenous knowledge, taken to refer to information about the properties of flora and fauna that remain unknown to mainstream science. But if we interpret the concept of indigenous knowledge in a broader sense, it refers to ways of perceiving the relations between people and their environment that arise from distinctive traditions with a long historical existence. In other words, the problem is not just the maintenance of institutions that still bear the marks of their colonial origin but the continuing disservice done to the fields of knowledge and

experience in which Africa's most enduring traditions of governance are located.

Many countries, and all ex-colonies, live with the legacy of institutions and ideas originally imposed or introduced from outside,
including some Asian countries that are now emerging as major
powers. If we pose a slightly revised question, as to why some
former colonies have to all appearances successfully assimilated
the colonial past to the extent of being acclaimed for their development, while others have not, a search for an answer will certainly
involve examining the record of strategic decisions taken at key
points of their history,[3] but it is also necessary to take into account
fundamental historical differences between societies. Many Asian
countries had histories of literacy, bureaucratic government and
record-keeping long before they were colonised, and some have
succeeded in fusing colonial institutions and practices and regimes
of knowledge with indigenous ones in a more or less creative fashion. This has often proved more difficult in Africa. However, we
also need to place Asia's new economic success in proper perspective, as the majority of India's population, for example, continues
to live at levels of poverty comparable to those in Africa. It is thus
unsatisfactory to regard some countries as developing successfully
while others stagnate. It becomes more important to understand
what may cause relatively wealthy strata to invest in their own
countries, and to investigate the nature of the political relationship
between them and their less favoured compatriots in a series of
cases, each of them unique. This book has evoked some of the factors involved in the case of sub-Saharan Africa.

At this juncture, it is worth making a short detour bringing to
attention the degree to which Africa's history has acquired a peculiar moral colouration. Tracing the historical trajectory of social and
political processes in Africa often causes people to suppose that
moral judgement is being passed, either positive or negative
depending on circumstances, even when no such intention is present. The reasons for such a reaction may be understood historically. European merchants who shipped slaves from Africa often
justified their business by claiming that the place was so barbarous
that transportation was preferable to staying behind, implying that
slave-trading was therefore not so bad after all. This was perhaps

the beginning of the myth of the Dark Continent. After Britain's abolition of the slave trade in 1807, the British public gradually took to regarding Africa as a moral burden generally, and this view spread widely with the diffusion of scientific theories of racism and human evolution in the nineteenth century. That it has continued into recent times is suggested by Tony Blair's famous description of Africa as 'a scar on the conscience of the world'.[4]

As with so many ideas associated with Europe's self-appointed civilising mission in Africa, the morally articulated drive to improve Africa has acquired a nationalist corollary. In the nationalist version, Africa is portrayed as uniquely victimised by a Western world intent on keeping Africa down. Today, the cult of victimhood is perceptible in the often-heard opinion that Africa is being carved up once again by great powers intent on securing its resources for themselves, this time in the search for oil. The implication is that nothing much has changed since the late nineteenth century except that the exploiters now include Chinese and other Asians. In reality, African governments play a leading role in deciding who gets access to the continent's natural resources, coveted by new players as well as by old colonial ones, and under what conditions.

This is one of many cases in which discussion of African affairs is framed within a rhetorical corpus that has departed so far from historical facts as to be ineffective as a guide to understanding. In some instances old clichés remain in circulation because they are embedded in the mission-statements of institutions. Sometimes, African leaders themselves use Western clichés about their continent for their own purposes, for telling the powerful what they want to hear is a standard technique in the strategy I have called political ju-jitsu. In the case of journalists, the mobilisation of standard phrases and ideas is often no more than a reaction to complexity. The world is easier to explain and to understand when it is presented in simple, recognisable images.

When it comes to the positions taken by outsiders towards Africa, though, there has been at least one striking change in recent decades. In the early years after African countries had acquired independence from colonial rule, liberals and left-wingers tended to be the greatest optimists about the future prospects of these countries, believing that political will alone could prevail and that liberation was unstoppable. Sceptics were suspected of nostalgia for colonial rule. Thereafter, the tables turned, with those on the political right claiming to be on the side of progress while leftists were reduced to condemning the injustice of what was happening. This switch is related to the fact that the economic and political reforms adopted in so many African countries in the last part of the twentieth century were sponsored by donor governments and by the international financial institutions, as a result of which these bodies acquired a vested interest in representing their own efforts as successful. They exuded an optimism every bit as vacuous as the systematic defamation sometimes called Afro-pessimism.

These observations on the ideological approaches commonly taken to Africa and its history may convince us that in order to acquire an accurate perception of the directions in which Africa has moved and is moving, it is necessary to dispense with several outdated ideas. Among these are the notions that Africa is a continent standing outside time, that it constitutes a particular moral burden on the West and that it is peculiarly susceptible to becoming a victim. Views of this type are by no means confined to the uneducated or ill-informed. They may be expressed by people of the standing of France's President Sarkozy, whose African keynote speech was quoted in an earlier chapter.[5] Nor are they expressed only by politicians and ideologues of the right. On the contrary, the idea that sub-Saharan Africa is perennially lagging behind in human progress, first enunciated in Europe in the days of the Atlantic slave trade, has received new life from its deployment by several generations of people passionately in favour of Africa's liberation. Politicians, polemicists, administrators and others intent on emancipation and development, both inside and outside Africa, have generally continued to assume, like their colonial predecessors, that Africa needs not just to make progress, but to catch up with the rich world in very specific ways that they are happy to prescribe.

This particular vision of Africa's place in time, and therefore in the world, is closely associated with nationalist historiography. The golden age of African nationalism, beginning in the mid-twentieth century, coincided with the appearance of the first professional academic historians of the continent, initially in universities in the US and the United Kingdom, and soon in Africa itself as well as other places.[6] They were often fixated on providing historical charters for the sovereign states then being created in the continent. 'The task was to establish that the African past had glorious achievements to its credit, ones by no means inferior to those of Europe', writes the historian Abolade Adeniji. 'Thus, if Europeans had established organised polities, monarchs, and cities, nationalist historiography felt challenged to prove that Africans, too, had produced the same'.[7] The error of this position consists in assuming that progress always takes the same forms, recognisable by reference to the course taken by the countries of the North Atlantic.

To say that Africa's history has been under-theorised due to a surfeit of political commitment sounds dry and boring, but the effect is palpable. It has resulted in a vision of an Africa that constantly fails to attain the goals that have been established for it. It is made to appear as the one continent that never develops, despite the obvious changes taking place there.

Instead of trying to view Africa's past as similar to that of Europe, it is more accurate and also more rewarding to acknowledge that some of the most fundamental characteristics of Africa's history are strikingly different from the main threads that run through European history, so often taken as the yardstick of progress.

Seen from this angle, past and present become hard to dissociate, as many of the most striking themes of Africa's history are recognisable in those states labelled as 'fragile'. Consequently, the nature of these states cannot be fully grasped without revisiting our views of Africa's history. A useful exercise is therefore to identify some of the features of African societies today with a view to investigating what relation they may have to progress and to development, neither of which can be interpreted in exactly the same way now as they were in the last century.

Progress and Development

We have noted how successive generations of both Europeans and of African nationalists after 1945 identified development in terms of building bureaucratic states that could fulfil their obligations under international law and of generating economic growth with a view to enhancing the lives of their citizens, making them more like Europeans in matters of taste and consumption. In the euphoria of decolonisation, these seemed obvious ways to make progress.

In recent decades various other requirements amounting to a new generation of rights have been added to the core concepts of development, including in regard to education, health and other benefits. Poverty reduction has also become a prominent concern of developers. This broader approach is often subsumed in the concept of 'human development', which the United Nations Development Programme defines as follows:[8]

Human Development is a development paradigm that is about much more than the rise or fall of national incomes. It is about creating an environment in which people can develop their full potential and lead productive, creative lives in accord with their needs and interests. Development is thus about expanding the choices people have to lead lives that they value. And it is thus about much more than economic growth, which is only a means—if a very important one—of enlarging people's choices.

If human development really means creating an environment in which people can lead their lives in conformity with their own needs and interests as they perceive them, then it implies allowing them the freedom to decide how to set about achieving this goal. If we once again consider how some Asian countries have developed, we may note that, as a former chief economist of the World Bank has shown, they acquired their current status very often by not following Western policy precepts.[9] It is fair to draw the conclusion that there is no single path to development, even if it is in regard to economic growth alone, as there was often thought to be in the heyday of modernisation and in the heroic age of social science.

Hence, searching for economic or social theories that have proved their worth elsewhere and that must now be applied to Africa to enhance its development is not recommended. A better way to proceed is by considering the condition of Africa's states. It is widely acknowledged that many of them do not have bureaucracies able to deliver public goods in the way that was expected of them when they acquired legal sovereignty in the mid-twentieth century. In recent years it has ceased to be quite so clear as in the past exactly what a robust state might look like. The Washington consensus of the late twentieth century posited that sustainable development was possible only in multiparty democracies with free markets in which transaction costs are kept low by application of the principles known as 'good governance'. Many of these qualities may be desirable on moral or philosophical grounds, but once again, Asian examples suggest that they can no longer be presented as the only way to develop, since a Beijing consensus[10] may be emerging on the compatibility of high economic growth and authoritarian politics. It is conceivable that some of Africa's more effective authoritarian states could turn out to be successful at providing high living standards to a sizeable minority of the population even while they leave the majority to fend for themselves. The economies of Africa as a whole were growing at an average of 5 per cent or more in the eight years to 2008[11] and were enjoying unprecedented success in acquiring finance from capital markets. They are now heading for similar growth levels once again. One may argue that this is not true development, but the lack of dogmatism implied by the UN's definition of human development makes it harder than before to be categorical on this point. If external actors believe that a country which is growing economically is failing to develop in some other respect, this is a point that they need to argue rather than state as fact.

A crucial change in this regard is the spectacular rise of Chinese influence in Africa, which has caused much reflection on its likely consequences for development.[12] China has declined invitations to join the existing donor club by becoming a member of the OECD's Development Assistance Committee. Instead, it has created its own distinctive style in dealing with Africa, characterised by generous grants and loans often tied to the construction of infrastructure and recompensed with access to minerals, and, importantly, by elaborate expressions of respect. Less attention has been given to the Africa policies of other emerging powers such as Brazil, India, Malaysia and South Korea. Strikingly little research has been done on the numerous Islamic networks that link Africa to the Middle East and that often implement development projects. Saudi Arabia, Iran and the United Arab Emirates all devote substantial attention to their relations with African countries, including in terms of concessionary finance and project financing, and Turkey seems set to join them. These and other Muslim countries are home to large numbers of private charitable organisations with active African policies, including programmes of proselytisation and mosque-building, but also in regard to more technical aspects of welfare, financed with the alms that pious Muslims are required to give.[13]

The religious character of so many Middle Eastern NGOs may provide them with a distinct advantage when they work in Africa, as Africans have always tended to imagine the invisible forces that shape their lives as being of a spiritual nature and they have developed techniques for channelling these for social purposes. This is a prime example of the indigenous knowledge that is often dismissed by Western policy-makers because it lacks obvious technical applications or that is even considered frankly dysfunctional. Yet the fact is that in many African countries people place the most confidence in religious leaders. In the BBC's 'Who runs your world?' poll conducted in 2005, no fewer than 85 per cent of Nigerians said that they trusted religious leaders more than any other type of authority, and a similar proportion said they were willing to give them more power.[14]

The political and the religious are both modes of exerting control over the relationships that compose a society; both are languages of power. The key point at issue is the conviction of exercising control over one's own destiny. In the case of Africa, this control is widely felt to have been lost by the act of colonisation and never fully regained, not even through the acquisition of a legal sovereignty that was obtained at a time when African societies were poorly equipped to generate or absorb capital. Postcolonial governments in Africa continued to place official emphasis on the techniques of colonial rule, and even when these became less effective over time, politicians and officials continued to make a show of using colonial-style techniques since these are the currency of international recognition. In the meantime, the historical mode of governance through control of the spirit world has been officially denigrated (but also manipulated and abused) to the extent that people have lost confidence in their ability to control their social worlds, which incorporate ancestors and other spiritual beings. It is interesting to consider in this light the proclamation of an African renaissance made by the former South African president Thabo

Mbeki (1999–2008) in an effort to convince people that Africans were finally assuming control of their own destiny. It could be said that Thabo Mbeki was correct to perceive at the very end of the last century that Africa was emerging from its postcolonial period into a new era but that he was unsuccessful in finding a political language suited to the times. He expressed himself in a mix of Leninism, neo-liberal economics and black power rhetoric, reflecting his own formative experiences,[15] that may have struck a chord with the black South African intelligentsia but probably not with many others. There are many community leaders in Africa who use vocabularies less familiar to the rest of the world than Mbeki's. An immediate objective of development policy-makers should be to listen to these voices with a view to understanding what they are saying. Comprehending contemporary Africa requires us to take Africans seriously, including their traditions of knowledge.[16]

There are growing signs that many people prefer the language of religion as a means of taking control of their destiny, in time-honoured fashion. However, it must be emphasised that this needs to be fused with the appropriate technical skills if Africa is to develop in most meanings that can be attached to the word 'development'. It is not clear whether or how this might happen. The need to find a workable fusion between indigenous traditions of governance that have a real popular basis and the technocracy essential for success in today's world is arguably the single greatest challenge to Africa's progress.

Africans before the late nineteenth century managed to govern themselves without literacy and therefore without written legal codes, without religious scriptures, without bureaucracies and, in fact, without entities that could accurately be described as states in the modern sense of the word. Exceptions, such as the Christian kingdom of Ethiopia, the Islamic sultanates and emirates of the Sahel or the Islamic city-states of the Swahili coast, rarely deployed a consistent apparatus of control over an extensive territory. This history remains highly relevant to Africa today, as the states that are of current concern on account of their perceived fragility show strong continuities with older forms of governance. Shifting and highly personalised political practices, the articulation of power through social networks, struggles between centres and peripheries, and access to an invisible world perceived as inhabited by individual spirits, are all old ways of organising public affairs that exist today in a globalised world in which Africans constitute some fourteen per cent of humanity.

In making these observations, one should avoid any inference that there exists a timeless Africa that could be revived if only the accretions of colonialism could be scraped off, like the barnacles from a ship's hull. This is impossible, since what has happened has happened. But most of all, it is not even desirable, for policy-makers concerned about the problems posed by Africa's 'fragile' states are right to suppose that the world would be a safer place if every country were endowed with a reasonable degree of regular government in an internationally validated form, implying at least a minimum level of bureaucratic efficiency. If any given country is to take its rightful place in global circuits of trade and diplomacy in the present century, it not only needs a minimally effective state at its core, but it needs such a state in a form that is also adapted to its own cultural contexts and historical heritage. This is what the South African poet Breyten Breytenbach calls 'an African modernity nourished from African roots and realities'.[17]

Emerging Development Strategies

It is no coincidence that the golden era of development in Africa, during the third quarter of the last century, was also the time when most of its countries acquired formal sovereignty. A number of factors converged to make this possible. Of the two Cold War superpowers, one was hostile to and the other unenthusiastic about the continuation of European colonial empires in Africa. African elites were keen to take control of new states and were able to mobilise large numbers of people to this end. In those days there was a high degree of consensus among social scientists about what was needed to modernise traditional societies in social, political and economic fields through comprehensive schemes of state-led engineering. '"Modernisation" and "westernisation" were lumped together and contrasted with "backwardness and tradition"'[18] in straightforward fashion, as one economist recalls. These intellectual certainties enabled policy-makers to work with clear plans. To achieve growth and to become modern required accepting a whole package of ethical beliefs and political forms in the distinctive styles circulating within the rival Western and Soviet blocs in programmes of development that have to be numbered among the coercive utopias[19] so characteristic of the twentieth century. Last but not least, the whole intellectual and political edifice of development and modernisation enjoyed substantial public support both inside and outside Africa.

The world has changed since then, but key academic disciplines have not adapted well. One leading intellectual, Achille Mbembe, goes as far as to assert that thinking that is still 'in thrall [to] theories of social evolutionism and ideologies of development and modernisation' has 'undermined the very possibility of understanding African economic and political facts'.[20] The main targets of his scorn are political science and development economics. It is rather alarming to note that these remain the key disciplines used by Western donors in the formulation of policy. If Mbembe's views have any merit, then it is not only development policy-makers that need to rethink some fundamental assumptions, but also professional economists and legions of university teachers.

Sure enough, recent years have seen a growing number of critiques of development by well-informed sources,[21] although it is disturbing to note the degree to which universities continue to produce graduates schooled in outdated views about development and the contribution of social science thereto. Also emerging is a popular opposition to development aid, particularly in Europe, that is motivated by a mixture of concern about immigration, opposition to high taxation and scepticism about the results of prior spending in Africa especially. The fact that European publics are experiencing increasing doubts about development aid is not unwholesome since, as we have seen, the view of Africa as a unique moral burden on the West is outdated and is actually an impediment to the type of international cooperation that is most required. Reservations about development assistance would be most damaging if they were to transmute into scepticism about any form of Africa policy at all on the part of European governments, as sometimes threatens to occur. Accordingly, there is a need to state why it is necessary for most European governments to have a policy on Africa and what part development assistance might play in this.

In the first instance, there is a pressing need for new thinking about Africa's place in the world, and this book is intended as a modest contribution in this direction. In the political field, it is clear that ignoring Africa cannot be a serious option for major governments, as too much is at stake in light of Africa's growing importance as a market, as a field of investment, and as a diplomatic partner in a multi-polar world. In regard specifically to development aid, which in the tradition of the Netherlands and several other donor countries has been presented to the public as a moral obligation, this has now become one of several instruments for the management of an interconnected globe, as a recent official report to the Dutch government points out.[22] Development aid has a role to play in managing such matters as international security, migration flows and trade in foodstuffs. As the intellectual certainties of old-fashioned modernisation theories recede, and as the trajectories of various African countries change, there is an increasing need for pragmatic consideration of policy on a country-by-country basis.[23] Policy-makers and politicians will increasingly need to be sparing in their appeal to morality since this brings with it an intellectual and political baggage that tends to render policy ineffective.

While development aid has often been presented to Western publics as a moral obligation, official aid to developing countries has also been understood as one element in a strategic approach to the maintenance of an orderly world. What is most required is to bring this vision up to date. Half a century ago, embracing Africa in an orderly world implied building bureaucratic capacity in the dozens of new sovereign states then under construction. In the heyday of the Washington consensus, it was interpreted as meaning support for democracy and free trade. Today, development policy-makers can no longer afford to be either this ambitious or this dogmatic. Rather than arriving in Africa with checklists of required reforms, with a view to perfecting institutions that were originally introduced into the continent in colonial times, they need to recognise that African countries have outlived their post-colonial phase and have acquired a new character. While this often strikes Europeans and North Americans in terms of state fragility, Africa's states are in many respects better understood as remarkably adaptable and even resilient. It becomes increasingly important for outsiders to investigate with an open mind how they can work with those African institutions that currently exist. Research in this field is urgently required, as many institutions and networks that function effectively are not formally part of the state. In combating desertification, for example, or in supporting medical care, or in trying to persuade young Africans that irregular migration to Europe is not a rite of passage,[24] there is a need for technically qualified personnel to work with actors and networks that fall outside the official ambit of African states but that also do not take the organisational form of classic NGOs.

Nor does this mean concentrating only on the local or national level. A search for more effective governance in Africa is inseparable from a search for global institutions able to deal with a world that may be facing problems associated with climate change and increased competition for natural resources. Ever since Africa was partitioned by the Concert of Powers in 1884–5, its governance has been inseparable from the international system in general, a fact that we ignore at our peril. For reasons described in earlier chapters, Africa occupies a very particular position in many international circuits of diplomacy and commerce, into which it is integrated often by unofficial or informal means. The financial crisis that began in 2007 has revealed to general view aspects of globalisation that had previously been overlooked or misinterpreted by influential commentators and by key regulatory authorities, who assumed that markets were self-correcting and that global systems were more coherent and effective than was actually the case. Changed circumstances reveal that there are a number of institutions vital to the world's diplomatic, legal and financial governance that are in need of repair or reform, from the UN Security Council to financial markets. Those who undertake the necessary reforms need to avoid the ideological excesses that had such unforeseen consequences in Africa in the era of structural adjustment.

In this regard, one of the errors made by many international commentators towards the end of the last century was to regard

Africa's wars at that time as localised emergencies, small wars of international concern only on humanitarian grounds, rather than a serious threat to international peace and security. Most observers were slow to appreciate that the growing 'fragility' of Africa's states was an early sign of a wider problem with the system of international governance that was put in place in or around 1945 and is now showing its age.[25] It was the realisation that small conflicts could spread that led the United Kingdom to send troops to Sierra Leone in 2000 and thereafter to maintain political and financial support for a restored government there. A perception that what Washington calls 'ungoverned spaces' could threaten the US itself was also the rationale for the various military cooperation programmes that successive US administrations have put in place in the Sahel since 2002.[26] Several areas south of the Sahara have become a favoured location for a variety of operators threatening international security, including armed political extremists, drug-traders, dumpers of toxic waste and other environmental criminals. The Saharan outlaws calling themselves Al Qaeda in the Islamic Maghreb may have assimilated networks responsible for bombing European cities in the 1990s.[27] Somalia has attracted militant Islamists from a variety of countries. The US, as the world's only military power with a global reach, has taken the lead in responding to the security vacuum in Africa as a whole by forming a separate military command, Africom, which has now toned down the grandiose statements of ambition which it announced at the time of its launch by the Bush administration. Conversely, European countries need to apply greater attention to this aspect of African affairs. The most promising (as well as the least expensive) approach available to them is to identify areas of piecemeal cooperation with the governments of African sovereign states as well as with regional organisations whenever matters of mutual concern permit.

While Africom exists in the first instance to serve the US national interest, several Western powers remain fitful supporters of military intervention in Africa on humanitarian grounds. Critics portray this as the continuation of a long European tradition that goes back to the medieval wars of religion, when the pope gave divine sanction to wars against heretics and unbelievers.[28] The successful British military intervention in Sierra Leone in 2000 and the popular campaign in the US calling for intervention in Darfur mark the high point of liberal military intervention championed by Western powers. This concept has subsequently been discredited and must now be treated with increasing reserve, all the more so as China's distrust of international military intervention is well known. In Africa, intervention of this nature is widely viewed not as the implementation of a growingly coherent and consistent body of international law, but as a cover for the interests of great powers.

However, it is not only human lives in Africa that are at stake, but security in Europe also. West Africa now poses a discernible threat to European countries in the form of the rapid growth in the trade in cocaine from Latin America to Europe via West African countries. International law-enforcement officials first began to notice a significant rise in bulk shipments of cocaine to and from West Africa in 2005. According to a former head of the UN Office on Drugs and Crime (UNODC) in West Africa,[29] the total seizures of cocaine in the region leapt from 1.2 tonnes in 2005 to 4.3 tonnes in the first seven months of 2007. In a situation report the same year, the UNODC gave even higher figures, reporting that the Spanish and British navies seized 9.9 tonnes of cocaine on five ships in international waters off West Africa in 2006.[30] The size of the drug trade in relation to the small budgets of many West African countries is striking, and it is clear that some politicians and officials in the region are complicit. How to cooperate more effectively with African governments on this issue is a matter requiring urgent attention in Europe, particularly for countries such as Spain, Italy, the UK and the Netherlands that import considerable quantities of illegal narcotics from Africa.

In regard to security as well as many other matters, by no means all African states fall in the same category. While some countries have governments that are too weak to enforce their will more than a few kilometres from the presidency, others are sturdy enough to continue in their present form for the foreseeable future in spite of major weaknesses in territorial control and their frequent lack of interest in their people's welfare. All things considered, it appears that there are now emerging a handful of African states with quite high rates of economic growth that are able to finance their capital requirements through the market and that, in principle, should therefore not need concessionary financing from donors. These countries can reasonably be expected not to need donor support for their state budget. Some show signs of developing a middle class that has the wherewithal to invest at home, and a few of them could conceivably be on the verge of spectacular economic development. But for every South Africa, Nigeria or Ghana, with the ability to tap capital markets, there is a Central African Republic, a Malawi or a Burundi—small countries with limited resources, little ability to absorb or generate capital and overwhelmingly low-producing agrarian economies. It would be unrealistic to expect that they can attract finance through capital markets within the foreseeable future. Rich countries need to make strategic decisions concerning countries like these, which rely on donor funding for a large part of their state budgets. As long as they continue receiving money from benefactors for this purpose, they may be able to get along in something approaching their present state. If such funding dries up, the most likely consequence is that the reach of their state apparatus will become still smaller, and they will fall under the influence of more powerful neighbours, as happened in the 1990s to Liberia, the DRC and many other imploded states. This need not necessarily be a catastrophe, but it could turn into one if influential parties are unprepared. No European country can afford to maintain an equal interest in all of Africa's sovereign states, and European governments are thus obliged to decide where to concentrate their attention for development purposes. In the case of the Netherlands, a government commission on policy has recommended restricting development aid in Africa to perhaps ten countries.[31] The Netherlands has obvious commercial interests in a handful of African countries, including Kenya, Nigeria and South Africa. The dramatic growth of the cocaine trade suggests that it will need to devote serious attention, at least in the security sector, to West Africa.

Major political problems in Africa will in future attract the attention not only of the traditional OECD donors and of the leading African states and the African Union but also of other interested parties from Asia and elsewhere. The entry or re-entry into Africa of powers from Asia especially has fundamentally changed the strategic environment. Countries with Indian Ocean shorelines increasingly look to the powers on its far shores as commercial partners. Other places, too, notably those with significant Muslim populations, are developing dense cultural and commercial contacts with the Middle East and with financial centres in the Gulf. Although no Asian power has demonstrated any military ambition towards Africa, China and other Asian powers, like Africa's partners in Europe and North America, also find themselves growingly preoccupied with the question of how to ensure a minimum of order required for conventional trade or diplomacy. This is clearest in the case of Somalia, where piracy receives condemnation from all quarters. The government of any country that aspires to be a great power necessarily has to protect its interests outside its own borders, and seeks ways of arranging matters to its advantage, and it may be expected that China at least will consider military dispositions in Africa in the foreseeable future as it is already doing in the eastern Indian Ocean. For, as a British diplomat reminds us, 'the weak still need the strong and the strong still need an orderly world'.[32]

In short, a major area of attention for policy-makers both in Europe and elsewhere in coming years will surely be attention to the many 'fragile' states that enjoy sovereignty but that do not satisfy the conditions required of them by great powers or in which disorder otherwise poses a threat to international security. Just as piracy in Somalia poses a threat to shipping using the Red Sea and a stretch of the western Indian Ocean, insecurity in other parts of the continent could also pose wider threats to the interests of world powers. The need for enhanced security overlaps with poor oversight in a number of technical fields, such as control of territorial waters and protection against over-fishing and piracy, interdiction of the movement of counterfeit or illicit goods and control of airspace, where Africa's fragile states and their international partners have both reason to cooperate and the means to do so. Unlike the US, where Africom has developed a strategic vision embracing the whole of Africa, European countries have been slow to produce realistic responses to the security vacuum that affects large parts of the continent. The appointment in 2009 of an EU foreign minister gives this body a chance of articulating a foreign policy more effectively than it has done to date. The most likely way forward lies in grouping small numbers of EU member states with a common interest in developing a policy under the EU label on specific issues, as France has been the initiator of EU interventions in the DRC and Chad. In the case of West Africa, countries with a particular interest in the drug trade via West Africa, including France, Italy, the Netherlands, Spain and the UK, may be able to initiate an EU foreign policy initiative that aims at negotiating long-term cooperation with West African countries in fields of maritime surveillance, air-traffic control and drug law enforcement. On wider issues of security, too, the EU could be more effective in working both with the emerging African regional security forces designated by the African Union and with the US. After all, current defence spending by EU members is substantially more than that of China.[33]

In the world now emerging, Europeans perhaps more than anyone else have an interest in upholding a system of rules. Europe has been at the forefront of creating multilateral agreements covering common interests for well over a century. While in the past these structures have been dominated by European states, newly emerging or re-emerging powers are now taking a full part in these arrangements and institutions. China has in recent years signalled its growing willingness to uphold international structures, such as by its commitment of troops to UN peacekeeping missions. It has urged a review of the IMF's quota system with a view to enhancing its own participation, providing funding to the Fund's concessional loan resources and increasing its subscriptions to the IMF and the World Bank,[34] where China now has the third biggest block of votes. This is to be welcomed inasmuch as it allows well established world institutions to adapt their role in accordance with shifts in the balance of power. From a European perspective, decision-making through the UN, a formally constituted body, is preferable to the growth of informal international decision-making notably through the 'G-system' composed of the G-2, the G-8, the G-20 and others. It is therefore in the long-term interest of Europe's two permanent members of the UN Security Council, the United Kingdom and France, to work for reform of the UN system, including membership of its Security Council, since an improved UN system will contribute to a better system of peacekeeping, which remains one of Africa's most important problems. And, we have said, it is therefore a problem for the rest of the world, too.

In their pursuit of an orderly world, European countries may be advised to attach a higher priority to pragmatic cooperation with sovereign states in matters of mutual concern rather than working to advance the grand designs of global jurisdiction that grew during the 1990s. This is a matter that is difficult to discuss without being suspected either of a crude cultural relativism or unconcern about human rights. Since the Helsinki Declaration of 1975 and the championing of human rights by the Carter administration in the US, international human rights legislation has grown fast and has been applied with particular enthusiasm to Africa. The last two decades have witnessed the establishment of international courts to judge persons indicted for war crimes in regard to the 1994 Rwandan genocide and the war in Sierra Leone that lasted from 1991 to 2002. The International Criminal Court has opened investigations into a number of suspects in Africa and has issued indictments against a number of Africans, of which the most controversial concerns the president of Sudan. Whereas many African countries were enthusiastic signatories of the treaty establishing the ICC, and artful presidents may still find international justice useful for tactical purposes, the tide of African opinion appears to be turning against it. Moreover, few of the Asian powers now exercising increasing influence in Africa are keen on international justice either. This strongly suggests that international justice has reached its limits, at least for the foreseeable future, and that policy-makers should not be intent on extending it beyond what currently exists. The ICC clearly needs to consolidate its achievements to date before it takes on more ambitious goals. Similarly, major powers should be cautious about giving greater substance to the Responsibility to Protect that was adopted by the UN General Assembly in 2005, or at least they should not do so unless they are confident that such a move has very widespread international support.

Indeed, it is not only in regard to international criminal law that the tide may be receding, but also to the spread of the rule of law in the classic Western tradition, including in regard to commercial law. The rise of Asian influence brings with it a distinctive style of doing business. Just as Western businesspeople and policy-makers operate with a set of assumptions about how to set about their work that is based on what has become normal in their own countries, so do Asian and Middle Eastern policy-makers and entrepreneurs work with the habits emanating from their own histories. Whether they are businesspeople, religious activists or entrepreneurs, people coming from Asia and the Middle East are often better adapted to current conditions in Africa than are their Western counterparts since they are more used to dealing with the characteristic circumstances of emerging markets, in which the rule of law does not always play a central role, and in which transaction costs are regulated not by the state but by private parties using informal methods.

In sum, the emerging framework for European aid is a much more country-specific, less ideological, more pragmatic approach than in the past. Individual European countries will need to identify partner-countries in Africa with reference to their strategic importance as well as to historic links or other strong connections between a donor country and an African partner. Even within this framework, development policy will need to be tailored to the requirements of each country. Individual donors will therefore select those sectors in which they feel themselves the best equipped to work. In the case of the Netherlands, perhaps half of official aid is currently devoted to the fields of health and education, and rather less to infrastructure, agriculture and commerce.[35] The attention given by China to infrastructure projects, to widespread acclaim within Africa, suggests that European countries may wish to reconsider this field which was a donor favourite in the distant past. They may consider supporting the construction of infrastructure linking regional markets and centres within Africa, where only about 10–12 per cent of international trade takes place with other African nations, rather than with an eye on facilitating export marketing channels. Enhanced attention to infrastructure, security and other matters would inevitably reduce the budgets available for welfare provision, but, as has been pointed out,[36] welfare projects do not automatically lead to structural improvement or greater self-reliance.

Individual Western governments as well as non-governmental organisations and institutions will surely continue to give attention to key areas of social and economic life in Africa according to their own traditions and interests. In some circumstances, it may be advantageous to both parties to build linkages between specific institutions, such as hospitals, so that African staff can undergo part of their training in Europe, to mutual advantage, while retaining a link with hospitals in their home countries that can remain adequately equipped if they have such partnership arrangements. We have suggested that a crucial field of development in coming years may be land and agriculture in Africa, where the continent's relative abundance of agricultural land is attracting high interest from external investors. Since the Netherlands has internationally recognised expertise in many fields of agricultural research, this is one field that should be investigated further, including by means of training and professional exchanges in specific countries and the provision of services in technical fields. It is likely that in some fields civic activists will cultivate relationships with counterparts in Africa in regard to the women's movement, trade union activism and many others. There will remain groups of people in North Atlantic countries who may feel strongly about the need to provide assistance to people in Africa with whom they have links of some sort, possibly professional, or based on shared interest. There is no reason why this should not continue, such as in the field of solidarity and humanitarian organisations, church and mission societies, and so on. Much of this work may take place independent of governments, reducing the extent to which non-governmental organisations are *de facto* used to transmit privatised policy.

Decolonising the Western Mind

During the centuries that Europeans dominated the globe in so many respects, transforming the world in the process, they generated an extraordinary self-confidence that in many cases transmuted into a conviction that Europe has a duty to civilise the rest of the world. This idea was implanted in North America also, where it grew to form a key component of the US self-image. Africa came to play a particular part in this ideological scheme since in recent times it has been both the world's poorest continent and the one that can be most convincingly seen as a historic victim of the West.

In this book, it has been argued that Africa's special role in this particular vision of the world dates from the late eighteenth century, and that the modern vision of development is a direct descendant of the aspiration of nineteenth-century evangelicals to bring 'civilisation' to Africa, as they called it then. Mere mention of this genealogy makes many people in the aid business uncomfortable, as the vision or vocation of developing the poor world is often part of an ideology of equality, and it is therefore galling to be compared to the missionaries and paternalists of the past. What Africa's developers in past and present have in common is the assumption that the West—never really an exact geographical area, but a way of thinking that developed historically in Western Europe and North America—is in the vanguard of human history and that poor countries need to catch up. The passage of time is seen as a race, or perhaps a stately procession, in which the laggards may be helped towards the front ranks.

It is here that the financial crash that began in 2007 has had such a powerful effect. It has helped to define the prospect of a future in which Asian powers in particular have far more influence in the world than in the immediate past. This in turn obliges Westerners to reconsider many fundamental assumptions they have made in the past about their own place in the world. Grudgingly or otherwise, Europeans and North Americans will have to accept that not all of the ideas that they have distilled from a reading of their own history are milestones that have to be passed by all mankind on its journey into the future. By the same token, they will have to accept more than they are accustomed to doing that there are things they can learn from others.

> The signs of the rainy season
> say exactly what everyone wants to hear.[37]

It is to avoid the error of saying exactly what people want to hear that, I have argued in this short book, we need to consider Africa's recent history in ways that have more power to explain things than either the Africa-as-victim theory or the Africa-as-incompetent one, with their sub-variants. Only then are we equipped to understand Africa's place in a fast-changing world and to read accurately the omens concerning what may happen in the foreseeable future.

NOTES

INTRODUCTION

1. http://www.africaneconomicoutlook.org/fileadmin/uploads/aeo/Spreadsheets/Demographic%20Indicators.xls [accessed 4 June 2010]
2. John Iliffe, *Africans: The History of a Continent* (1995; 2nd edition, Cambridge University Press, 2007), p. 2.
3. http://www.africaneconomicoutlook.org/fileadmin/uploads/aeo/Spreadsheets/Demographic%20Indicators.xls [accessed 4 June 2010].
4. See the Mo Ibrahim Foundation website at www.moibrahimfoundation.org [accessed 20 May 2010].
5. William Wallis, 'Emerging Groups Make "African Lions" Roar', *Financial Times*, 1 June 2010.
6. Gerrie ter Haar, *Halfway to Paradise: African Christians in Europe* (Cardiff Academic Press, 1998).
7. Nick Wadhams, 'European Flight Paralysis Exacts High Price on the Kenyan Flower Trade', *The Guardian* [London], 20 April 2010.
8. A.G. Hopkins, 'The New Economic History of Africa', *Journal of African History*, 50, 2 (2009), pp. 162–3, noting Africa's relative wealth in 1500.
9. Simon Mpondo, 'The Season of the Rains', in Gerald Moore and Ulli Beier (eds), *The Penguin Book of Modern African Poetry* (1963; 3rd edn, Penguin, Harmondsworth etc., 1984), pp. 49–50.
10. Peter Cain and A.G. Hopkins, *British Imperialism: Innovation and Expansion* (Longman, London etc., 1993), p. 313.
11. Nicholas Stern, 'A Changed Africa still Needs our Help to Grow', *Financial Times*, 31 May 2010.
12. Stefan Halper, *The Beijing Consensus: How China's Authoritarian Model will Dominate the 21st Century* (Basic Books, New York, 2010).
13. Talk by Paul Mathieu of the UN Food and Agriculture Organisation, ministry of foreign affairs, The Hague, 16 December 2009.

14. Quoted in Pal Nyiri, *Foreign Concessions: The Past and Future of a Form of Shared Sovereignty* (inaugural lecture, VU University Amsterdam, 2009), p. 1.

15. 'The ANC: the Struggle for Control', Politicsweb, 23 July 2009, http://www.politicsweb.co.za/politicsweb/view/politicsweb/en/page71619?oid=137334&sn=Detail [accessed 16 August 2009].

16. Cf. Stephen Ellis and Gerrie ter Haar, *Worlds of Power: Religious Thought and Political Practice in Africa* (Hurst & Co., London, 2004).

17. Barry Sautman and Yan Hairong, 'The Forest for the Trees: Trade, Investment and the China-in-Africa Discourse', *Pacific Affairs*, 81, 1 (2008), pp. 9–29.

18. Philip Snow, *The Star Raft: China's Encounter with Africa* (Weidenfeld and Nicolson, London, 1988).

1. AFRICA IN TIME

1. The English translation is from the website of the Royal African Society at http://www.royalafricansociety.org/index.php?option=com_content& task=view&id=416. The French original may be found at http://www.elysee.fr/elysee/elysee.fr/francais/interventions/2007/juillet/allocution_a_l_universite_de_dakar.79184.html [both sites accessed 22 May 2010].

2. Finn Fuglestad, *The Ambiguities of History: The Problem of Ethnocentrism in Historical Writing* (Oslo Academic Press, 2005), esp. pp. 10–6.

3. S.J.S. Cookey, *King Jaja of the Niger Delta: His Life and Times, 1821–1891* (NOK publishers, New York, 1974).

4. *The Guardian*, Lagos, 13 July 2008: http://www.guardiannewsngr.com/sunday_magazine/article27//indexn3_html?pdate=130708&ptitle=Remembering%20Adam%20Fiberesima%20Of%20The%20Opera%20Opu%20Jaja%20Fame&cpdate=150708 [accessed 15 July 2008].

5. A brief history of Rivers State is included on the official website: http://www.riversstatenigeria.net/index.php?option=com_content&view=article&id=8&Itemid=9 [accessed 16 July 2008].

6. United Nations Office on Drugs and Crime, *Transnational Trafficking and the Rule of Law in West Africa: A Threat Assessment* (UNODC, Vienna, 2009), p. 26.

7. '"Blood Oil" Dripping from Nigeria', BBC News, 27 July 2008: http://newsvote.bbc.co.uk/mpapps/pagetools/print/news.bbc.co.uk/2/hi/africa/7519302.stm [accessed 28 July 2008]. A senior official of the Nigerian Drug Law Enforcement Agency doubts that cocaine is traded in the Niger Delta: see comments by Victor Cole-Showers at a conference in Washington, DC on 28 May 2009: http://www.wilsoncenter.org/

ondemand/index.cfm?fuseaction=media.play&mediaid=8D70
866F-A33B-FE56–0050236EBFFE0EB5 [accessed 6 August 2009].

8. AfricaFocus Bulletin, 5 June 2010, supplied by email: see www.africa-focus.org

9. E.g. Sebastian Junger, 'Blood Oil', *Vanity Fair*, February 2007: http://www.vanityfair.com/politics/features/2007/02/junger200702 [accessed 16 July 2008].

10. Toyin Falola and Matthew M. Heaton, *A History of Nigeria* (Cambridge University Press, 2008), p. 238.

11. Quoted in Henry L. Bretton, *Power and Stability in Nigeria: The Politics of Decolonization* (Frederick A. Praeger, New York, 1962), p. 127.

12. Quoted in James Booth, *Writers and Politics in Nigeria* (Hodder and Stoughton, London, 1981), p. 23.

13. John Peel, *Religious Encounter and the Making of the Yoruba* (Indiana University Press, Bloomington, IN, 2000).

14. See e.g. Bruce Berman and John Lonsdale, *Unhappy Valley: Conflict in Kenya and Africa* (2 vols, James Currey, London, 1992). For a succinct summary, John Lonsdale, 'Moral Ethnicity and Political Tribalism', in Preben Kaarsholm and Jan Hultin (eds), *Inventions and Boundaries: Historical and Anthropological Approaches to the Study of Ethnicity and Nationalism* (Occasional paper 11, International Development Studies, Roskilde University, 1994), pp. 131–50.

15. Helen Callaway and Dorothy O. Helly, 'Crusader for Empire: Flora Shaw/Lady Lugard', in Nupur Chaudhuri and Margaret Strobel (eds), *Western Women and Imperialism: Complicity and Resistance* (Indiana University Press, Bloomington, IN, 1992), pp. 79–97.

16. Sir F.D. Lugard, 'Report by Sir F.D. Lugard on the Amalgamation of Northern and Southern Nigeria, and Administration, 1912–1919', in A.H.M. Kirk-Greene (ed.), *Lugard and the Amalgamation of Nigeria: A Documentary Record* (Frank Cass, London, 1968), p. 67.

17. Ibid.

18. I.F. Nicolson, *The Administration of Nigeria 1900–1960: Men, Methods and Myths* (Clarendon Press, Oxford, 1969), p. 8.

19. An important, and hotly contested, essay on this subject is Achille Mbembe, 'A propos des écritures africaines de soi', *Politique africaine* 77 (2000), pp. 16–43. A subsequent English version, translated by Steven Rendall, published in *Public Culture* 14, 1 (2002), pp. 239–73, is significantly different in content.

20. See notably Adam Hochschild, *King Leopold's Ghost: A Story of Greed, Terror, and Heroism in Colonial Africa* (Houghton Mifflin, Boston, MA, etc., 1998). It was largely in response to the worldwide revulsion caused by this account of the Congo Free State that the Africa Museum

in Tervuren, Belgium, organised an exhibition that aimed to offer a more nuanced view of colonial history. See the catalogue edited by Jean-Luc Vellut et al, *Het Geheugen van Congo: De koloniale tijd* (Koninklijk Museum voor Midden-Africa, Tervuren, 2005); also Jan-Bart Gewald, 'More than Red Rubber and Figures Alone: a Critical Appraisal of the Memory of the Congo Exhibition at the Royal Museum for Central Africa, Tervuren, Belgium', *International Journal of African Historical Studies*, 39, 3 (2006), pp. 471–86.

21. The story of Britain, Sierra Leone and the American revolution is brilliantly told by Simon Schama, *Rough Crossings: Britain, the Slaves and the American Revolution* (BBC Books, London, 2005).

22. Obafemi Awolowo, *The Path to Nigerian Freedom* (Faber and Faber, London, 1947), pp. 47–8.

23. Jacob F. Ade Ajayi, 'Continuity of African Institutions under Colonial Rule', in Toyin Falola (ed.), *Tradition and Change in Africa: The Essays of J.F. Ade Ajayi* (Africa World Press, Trenton, NJ, 2000), p. 158. The original version of this essay was published in 1965.

24. See e.g. E.E. Osaghae, 'The State of Africa's Second Liberation', *Interventions*, 7, 1 (2005), pp. 1–20.

25. J.C. Anene, 'Jaja of Opobo', in K.O.Dike (ed), *Eminent Nigerians of the Nineteenth Century: A Series of Studies Originally Broadcast by the Nigerian Broadcasting Corporation* (Cambridge University Press, 1960), p. 25.

26. Cf. Catherine Coquery-Vidrovitch, 'De la périodisation en histoire africaine: peut-on l'envisager?', *Afrique et histoire*, 2 (2004), pp. 31–65.

27. Geoffrey Barraclough, *An Introduction to Contemporary History* (1964; Pelican edn., London, 1967), p. 20. Emphasis in the original. Barraclough, on p. 23 of the same text, makes probably the first recorded use of the term 'post-modern'.

28. Frederick Cooper, *Africa Since 1940: The Past of the Present* (Cambridge University Press, 2002), a standard work on Africa's contemporary history, takes 1940 as its starting-point.

29. William Pfaff, 'Mac Bundy Said He was "All Wrong"', *New York Review of Books*, LVII, 10 (10 June 2010), p. 59; cf. Wm. Roger Louis and Ronald Robinson, 'The U.S. and the End of British Empire in Tropical Africa', in Prosser Gifford and Wm. Roger Louis (eds), *The Transfer of Power in Africa: Decolonization, 1940–1960* (Yale University Press, New Haven and London, 1982), pp. 31–55.

30. The text of the speech is available at http://www.bartleby.com/124/pres53.html [accessed 6 August 2008].

31. UNCTAD statistics quoted by Adam Habib, 'Advancing African Development: the Necessity for Aid and Trade', African Arguments

blog: http://africanarguments.org/2009/03/advancing-african-development-the-necessity-for-aid-and-trade/ [accessed 6 August 2009].

32. See e.g. William Ellis, *History of Madagascar* (2 vols, Fisher and Son, London and Paris, 1838), I, p. 82. Gilbert Rist (trans. Patrick Camiller), *The History of Development: From Western Origins to Global Faith* (1997; new edn, Zed Books, London and New York, 2002), actually traces the idea of development to antiquity.

33. There is a case to be made for Western Sahara being in effect a colony of Morocco, while South Africa itself, legally speaking, ceased to be a colony in 1910.

34. W.R. Crocker, *Australian Ambassador: International Relations at First Hand* (Melbourne University Press, Carlton, Victoria, 1971), pp. 21–22.

35. Kwame Nkrumah, *The Autobiography of Kwame Nkrumah* (Thomas Nelson, Edinburgh, 1957), p. 164.

36. William Wallis and Tom Burgis, 'Attitudes Change to Business in Region', *Financial Times*, 4 June 2010.

37. Mark Mazower, *Dark Continent: Europe's Twentieth Century* (Penguin, London, 1998), p. 51.

38. Alan Burns, *In Defence of Colonies* (Geo. Allen & Unwin, London, 1957), p. 17.

39. Stephen W. Smith, 'Nodding and Winking', *London Review of Books*, 32, 3 (11 Feb. 2010), pp. 10–2.

40. '50 ans Françafrique cétro', special edition: www.afrique2010.fr [accessed 5 June 2010].

41. Crawford Young, 'The End of the Post-colonial State in Africa? Reflections on Changing African Political Dynamics', *African Affairs*, 103, 410 (2004), pp. 23–49.

42. I. William Zartman (ed.), *Collapsed States: The Disintegration and Restoration of Legitimate Authority* (Lynne Rienner, Boulder, CO, 1995).

43. In regard to Africa, see Achille Mbembe, *On the Postcolony* (University of California Press, Berkeley, 2001); also, Rita Abrahamsen, 'African Studies and the Postcolonial Challenge', *African Affairs*, 102, 407 (2003), pp. 189–210.

44. Peter Gowan, *The Global Gamble: Washington's Faustian Bid for World Dominance* (Verso, London and New York, 1999).

45. James Ferguson, *Global Shadows: Africa in the Neoliberal World Order* (Duke University Press, Durham, NC and London, 2006), esp. chaps. 1 and 8.

46. Mark Duffield, *Global Governance and the New Wars: The Merging of Development and Security* (Zed Books, London etc., 2001).

47. Interview with Dr Michael Power, Cape Town, 3 February 2009.

2. A WORLD OF LIGHT AND SHADE

1. Cf. Jean-François Bayart, 'Africa in the World: a History of Extraversion', *African Affairs*, 99, 395 (2000), pp. 217–67.
2. Quoted by Rana Foroohar, 'Where the Money is', *Newsweek International*, 5 Sept. 2005: http://kennethandersonlawofwar.blogspot.com/2005/08/newsweek-international-on-ngos-as.html [accessed 6 August 2009].
3. Michael A. Cohen, Maria Figueroa Küpçü, Parag Khanna, 'The New Colonialists', *Foreign Policy* (16 June 2008): http://www.foreignpolicy.com/story/cms.php?story_id=4351 [accessed 16 August 2009].
4. http://www.gatesfoundation.org/about/Pages/foundation-fact-sheet.aspx [accessed 30 December 2008].
5. Of which 192 are members of the UN. Only the Vatican is not.
6. See chapter 1, p. 16.
7. The phrase is used by Manuel Castells, *End of Millennium* (1998; 2nd edn, Blackwell, Oxford, 2000), p. 72, part III of *The Information Age*. Chapter 2 concerns what Castells calls 'the Rise of the Fourth World', and pp. 82–128 specifically concern Africa.
8. Global Financial Integrity, 'Illicit Financial Flows from Africa: Hidden Resource for Development' (internet publication, Washington DC, 2010), p. 5: www.gfip. org [accessed 1 May 2010].
9. A pseudonym used in the present text. Author's interview, Spain, 5 November 2009.
10. Namvula Rennie, 'The Lion and the Dragon: African Experiences in China', *Journal of African Media Studies*, 1, 3 (2009), pp. 379–414.
11. People's Daily online 11 March 2010: www.english.peoplesdaily.com.cn/90001/90777/908555/6915525.html [accessed 14 May 2010].
12. Police source.
13. UNHCR, '2008 Global Trends: Refugees, Asylum-seekers, Returnees, Internally Displaced and Stateless Persons', June 2009, p. 7: http://www.unhcr.org/statistics.html [accessed 1 June 2010].
14. Jean-François Bayart, Stephen Ellis and Béatrice Hibou, *The Criminalization of the State in Africa* (James Currey and the International African Institute, Oxford, 1999).
15. Gérard Prunier, *From Genocide to Continental War: The 'Congolese' Conflict and the Crisis of Contemporary Africa* (Hurst & Co., London, 2009), esp. pp. 13–4.
16. BBC News, 28 August 2010, 'Rwanda Threatens UN over DR Congo "Genocide" Report': http://www.bbc.co.uk/news/world-africa-11122650 [accessed 18 October 2010].

17. Prunier, *From Genocide to Continental War*, p. 459, note 10.

18. Stephen Ellis, 'Africa and International Corruption: the Strange Case of South Africa and Seychelles', *African Affairs*, 95, 379 (1996), pp. 165–96.

19. Ibid, p. 192.

20. The classic work is Walter Rodney, *How Europe Underdeveloped Africa* (Bogle-L'Ouverture, London, 1972). Another influential figure in spreading dependency theory in Africa was the Egyptian economist Samir Amin, the first executive secretary of the Council for the Development of Social Science Research in Africa (Codesria), Africa's leading social science research organisation. Codesria has been hooked ever since.

21. Quoted by Arthur Smithies in his memorial of Schumpeter, *American Economic Review*, 40, 4 (1950), p. 644.

22. Bayart, 'Africa in the World'.

23. Guy Arnold, *Africa: A Modern History* (Atlantic Books, London, 2005), pp. 935–6.

24. Cf. Tom Porteous, *Britain in Africa* (Zed Books, London etc., 2008).

25. Claude Ake, *Democracy and Development in Africa* (The Brookings Institution, Washington, DC, 1996), p. 1.

26. James Ferguson, *The Anti-Politics Machine: 'Development', Depoliticization, and Bureaucratic Power in Lesotho* (Cambridge University Press, 1990).

27. The best single book on how the Atlantic slave trade worked is Joseph C. Miller, *Way of Death: Merchant Capitalism and the Angolan Slave Trade, 1730–1830* (University of Wisconsin Press, Madison, WI, 1996).

28. Cooper, *Africa Since 1940*, ch.7.

29. Rémi Brague, *The Law of God: The Philosophical History of an Idea* (trans. Lydia G. Cochrane, University of Chicago Press, 2007), pp. 2, 12–13.

30. John Darwin, *After Tamerlane: The Global History of Empire* (Allen Lane, London, 2007), p. 237.

31. Walter Bagehot, 'The Danger of Lending to Semi-civilized Countries', in Norman St John Stevas (ed.), *The Collected Works of Walter Bagehot*, vol. 10 (*The Economist*, London, 1978), p. 419.

32. E.g. Bayart et al., *The Criminalization of the State in Africa*; Patrick Chabal and Jean-Pascal Daloz, *Africa Works: Disorder as Political Instrument* (James Currey and the International African Institute, Oxford, 1999).

33. This section borrows heavily from Stephen Ellis, 'Government by Graft: the Roots of Corruption in Africa', *Current History*, 105, 691 (May 2006), pp. 203–8.

34. An excellent overview is Malte Gephart, *Contextualizing Conceptions of Corruption: Challenges for the International anti-Corruption Campaign*

(Working Paper no. 115, German Institute of Global and Area Studies, Hamburg, 2009).

35. *Notre Voie* [Abidjan], no. 1929, 2 Nov. 2004.

36. Ike Okonta, 'Nigeria: Chronicle of a Dying State', *Current History*, 104, 682 (May 2005), p. 205.

37. Achille Mbembe, 'An Essay on the Political Imagination in Wartime', *Codesria Bulletin*, 2–4 (2000), pp. 6–21.

38. Estimate by Tax Justice Network: http://www.afrika.no/Detailed/ 11605.html [accessed 5 December 2009]; also, Global Financial Integrity, 'Illicit Financial Flows', p. 6.

39. World Bank, 'World Development Indicators Database', 19 April 2010: http://siteresources.worldbank.org/DATASTATISTICS/Resources/ GDP. pdf [accessed 1 June 2010].

40. Quoted in James Myburgh, 'Who is Kgalema Motlanthe?', 25 September 2008: http://www.politicsweb.co.za/politicsweb/view/politicsweb/en/page71619?oid=104369&sn=Detail [accessed 5 December 2009].

41. Andrew Feinstein, *After the Party: A Personal and Political Journey Inside the ANC* (Jonathan Ball, Johannesburg, 2007), esp. p. 177.

42. Author's interview, Johannesburg, 27 October 2009.

43. *Report of the Foster-Sutton Tribunal of Inquiry into Allegations of Improper Conduct by the Premier of the Eastern Region of Nigeria* (Her Majesty's Stationery Office, London, 1957).

44. National Archives and Records Administration, Maryland (NARA II), subject numeric files, RG59, Nigeria POL 15–4, 1/1/64, box 2525: Birney A. Stokes to Dept of State, 26 Jan. 1966.

45. Henry L. Bretton, *Power and Politics in Africa* (Longman, London, 1973), p. 129.

46. Raymond W. Baker, *Capitalism's Achilles Heel: Dirty Money and How to Renew the Free-market System* (John Wiley and Sons, New York, 2005), pp. 11–12.

47. Ronen Palan, Richard Murphy and Christian Chavagneux, *Tax Havens: How Globalization Really Works* (Cornell University Press, Ithaca, NY, 2010).

48. Ibid., p. 79.

49. Ronen Palan, *The Offshore World: Sovereign Markets, Virtual Places, and Nomad Millionaires* (Cornell University Press, London and Ithaca, 2003), p. 7.

50. European Commission, working document, SEC (2008) 196: 'An Examination of the Links between Organised Crime and Corruption' (unpublished).

51. 'Nigeria Suspends Siemens Dealings', BBC News, 6 December 2007, http://news.bbc.co.uk/2/hi/business/7130315.stm [accessed 16 August 2009].

52. 'Nigeria: the Gas Ghost Keeps Haunting', *Africa Confidential*, 49, 10 (9 May 2008), p. 1.

53. Michael Peel, 'The Global Graft Connection', *Financial Times*, 8 June 2010.

54. Quoted in John Ikubaje, *Corruption and Anti-Corruption: Revenue Transparency in Nigeria's Oil Sector* (Joe-tolalu and Associates, Lagos, 2005), p. 3.

55. John Hatchard, 'Combating Transnational Crime in Africa: Problems and Perspectives', *Journal of African Law*, 50, 2 (2006), p. 154.

56. United Nations Office on Drugs and Crime, *Cocaine Trafficking in West Africa: The Threat to Stability and Development (with special reference to Guinea-Bissau)* (UNODC, Vienna, 2007).

57. Flemming Quist, 'Drug Trafficking in West Africa 2000–2004 in an International Perspective', UNODC workshop on West African organised crime, Dakar, 2–3 April 2004.

58. Author's interview with UNODC official, London, 24 November 2009 and publicised remarks to the UN Security Council by UNODC chief Antonio Maria Costa, 9 December 2009.

59. Testimony of Thomas Harrigan to the Senate Committee on Foreign Relations, subcommittee on Africa, 23 June 2009: http://www.justice.gov/dea/pubs/cngrtest/ct062309.pdf [accessed 3 June 2010].

60. UNODC, *Cocaine Trafficking in West Africa*, p. 28.

61. Author's interview with UNODC official, London, 24 November 2009.

62. Global Financial Integrity, 'Illicit Financial Flows', p. 1. The figure of $1.8 trillion is adjusted.

63. Loretta Napoleoni, *Modern Jihad: Tracing the Dollars Behind the Terror Networks* (Pluto Press, London, 2003).

64. John K. Cooley, *Unholy Wars* (2001; new edn, Pluto Press, London, 2002), p. 90.

65. United States Senate, Permanent subcommittee on investigations of the Committee on Governmental Affairs, *Private Banking and Money Laundering: A Case Study of Opportunities and Vulnerabilities* (US Government Printing Office, Washington DC, 2000).

66. Francisco E. Thoumi, 'The Rise of Two Drug Tigers: the Development of the Illegal Drugs Industry and Drug Policy Failure in Afghanistan and Colombia', in F. Bovenkerk and M. Levi (eds), *The Organized Crime Community: Essays in Honor of Alan A. Block*, Studies of Organ-

ised Crime no. 6 (Spring Science and Business, New York, 2007), p. 126.

67. Robert I. Friedman, *Red Mafiya:How the Russian Mob has Invaded America* (Little, Brown, and Co., New York, 2000), pp. 57–8.

68. Misha Glenny, *McMafia: Seriously Organised Crime* (Vintage, London, 2009), part 1. In his introduction, on p. 3, Glenny suggests that the rot set in earlier, in the first half of the 1980s.

69. Eva Joly, *Est-ce dans ce monde-là que nous voulons vivre?* (Eds. Les Arènes, Paris, 2003), p. 190.

70. Cf. Feinstein, *After the Party*, pp. 252–3.

71. Michael Klare, *Blood and Oil* (2004; Penguin edn, London, 2005), esp. ch.2.

72. Joly, *Est-ce dans ce monde-là?*, p. 208 et seq.

73. Ibid., p. 215.

74. Ibid., pp. 206–56.

75. Ibid., pp. II-III, 209–10.

76. 'How the Super-rich just Get Richer', BBC News, 29 November 2007.

77. Stanley Cohen, 'Politics and Crime: Spot the Difference', *British Journal of Sociology*, 47, 1 (2001), pp. 1–21.

78. Charles Tilly, 'War Making and State-making as Organized Crime', in Peter Evans, Dietrich Rueschemeyer and Theda Skocpol (eds), *Bringing the State Back In* (Cambridge University Press, 1985), pp. 169–87.

79. Giorgio Blundo and Jean-Pierre Olivier de Sardan (eds), *Etat et corruption en Afrique: une anthropologie comparative des relations entre fonctionnaires et usagers* (Karthala, Paris, 2007).

80. Stanislav Andreski, *The African Predicament: A Study in the Pathology of Modernisation* (Michael Joseph, London, 1968), p. 109.

81. Gideon Rachman, 'Indian Democracy has an Ugly Side', *Financial Times*, 19 March 2009.

82. Michaela Wrong, *It's Our Turn To Eat: The Story of a Kenyan Whistle-blower* (Fourth Estate, London, 2009).

83. Ibid., pp. 223–4, 255–78.

84. On Nigeria, see Andrew Apter, *The Pan-African Nation: Oil and the Spectacle of Culture in Nigeria* (University of Chicago Press, Chicago, 2005); and Daniel J. Smith, *A Culture of Corruption: Everyday Deception and Popular Discontent in Nigeria* (Princeton University Press, 2007).

85. English translation in the possession of the author.

86. For a survey of the literature, see Daniel Large, 'Beyond "Dragon in the Bush": the Study of China-Africa Relations', *African Affairs* 107, 426 (2008), pp. 45–61.

87. http://news.xinhuanet.com/english/2009–11/09/content_12413128.htm [accessed 11 Dec.2009].

88. Barney Jopson, 'Chinese Copper Entrepreneurs Flee', *Financial Times*, 20 February 2009.

89. Author's interviews, Beijing, April 2009.

90. The newsletter *Africa-Asia Confidential* publishes information on Asian-African business relations in particular: www.africa-asia-confidential.com

91. Author's discussion with African business analyst, Addis Ababa, 19 August 2009.

92. *Cape Times*, 6 November 2009, quoted in Dot Keet, 'Practical and Tactical Challenges, and Strategic Perspectives for African Engagement with China' (unpublished conference paper, 2010).

93. National Intelligence Council, 'Mapping sub-Saharan Africa's Future', conference report, March 2005, p. 8: http://www.dni.gov/nic/confreports_africa_future.html [accessed 28 December 2008].

94. Mbembe, 'A propos des écritures africaines de soi', pp. 25–6.

95. Christopher Clapham, 'Fitting China in', Brenthurst Discussion Papers 8/2006: www.thebrenthurstfoundation.org [accessed 7 August 2009].

96. J.H. Mensah, quoted in William Wallis and Tom Burgis, 'Continent Drives a Harder Bargain', *Financial Times*, 14 June 2010.

97. Information supplied by US law enforcement officials, Chicago, 29 July 2009.

98. Glenny, *McMafia*, p. 382.

99. Ibid, pp. 359–68.

100. Interview with Dr Michael Power, Cape Town, 3 February 2009.

3. MONEY AND LAND

1. United Nations Conference on Trade and Development, *World Investment Report 2009* (UN, New York and Geneva, 2009), p. 42: http://unctad.org/en/docs/wir2009_en.pdf [accessed 1 June 2010]. Some observers consider these figures to be underestimates since they fail to capture financial movements outside formal banks, notably by African and Asian traders.

2. International Monetary Fund, 'World Economic Outlook Database', October 2009: http://www.imf.org/external/pubs/ft/weo/2009/02/weodata/weoreptc.aspx?sy=2007&ey=2014&scsm=1&ssd=1&sort=country&ds=.&br=1&c=001%2C110%2C163%2C119%2C203%2C123%2C998%2C200%2C605%2C603%2C904%2C901%2C505%2C511%2C405%2C205&s=NGDP_RPCH&grp=1&a=1&pr.x=62&pr.y=7 [accessed 2 June 2010]

3. Dilip Ratha, Sanket Mohapatra, and Ani Silwal, *Migration and Development Brief 11* (World Bank, Washington, DC, 3 November 2009).

4. Peter Guest, 'Africa is a Glimmer of Hope in Global Gloom', *Financial Times*, 3 November 2008.

5. Matthew Green, 'Brussels Takes on Gazprom in Nigeria', *Financial Times*, 17 September 2008.

6. Jedrzej George Frynas and Manuel Paulo, 'A New Scramble for African Oil? Historical, Political and Business Perspectives', *African Affairs* 106, no. 423 (2007), pp. 229–51.

7. Nicholas Shaxson, *Poisoned Wells: The Dirty Politics of African Oil* (Palgrave Macmillan, New York etc., 2007), pp. 1–2.

8. Peter York, *Dictators' Homes* (Atlantic Books, London, 2005), pp. 62–7, includes some photos.

9. Author's interview, Geneva, 30 January 2008.

10. Global Financial Integrity, 'Illicit Financial Flows from Africa', p. 36.

11. Author's interview with diplomatic sources, Lusaka, 17 November 2008.

12. Author's interviews, Nairobi, 10 November 2008.

13. John Gill, 'UK Looks Set to Benefit from Nigerian Student Boom', *Times Higher Education Supplement*, 11 December 2008.

14. Quoted in David Oakley, 'Ecobank Plans Africa's Biggest Rights Issue to Fund Growth', *Financial Times*, 21 August 2008.

15. 'Rwanda produceert mobiele telefoons', IPS, 6 Oct. 2008: www.afrikanieuws.nl/site/list_messages/20889 [accessed 17 Oct. 2008].

16. Julien-Pierre Du Maine de la Josserie, 'Idée de la Côte occidentale de Madagascar, depuis Ancouala au nord, jusqu'à Mouroundava désigné par les Noirs sous le nom Menabe', *Annales des voyages, de la géographie, et de l'histoire*, XI (1810), p. 48. This describes a journey in 1792.

17. Author's interview, Dubai, 6 April 2009.

18. Chibuike Uche, 'Bank of England versus the IBRD: did the Nigerian Colony Deserve a Central Bank?', *Explorations in Economic History*, 34, 2 (1997), p. 226.

19. William Wallis, 'Emerging Groups Make "African Lions" Roar', *Financial Times*, 1 June 2010.

20. Author's interview with African hedge-fund manager, London, 8 September 2008.

21. Robin Luckham et al., *The Middle Classes and their Role in National Development* (CDD/ODI Policy Brief no. 3, Centre for Democracy and Development, Accra, 2005), p. 6.

22. See the 2009 annual report at http://www.ecobank.com [accessed 22 June 2010].

23. Author's interview with asset manager, Accra, 28 August 2008.

24. Joseph Coomson, 'Ghana: London Stock Exchange Welcomes Country's Eurobond Issue', *Ghanaian Chronicle*, 9 October 2007.

25. Ghana News Agency, 17 December 2007: http://business.africanpath.com/article.cfm?articleID=48224 [accessed 24 September 2008]

26. 'Sonangol Holds 9.96 pct of BCP—Report', Reuters, 13 May 2008: http://www.reuters.com/article/rbssFinancialServicesAndRealEstateNews/idUSL1353908220080513 [accessed 24 September 2008].

27. 'Stash the Cash', *Africa Confidential*, 49, 6 (14 March 2008), p. 10. On Sonangol, see Ricardo Soares de Oliveira, 'Business Success, Angola-style: Postcolonial Politics and the Rise and Rise of Sonangol', *Journal of Modern African Studies*, 45, 4 (2007), pp. 595–619.

28. Reuters, 10 June 2008: http://business.smh.com.au/business/ipo-rocks-east-africa-20080610-2o88.html [accessed 24 September 2008].

29. David C. Nellor, 'The Rise of Africa's "Frontier" Markets', *Finance & Development* (Sept. 2008), pp. 30–3.

30. Han Koch, 'Afrikaanse beurzen in opkomst', *Trouw* [Amsterdam], 5 June 2008.

31. Alec Russell, 'A Real African Strategy Bucks the "Briefcase Banking" Trend', FT.com, 6 August 2007: www.ft.com/cms/s/6442dd7a [accessed 17 July 2008].

32. Quoted by Paul Trewhela, 'The Split in the ANC', 1 June 2010: www.politicsweb.co.za [accessed 2 June 2010].

33. Paul Trewhela, 'Malema, China and the "Mugabe Turn"', 17 April 2010, www.politicsweb.co.za [accessed 2 June 2010].

34. John Vandaele, 'China outdoes Europeans in Congo', Asia Times online, 12 Feb. 2008: http://www.atimes.com/atimes/China_Business/JB12Cb01.html [accessed 24 September 2008].

35. Antoine Roger Lokongo, 'Sino-DRC Contracts to Thwart the Return of Western Patronage', Pambazuka News, 422 (5 March 2009): http://www.pambazuka.org/en/category/africa_china/54567 [accessed 16 August 2009]; William Wallis, 'China Pact Threat to Congo IMF Aid', *Financial Times*, 15 May 2009.

36. 'Quiet President, Worried Country', *Africa Confidential*, 49, 12 (6 June 2008), p. 5.

37. Matthew Green and Jamil Anderlini, 'China's CDB Seals Nigerian Deal', FT.com, 30 October 2007: www.ft.com/cms/s/95491 [accessed 17 July 2008].

38. Tom Burgis, 'Brokers Resist Nigerian Watchdog', *Financial Times*, 7 June 2010; BBC News, 'Nigeria's Iron Lady Takes on Fraudsters', 1 July 2010: http://news.bbc.co.uk/2/hi/world/africa/10464725.stm

39. http://www.grofin.com/home.asp?PID=152&ToolID=2&ItemID=299 [accessed 11 August 2009].

40. www.ghanahomeloans.com [accessed 23 September 2008].

41. Nicholas Stern, 'A Changed Africa Still Needs our Help to Grow', *Financial Times*, 30 May 2010.

42. William Wallis, 'Humble Fare that Fed Trading Empire', *Financial Times*, 1 September 2008.

43. Author's interview with Dr Michael Power, Cape Town, 3 February 2009.

44. http://portal.pohub.com/portal/page?_pageid=761,264604&_ dad=pogprtl&_schema=POGPRTL [accessed 25 February 2009]; author's interviews, Dubai, 6 April 2009.

45. John Gray, 'We Simply do not Know!', *London Review of Books*, 31, 22 (19 Nov. 2009), p. 14.

46. Hernando de Soto, *The Mystery of Capital: Why Capitalism Triumphs in the West and fails Everywhere Else* (Basic Books, New York, 2000), p. 1.

47. Italics in original. Sayre P. Schatz, *Development Bank Lending in Nigeria: The Federal Loans Board* (Nigerian Institute of Social and Economic Research and Oxford University Press, Ibadan and London, 1964), p. 91.

48. Cf. Douglas Rimmer, 'Learning About Economic Development from Africa', *African Affairs*, 102, 408 (2003), pp. 469–91.

49. Talk by Paul Mathieu of the UN Food and Agriculture Organisation, ministry of foreign affairs, The Hague, 16 December 2009.

50. Bernard Berendsen (ed.), *Emerging Global Scarcities and Power Shifts* (KIT Publishers, Amsterdam, 2009).

51. G. Pascal Zachary, 'The Coming Revolution in Africa', *The Wilson Quarterly*, 32, 1 (2008): www.wilsoncenter.org [accessed 10 December 2008].

52. Peter M. Lewis, *Growing Apart: Oil, Politics, and Economic Change in Indonesia and Nigeria* (University of Michigan Press, Ann Arbor, MI, 2007).

53. On 'urban bias', see esp. Robert H. Bates, *Markets and States in Tropical Africa: The Political Basis of Agricultural Policies* (California University Press, Berkeley, CA, 1981).

54. Cf. Christian Geffray, *La Cause des armes au Mozambique: anthropologie d'une guerre civile* (Karthala, Paris, 1990).

55. The World Bank, *World Development Report, 2007: Development and the Next Generation* (The World Bank, Washington DC, 2006).

56. Zachary, 'The Coming Revolution in Africa'.

57. Javier Blas and Andrew England, 'Foreign Fields', *Financial Times*, 20 August 2008.

58. Lorenzo Cotula, Sonja Vermeulen, Rebecca Leonard and James Keeley, *Land Grab or Development Opportunity? Agricultural Investment and International Land Deals in Africa* (IIED, FAO and IFAD, Rome, 2009): ftp://ftp. fao.org/docrep/fao/011/ak241e/ak241e.pdf [accessed 6 August 2009].

59. Javier Blas, 'Chunk of Madagascar Rented by Daewoo to Grow Food for S Korea', *Financial Times*, 19 November 2008.

60. Ibid.; see the remarks by Didier Galibert to the French National Assembly on 6 May 2009: http://www.assemblee-nationale.fr/13/cr-cafe/08–09/c0809054.asp [accessed 6 August 2009].

61. Javier Blas, 'Saudis get First Taste of Foreign Harvest', *Financial Times*, 5 March 2009.

62. Javier Blas and William Wallis, 'US Investor sees Profit in Sudan', *Financial Times*, 10–11 January 2009.

63. Eric de la Chesnais, 'Le grand monopoly mondial des terres agricoles', *Le Figaro*, 16 November 2009.

64. Peter Geschiere et al. (eds), 'Autochthony and the Crisis of Citizenship', special number of *African Studies Review*, 49, 2 (2006); Peter Geschiere, *The Perils of Belonging: Autochthony, Citizenship, and Exclusion in Africa and Europe* (University of Chicago Press, 2009).

65. Catherine Boone, 'Property and Constitutional Order: Land Tenure Reform and the Future of the African State', *African Affairs*, 106, 425 (2007), pp. 557–86.

66. Joseph Ayee et al., 'Land-related Conflicts in Ghana: the Causes, Dynamics and Policy Implications in the Greater Accra and Eastern Regions' (Consortium for Development Partnerships, Codesria, Dakar, unpublished paper).

67. 'Ghana: Look North', *Africa Confidential*, 49, 19 (19 Sept. 2008), p. 10.

68. Rudolf ten Hoedt, 'Reportage: wie plukt de vruchten?', *Internationale* online, July 2010: http://www.isonline.nl/?node_id=65786.

69. Tom Burgis, 'Angola Launches $6 bn Agriculture Expansion', *Financial Times*, 4–5 October 2008.

70. Ibid.

71. Author's interview with official of the Zambian National Farmers' Union, Lusaka, 17 November 2008.

72. 'Malawi: Subsidising Agriculture is not enough', IRIN, 5 February 2008: http://www.irinnews.org/report.aspx?ReportID=76591 [accessed 1 December 2008].

73. Javier Blas, 'China Rules out Pursuit of Africa Farmland', *Financial Times*, 21 April 2009.

74. http://houseofchiefs.blogspot.com, 14 March 2009 [accessed 4 April 2009]. See also Sarah Monks, 'Scramble for Africa', *South China Morning Post*, 19 August 2008.

75. 'Malawi: Subsidising Agriculture is not enough', IRIN, 5 February 2008: http://www.irinnews.org/report.aspx?ReportID=76591 [accessed 1 December 2008]

76. Camilla Toulmin, *Climate Change in Africa* (Zed Books, London and New York, 2009).

77. Calestous Juma, Chair's summary, paragraph 1.3, 'Growing Prosperity: Agriculture, Economic Renewal and Development' (draft report, OECD, Paris, 2009).

4. HOW TO BE A HEGEMON

1. BBC News, 'African View: Big Men do not Die', 18 June 2009: http://news.bbc.co.uk/2/hi/africa/8107876.stm [accessed 22 June 2009].

2. Eyadema's career has been brilliantly described in the form of a novel, by Ahmadou Kourouma, *En attendant le vote des bêtes sauvages* (Seuil, Paris, 1998). An academic study is Comi M. Toulabor, *Le Togo sous Eyadema* (Karthala, Paris, 1986).

3. Bayart et al, *The Criminalization of the State in Africa*, pp. 20–2.

4. Craig Jacobs, 'Hobnobbing with SA's Rich and Famous', *Sunday Times* [Johannesburg], 25 October 2009.

5. See e.g. the video 'Ellen Johnson Sirleaf, Africa's First Elected Female President, Lifting up Liberia' http://www.huffingtonpost.com/2009/04/01/ellen-johnson Sirleaf-afr_n_182000.html [accessed 5 December 2009].

6. Ellen Johnson Sirleaf, *This Child Will be Great: Memoir of a Remarkable Life by Africa's First Woman President* (HarperCollins, New York, 2009).

7. Garba Deen Muhammad, 'Cecilia Ibru's Flippancies', *Sunday Trust* [Abuja] 28 October 2007.

8. Chapter 2, p. 51.

9. Jean-François Bayart, 'Les chemins de traverse de l'hégémonie coloniale en Afrique de l'ouest francophone: anciens esclaves, anciens combattants, nouveaux musulmans', *Politique africaine*, 105 (2007), pp. 202–6.

10. Jean-François Bayart, 'Hégémonie et coercition en Afrique sub-saharienne: la « politique de la chicotte »', *Politique africaine*, 110 (2008), p. 126.

11. See the preface to the second edition of Jean-François Bayart, *The State in Africa* (Polity Press, Cambridge, 2009).

12. Marshall Sahlins, *Apologies to Thucydides: Understanding History as Culture and Vice Versa* (University of Chicago Press, 2004), pp. 138–9.

13. Iliffe, *Africans: The History of a Continent*, p. 2.

14. On urban population, African Development Bank, *Human Development Indicators*, 2007, http://www.afdb.org/portal/page?_pageid=473,189 04239&_dad=portal&_schema=PORTAL [accessed 27 November 2008]; on total population, African Development Bank et al., *African Statistical Yearbook 2009* (ADB et al, Tunis etc., 2009), p. 30, from which I have extrapolated the figure of a billion.

15. Moses Nagbe, *Bulk Challenge* (Champion Publications, Cape Coast, Ghana, 1996), pp. 53–4.

16. Andrew Jack, 'In the Family Way', *Financial Times*, 10 December 2009.

17. The best-known African novels of social change in English are by Chinua Achebe, especially his trilogy beginning with *Things Fall Apart* (Heinemann, London, 1958).

18. On colonial military service by ex-slaves, see Gregory Mann, *Native Sons: West African Veterans and France in the Twentieth Century* (Duke University Press, Durham, NC, 2006); for a theoretical discussion, Bayart, 'Les chemins de traverse de l'hégémonie coloniale en Afrique de l'Ouest francophone'.

19. Lonsdale, 'Moral Ethnicity and Political Tribalism'.

20. William Reno, *Corruption and State Politics in Sierra Leone* (Cambridge University Press, 1995), esp. pp. 2–3 on 'shadow states'; Ferguson, *Global Shadows*. Glenny, *McMafia*, p. 8, analyses the 'shadow economies' of globalisation. Interestingly, the notion of a 'shadow' government was used already 50 years ago by Jean Suret-Canale, 'La Guinée dans le système colonial', *Présence africaine*, 29 (1959–60), p. 97.

21. Reno, *Corruption and State Politics*, p. 12.

22. Ibid., p. 3.

23. Stephen Ellis, 'The Okija Shrine: Death and Life in Nigerian Politics', *Journal of African History*, 49, 3 (2008), pp. 445–66.

24. International Marketing Council of South Africa, 'SA Men Get State Pensions Earlier', 16 July 2008: http://www.southafrica.info/services/government/pension-160708.htm [accessed 1 December 2008].

25. As revealed by the COSATU survey compiled by the sociology department at Wits University in 2008: Sociology of Work workshop, Johannesburg, 17–18 December 2008.

26. William Reno, 'Anti-Corruption Efforts in Liberia: Are they Aimed at the Right Targets?', *International Peacekeeping*, 15, 3 (2008), p. 394.

27. Lant Pritchett and Michael Woolcock, 'Solutions when the Solution is the Problem: Arraying the Disarray in Development', *World Development*, 32, 2 (2004), p. 193.

28. Ibid.

29. http://www.unbotswana.org.bw/undp/poverty.html [accessed 19 December 2009].

30. William Wallis and Tom Burgis, 'Attitudes Change to Business in Region', *Financial Times*, 4 June 2010.

31. Karl Polanyi, *The Great Transformation* (1944; Octagon Books, New York, 1975), p. 162.

32. National Intelligence Council, 'Mapping sub-Saharan Africa's Future', conference report, March 2005, p. 8: http://www.dni.gov/nic/confreports_africa_future.html [accessed 22 December 2008].

33. Ricardo Soares de Oliveira, *Oil and Politics in the Gulf of Guinea* (Hurst & Co., London, 2007), pp. 79–83.

34. Soares de Oliveira, 'Business Success, Angola-style'.

35. Soares de Oliveira, *Oil and Politics in the Gulf of Guinea*, pp. 20–1. The memorable phrase 'successful failed state' seems to have been invented by Gérard Prunier and Rachel Gisselquist.

36. Phillip Bobbitt, *The Shield of Achilles: War, Peace and the Course of History* (Penguin, London, 2002), p. xxvi and *passim*; Robert Cooper, 'The Post-modern State', in Mark Leonard (ed.), *Re-Ordering the World: The Long-term Implications of 11 September* (The Foreign Policy Centre, London, 2002), pp. 11–20.

37. De Soto, *The Mystery of Capital*, p. 1.

38. Mary Douglas, quoted in Richard Seaford, *Money and the Early Greek Mind: Homer, Philosophy, Tragedy* (Cambridge University Press, 2004), p. 8, note 32.

39. Ellis and Ter Haar, *Worlds of Power*, p. 14.

40. John Lonsdale, 'States and Social Processes in Africa: A Historiographical Survey', *African Studies Review*, 24, 2–3 (1981), p. 139.

41. Biko Agozino, 'Crime, Criminology and post-Colonial theory: Criminological Reflections on West Africa', in James Sheptycki and Ali Wardak (eds), *Transnational and Comparative Criminology* (Glasshouse Press, London, 2005), p. 125.

42. Brague, *The Law of God*, p. 2.

43. Ibid, pp. 12–3.

44. Simeon O. Eboh, 'Law and Order in the Society: The Nigerian Experience', *The Nigerian Journal of Theology*, 18 (2004), p. 24.

45. Kwasi Wiredu, 'Modes of Thought in African Philosophy', in John Middleton (editor-in-chief), *Encyclopaedia of Africa South of the Sahara* (4 vols, Charles Scribner's Sons, New York, 1997), 3, p. 171.

46. Polycarp Ikuenobe, 'Moral Thought in African Cultures? A Metaphilosophical Question', *African Philosophy*, 12, 2 (1999), pp. 109–16.

47. Brague, *The Law of God*, p. 239.

48. Eboh, 'Law and Order in the Society', p. 24.

49. Filip De Boeck, comment in 'Ethnographic Sorcery', *African Studies Review* 51, 3 (2008), p. 143.

50. 'Introduction', pp. xxii–xviii, in Jacob Olupona (ed.), *African Spirituality: Forms, Meanings and Expressions* (Crossroad Publishing, New York, 2000).

51. Mbembe, 'An Essay on the Political Imagination in Wartime', esp. pp. 7–8.

52. Ruth Marshall, *Political Spiritualities: The Pentecostal Revolution in Nigeria* (University of Chicago Press, 2009).

53. Cf. Jean and John L. Comaroff (eds), *Modernity and its Malcontents: Ritual and Power in Postcolonial Africa* (University of Chicago Press, 1993).

54. 'The Year the God of Finance Failed', *Financial Times*, 27–28 December 2008.

55. James Buchan, *Frozen Desire: The Meaning of Money* (Farrar, Straus, and Giroux, New York, 1997), pp. 61 (quotation), 112–14, 138–9.

56. Seaford, *Money and the Early Greek Mind*.

57. Presidential address to the Classical Association by Richard Seaford, summarised as 'World without Limits', *Times Literary Supplement*, 19 June 2009.

58. See e.g. India's Honey Bee network: www.sristi.org/hbnew/aboutus.php [accessed 10 December 2009].

59. Toulmin, *Climate Change in Africa*.

5. MATTERS OF STATE

1. Paul Kennedy, *The Parliament of Man: The United Nations and the Quest for World Government* (Penguin edn., London, 2007), pp. 69–71. The quotation is on p. 76.

2. Ferguson, *Global Shadows*, ch.3.

3. Strobe Talbott, *The Russia Hand: A Memoir of Presidential Diplomacy* (Random House, New York, 2002), p. 85.

4. Darwin, *After Tamerlane*.

5. Rigsarkivet, Copenhagen, Denmark: archives of the Vestindisk-Guineisk Kompagni, boxes 219–21, journal of Charles Barrington, pt. IV, p. 69, entry for 20/31 Jan. 1738.

6. Soares de Oliveira, *Petroleum and Politics*, p. 30.

7. Quoted in Robert A. Smith, *The Emancipation of the Hinterland* (The Star Magazine and Advertising Services, Monrovia, 1964), p. 5.

8. Eric D. Weitz, 'From the Vienna to the Paris System: International Politics and the Entangled Histories of Human Rights, Forced Deportations, and Civilizing Missions', *American Historical Review*, 113, 5 (2008), p. 1321.

9. John D. Hargreaves, *West Africa Partitioned* (2 vols., Macmillan, London, 1974), I, p. 40.

10. Gerard Kreijen, 'State Failure, Sovereignty and Effectiveness: Legal Lessons from the Decolonization of sub-Saharan Africa' (PhD thesis, University of Leiden, 2003).

11. Christopher Andrew and Vasili Mitrohkin, *The Mitrohkin Archive II: The KGB and the World* (Allen Lane, London, 2005), ch. 23, esp. pp. 480–1.

12. Stephen Ellis, *The Mask of Anarchy: The Destruction of Liberia and the Religious Dimension of an African Civil War* (Hurst & Co., London, 1999).

13. http://www.pbs.org/newshour/bb/white_house/january97/albright_1–24.html [accessed 27 December 2008].

14. Stewart Patrick and Kaysie Brown, *Greater than the Sum of its Parts? Assessing 'Whole of Government' Approaches to Fragile States* (International Peace Academy, New York, 2007), p. 4.

15. Mohamed Ahmed, 'Pirate Stock Exchange Helps Fund Hijackings', Reuters, 1 December 2009.

16. Information supplied by J. Peter Pham, Senior Fellow and Director, Africa Project National Committee on American Foreign Policy, 17 August 2009.

17. Béatrice Hibou (ed.), *The Privatisation of the State* (Hurst & Co., London, 2005).

18. Quoted in Bayart, 'Hégémonie et coercition en Afrique sub-saharienne', p. 123.

19. Interview with Inspector General of Police Tafa Balogun, *Tell* [Lagos], 6 September 2004.

20. The charge sheet is published at http://www.nairaland.com/nigeria/topic-42.0.html [accessed 27 April 2010].

21. E.g. Basil Davidson, *The Black Man's Burden: Africa and the Curse of the Nation-state* (James Currey, London, 1992).

22. G.W.F. Hegel, *Lectures on the Philosophy of World History* (1830; trans. and introduced by H.B. Nisbet and Duncan Forbes, Cambridge University Press, 1975), esp. p. 174.

23. E.g. Osaghae, 'The State of Africa's Second Liberation', p. 11.

24. See e.g. the essays by Paul Tiyambe Zeleza and Godwin R. Murunga in *Codesria Bulletin*, 1 & 2 (2004).

25. E.g. B.A. Ogot, 'The Historical Development of African Societies, 1500–1800', in UNESCO, *General History of Africa*, V (Heinemann/Unesco/University of California Press, London etc., 1992), p. 895.

26. Cf. Bayart, 'Africa in the World'.

27. Public address by Fatou Bensouda, Africa-Europe Group on International Studies (AEGIS) conference, Leiden, 12 July 2007.

28. See Chapter 2, p. 38.

29. Ronald Robinson, 'Non-European Foundations of European Imperialism: Sketch for a Theory of Collaboration', in E.R.J. Owen and R.B. Sutcliffe (eds), *Studies in the Theory of Imperialism* (Longman, London, 1972), pp. 117–42.

30. Robert H. Bates, *When Things Fell Apart: State Failure in Late-century Africa* (Cambridge University Press, 2008).

31. Mushtaq H. Khan, 'Governance and Growth: History, Ideology and Methods of Proof', unpublished paper.

32. David Sogge, *State Weakness: Seen from Another Perspective* (Working Paper 64, Fundacion para las Relaciones Internacionales y el Dialogo Exterior, Madrid, 2008), p. 2. Italics in original.

33. Jeff Herbst, *States and Power in Africa: Comparative Lessons in Authority and Control* (Princeton University Press, 2000), p. 19.

34. Prunier, *From Genocide to Continental War*.

35. Simon Chesterman, 'The UN Security Council and the Rule of Law', Institute for International Law and Justice, New York University, 2008: http://papers.ssrn.com/sol3/papers.cfm?abstract_id=1279849 [accessed 14 March 2009].

36. Dennis Tull and Andreas Mehler, 'The Hidden Costs of Power-sharing: Reproducing Insurgent Violence in Africa', *African Affairs*, 104, 416 (2005), pp. 375–98.

37. Chesterman, 'The UN Security Council'.

38. Interview with former head of UN peacekeeping Jean-Marie Guéhenno, *NRC Handelsblad* [Rotterdam], 15 November 2008.

39. Harvey Morris, 'UN Considers Future of its Thin Blue Line', *Financial Times*, 4 August 2009.

40. Alex de Waal, 'Mission without End? Peacekeeping in the African Political Marketplace', *International Affairs*, 85, 1 (2009), pp. 99–113. The notion of a political marketplace was discussed at a conference at Tufts University, Boston, on 3–4 December 2009.

41. Human Security Centre, *Human Security Report 2005: War and Peace in the 21st century* (Oxford University Press, New York, 2005). This has

given rise to a debate on the number of deaths in Congo, but the general decline in the number of African wars is indisputable.

42. Cf. Herbst, *States and Power in Africa*, pp. 264–72.

43. Cf. Mahmood Mamdani, *Saviors and Survivors: Darfur, Politics, and the War on Terror* (Pantheon Books, New York, 2009), pp. 273–88.

44. The precise numbers remain a matter of debate. See Human Security Report, 'The Shrinking Costs of War', chapter 3: http://www.hsr-group. org/docs/Publications/HSR2009/2009HumanSecurityReport_Pt2_3_DeathTollDemocraticRepublicCongo.pdf

45. As the present author did when recruited by the British organisation Voluntary Service Overseas to work as a teacher in central Africa in 1971.

46. Robert Wright, 'Piracy Brings Rich Booty to Somali Shores', *Financial Times*, 3 March 2009; see also 'Gouverner la mer: Etats, pirates, sociétés', special number, *Politique africaine*, 116 (2009).

47. International Crisis Group, *Somalia: To Move Beyond the Failed State* (Africa Report no. 147, Nairobi/Brussels, 23 December 2008), p. 22.

48. Stephen Ellis, 'How to Rebuild Africa', *Foreign Affairs*, 84, 5 (2005), pp. 135–48.

49. Andre Le Sage, 'Africa's Irregular Security Threats: Challenges for U.S. Engagement', Institute for National Strategic Studies, National Defense University, Washington DC, *Strategic Forum*, 255 (May 2010).

50. Clapham, 'Fitting China in'.

51. Bayart, 'Africa in the World'.

6. TWENTY-FIRST CENTURY DEVELOPMENT

1. A good summary of a radical view is Osaghae, 'Africa's Second Liberation'.

2. Shaxson, *Poisoned Wells*, p. 76.

3. Currently the subject of the research project Tracking Development, sponsored by the Netherlands Ministry of Foreign Affairs.

4. Porteous, *Britain in Africa*, p. 42.

5. Chapter 1, p. 9.

6. Joseph C. Miller, 'History and Africa/Africa and History', *American Historical Review*, 104, 1 (1999), pp. 1–32.

7. Abolade Adeniji, 'Universal History and the Challenge of Globalization to African Historiography', *Radical History Review*, 91 (2005), p. 100.

8. UNDP, 'Human Development Reports': http://hdr.undp. org/en/humandev/ [accessed 24 June 2010].

9. Joseph Stiglitz, *Globalization and its Discontents* (W.W. Norton & Co., New York, 2002), p. 91.

10. Halper, *The Beijing Consensus*.

11. http://www.africaneconomicoutlook.org/fileadmin/uploads/aeo/ Spreadsheets/Basic%20indicators%202008.xls [accessed 11 June 2010].

12. Arjan de Haan, *Will China Change International Development As We Know It?* (ISS Working Paper 475, Institute of Social Studies, The Hague, 2009).

13. Jonathan Benthall and Jérôme Bellion-Jourdan, *The Charitable Crescent: Politics of Aid in the Muslim World* (I.B. Tauris, London, 2003).

14. 'Africans Trust Religious Leaders', BBC News, 14 September 2005: http://news.bbc.co.uk/2/hi/africa/4246754.stm [accessed 10 June 2010].

15. Cf. Mark Gevisser, *Thabo Mbeki: The Dream Deferred* (Jonathan Ball, Johannesburg, 2007).

16. Stephen Ellis and Gerrie ter Haar, 'Religion and Politics: Taking African Epistemologies Seriously', *Journal of Modern African Studies*, 45, 3 (2007), pp. 385–401.

17. Breyten Breytenbach, 'Mandela's Smile: Notes on South Africa's Failed Revolution', *Harpers Magazine* (December 2008): http://www. thetruthseeker.co.uk/article.asp?ID=9848 [accessed 28 May 2009].

18. Deepak Lal, *Unintended Consequences: The Impact of Factor Endowments, Culture and Politics on Long-run Economic Performance* (The MIT Press, Cambridge, MA, 1998), p. 177.

19. The phrase is used by Zbigniew Brzezinski, *Out of Control: Global Turmoil on the Eve of the Twenty-first Century* (Charles Scribner's Sons, New York, 1993).

20. Achille Mbembe, *On the Postcolony* (University of California Press, Berkeley and Los Angeles, 2001), p. 7.

21. E.g. William Easterly, *The White Man's Burden: Why the West's Efforts to Aid the Rest Have Done So Much Ill and So Little Good* (Penguin Books, New York etc., 2006). Particularly highly publicised is Dambisa Moyo, *Dead Aid: Why Aid isn't Working and how there is Another Way for Africa* (Allen Lane, London, 2009).

22. Wetenschappelijke Raad voor het Regeringsbeleid, *Minder pretentie, meer ambitie: ontwikkelingshulp die verschil maakt* (WRR and Amsterdam University Press, The Hague and Amsterdam, 2010), pp. 44–53.

23. Ibid, pp. 11–2.

24. Cf. UN Office on Drugs and Crime, *The Role of Organized Crime in the Smuggling of Migrants from West Africa to the European Union* (UNODC, Vienna, forthcoming).

25. An exception was Larry Minear, Colin Scott and Thomas Weiss, *The News Media, Civil War, and Humanitarian Action* (Lynne Rienner, Boulder, CO and London, 1996), pp. 147–50.

26. http://www.globalsecurity.org/military/ops/pan-sahel.htm [accessed 24 June 2010].

27. James D. Le Sueur, *Between Terror and Democracy: Algeria since 1989* (Fernwood Publishing etc., Black Point, Nova Scotia etc., 2010), pp. 122–42.

28. Danilo Zolo, *Victors' Justice: From Nuremburg to Baghdad* (2006; English translation by M.W. Weir, Verso, London, 2009).

29. Antonio L. Mazzitelli, 'Transnational Organized Crime in West Africa: The Additional Challenge', *International Affairs*, 83, 6 (2007), p. 1075.

30. UNODC, 'Cocaine Trafficking in Western Africa, Situation Report', October 2007, pp. 3–5: http://www.google.com/search?hl=en&q=U NODC+Situation+Report%E2%80%99%2C+October+2007&btnG=Sea rch [accessed 24 November 2008].

31. WRR, *Minder pretentie, meer ambitie*, p. 13.

32. Cooper, 'The Post-modern State', p. 17.

33. Mark Leonard, director of the European Council on Foreign Relations, in a lecture at the Vrije Universiteit Amsterdam, 10 June 2010, stated that EU defence spending was four times that of China. An internet search suggests that most sources would place EU's military budgets combined as closer to twice China's.

34. Statement by Zhou Xiaochuan, governor, People's Bank of China, IMF International Monetary and Financial Committee, 24 April 2010: http://www.imf.org/External/spring/2010/imfc/statement/eng/ chn.pdf [accessed 10 June 2010].

35. WRR, *Minder pretentie, meer ambitie*, p. 11, is mistaken in attributing 75 per cent to welfare.

36. Ibid.

37. Mpondo, 'The Season of the Rains'.

BIBLIOGRAPHY

Unpublished Documents

Ayee, Joseph et al., 'Land-related Conflicts in Ghana: the Causes, Dynamics and Policy Implications in the Greater Accra and Eastern Regions' (Consortium for Development Partnerships, Codesria, Dakar).

Congress of South African Trade Unions (COSATU) survey, 2008 (department of sociology, University of the Witwatersrand, Johannesburg).

European Commission, working document, SEC (2008) 196: 'An Examination of the Links between Organised Crime and Corruption'.

Juma, Calestous, 'Growing Prosperity: Agriculture, Economic Renewal and Development' (draft report, Organisation for Economic Cooperation and Development, Paris, 2009).

Keet, Dot, 'Practical and Tactical Challenges, and Strategic Perspectives for African Engagement with China' (2010).

Khan, Mushtaq H., 'Governance and Growth: History, Ideology and Methods of Proof', School of Oriental and African Studies, London.

Kreijen, Gerard, 'State Failure, Sovereignty and Effectiveness: Legal Lessons from the Decolonization of sub-Saharan Africa' (PhD thesis, University of Leiden, 2003).

National Archives and Records Administration, Maryland (NARA II), USA: subject numeric files RG59, Nigeria POL 15–4, 1/1/64, box 2525: Birney A. Stokes to Dept of State, 26 Jan. 1966.

Quist, Flemming, 'Drug Trafficking in West Africa 2000–2004 in an International Perspective' (paper presented at United Nations Office on Drugs and Crime workshop on West African organised crime, Dakar, Senegal, 2–3 April 2004).

Rigsarkivet, Copenhagen, Denmark: archives of the Vestindisk-Guineisk Kompagni, boxes 219–21, journal of Charles Barrington, 1738.

Newspapers, magazines, press agencies

Africa-Asia Confidential, London.

Africa Confidential, London.

Cape Times, Cape Town.

Financial Times, London.

Figaro, Paris.

Ghana News Agency, Accra.

Ghanaian Chronicle, Accra.

Guardian, Lagos.

Guardian, London.

Notre Voie, Abidjan.

NRC Handelsblad, Rotterdam.

Reuters New Agency, London.

South China Morning Post, Hong Kong.

Sunday Times, Johannesburg.

Sunday Trust, Abuja.

Tell, Lagos.

Trouw, Amsterdam.

Internet Sites and Publications

AfricaFocus Bulletin, 5 June 2010, published online by www.africafocus. org.

African Development Bank, *Human Development Indicators*, 2007: http:// www.afdb.org / portal / page?_pageid=473,18904239&_dad=portal&_ schema=PORTA.

African Economic Outlook: http://www.africaneconomicoutlook.org.

Afrique 2010: http://www.afrique2010.fr.

Assemblée Nationale, France: http://www.assemblee-nationale.fr/.

Bartleby http://www.bartleby.com/124/pres53.html.

BBC News: http://news.bbc.co.uk.

Bill and Melinda Gates Foundation: http://www.gatesfoundation.org/ about/Pages/foundation-fact-sheet.aspx.

Chesterman, Simon, 'The UN Security Council and the Rule of Law', Institute for International Law and Justice, New York University, 2008: http://papers.ssrn.com/sol3/papers.cfm?abstract_id=1279849.

Clapham, Christopher, 'Fitting China in', Brenthurst Discussion Papers 8/2006: http://www.thebrenthurstfoundation.org.

Cohen, Michael A., Maria Figueroa Küpçü and Parag Khanna, 'The New Colonialists', *Foreign Policy* (16 June 2008): http://www.foreignpolicy. com/story/cms.php?story_id=4351.

Dubai Ports World: http://portal.pohub.com/portal/page?_pageid=761, 264604&_dad=pogprtl&_schema=POGPRTL.

Ecobank: http://www.ecobank.com.

Foroohar, Rana, 'Where the Money is', *Newsweek International*, 5 Sept. 2005: http://kennethandersonlawofwar.blogspot.com/2005/08/newsweek-international-on-ngos-as.html.

Financial Times, FT.com: http://www.ft.com.

French Republic, presidency: http://www.elysee.fr/elysee/elysee.fr/francais/interventions/2007/juillet/allocution_a_l_universite_de_dakar.79184.html.

Ghana Home Loans: http://www.ghanahomeloans.com.

Global Financial Integrity, 'Illicit Financial Flows from Africa: Hidden Resource for Development' (internet publication, Washington DC, 2010), p. 5: www.gfip. org.

GroFin: http://www.grofin.com.

Habib, Adam, 'Advancing African Development: the Necessity for Aid and Trade', African Arguments blog: http://africanarguments.org/2009/03/advancing-african-development-the-necessity-for-aid-and-trade/.

Honey Bee network: http://www.sristi.org/hbnew/aboutus.php.

House of Chiefs, Zambia: http://houseofchiefs.blogspot.com.

Huffington Post: http://www.huffingtonpost.com.

Human Security Report, 'The Shrinking Costs of War': http://www.hsr-group. org/docs/Publications/HSR2009/2009HumanSecurityReport_Pt2.

Integrated Regional Information Networks, United Nations Office for the Coordination of Humanitarian Affairs (IRIN): http://www.irinnews. org. Inter Press Service news agency (IPS): http://www.afrikanieuws. nl/site/list_messages/20889.

International Marketing Council of South Africa: http://www.southafrica. info/services/government/pension-160708.htm.

International Monetary Fund, 'World Economic Outlook Database', October 2009: http://www.imf.org/external/pubs/ft/weo/2009.

King, Martin Luther, 'Beyond Vietnam: a Time to Break Silence', published at http://www.hartford-hwp. com/archives/45a/058.html.

Lokongo, Antoine Roger, 'Sino-DRC Contracts to Thwart the Return of Western Patronage', Pambazuka News, 422 (5 March 2009): http://www.pambazuka.org/en/category/africa_china/54567.

Mo Ibrahim Foundation: http://www.moibrahimfoundation.org.

Myburgh, James, 'Who is Kgalema Motlanthe?', 25 September 2008: http://www.politicsweb.co.za/politicsweb/view/politicsweb/en/page71619?oid=104369&sn=Detail.

Nairaland: http://www.nairaland.com.

National Intelligence Council, Washington DC, 'Mapping sub-Saharan Africa's Future', 2005: http://www.dni.gov/nic/confreports_africa_future.html.

People's Daily online, China: http://www.english.peoplesdaily.com.cn/90001/ 90777/908555/6915525.html.

Politicsweb, South Africa: http://www.politicsweb.co.za/politicsweb/view/politicsweb/en/page71619?oid=137334&sn=Detail.

Rivers State, Nigeria: http://www.riversstatenigeria.net.

Royal African Society: http://www.royalafricansociety.org/index.php?option=com_content&task=view&id=416.

Tax Justice Network: http://www.afrika.no/Detailed/11605.html.

Ten Hoedt, Rudolf, 'Reportage: wie plukt de vruchten?', *Internationale Samenwerking* online, July 2010: http://www.isonline.nl/?node_id=65786.

Trewhela, Paul, 'Malema, China and the "Mugabe Turn"', 17 April 2010, http://www.politicsweb.co.za.

Trewhela, Paul, 'The Split in the ANC', 1 June 2010: http://www.politicsweb.co.za.

United Nations Conference on Trade and Development, *World Investment Report 2009* (UN, New York and Geneva, 2009): http://unctad.org/en/docs/wir2009_en.pdf.

United Nations Development Programme, Botswana: http://www.unbotswana.org.bw/undp/poverty.html.

United Nations Development Programme, 'Human Development Reports': http://hdr.undp. org/en/humandev/.

United Nations High Commissioner for Refugees, '2008 Global Trends: Refugees, Asylum-seekers, Returnees, Internally Displaced and Stateless Persons', June 2009: http://www.unhcr.org/statistics.html.

United Nations Office on Drugs and Crime, 'Cocaine Trafficking in Western Africa, Situation Report', October 2007: http://www.google.com/search?hl=en&q=UNODC+Situation+Report%E2%80%99%2C+October+2007&btnG=Search.

United States Senate Committee on Foreign Relations, subcommittee on Africa, testimony of Thomas Harrigan (Drug Enforcement Administration), 23 June 2009: http://www.justice.gov/dea/pubs/cngrtest/ct062309.pdf.

Uys, Stanley, 'The ANC: the Struggle for Control', Politicsweb, 23 July 2009, http://www.politicsweb.co.za/politicsweb/view/politicsweb/en/page71619?oid=137334&sn=Detail.

Vandaele, John, 'China Outdoes Europeans in Congo', Asia Times online, 12 Feb. 2008: http://www.atimes.com/atimes/China_Business/JB12Cb01.html.

Woodrow Wilson Center for International Studies, Washington DC:
http://www.wilsoncenter.org.

World Bank, 'World Development Indicators Database', 19 April 2010:
http://siteresources.worldbank.org.

Xinhua news agency: news.xinhuanet.com/english.

Zhou Xiaochuan, statement to the IMF International Monetary and Financial Committee, 24 April 2010: http://www.imf.org/External/spring/
2010/imfc/statement/eng/chn.pdf.

Published Books and Articles

Abrahamsen, Rita, 'African Studies and the Postcolonial Challenge', *African Affairs*, 102, 407 (2003), pp. 189–210.

Achebe, Chinua, *Things Fall Apart* (Heinemann, London, 1958).

Ade Ajayi, Jacob F., 'Continuity of African Institutions under Colonial
Rule', in Toyin Falola (ed.), *Tradition and Change in Africa: The Essays of
J.F. Ade Ajayi* (Africa World Press, Trenton, NJ, 2000), pp. 153–63.

Adeniji, Abolade, 'Universal History and the Challenge of Globalization
to African Historiography', *Radical History Review*, 91 (2005), pp. 98–103.

African Development Bank et al., *African Statistical Yearbook 2009* (ADB et
al., Tunis etc., 2009).

Agozino, Biko, 'Crime, Criminology and Post-colonial Theory: Criminological Reflections on West Africa', in James Sheptycki and Ali Wardak
(eds), *Transnational and Comparative Criminology* (Glasshouse Press, London, 2005), pp. 117–34.

Ake, Claude, *Democracy and Development in Africa* (The Brookings Institution, Washington DC, 1996).

Andreski, Stanislav, *The African Predicament: A Study in the Pathology of
Modernisation* (Michael Joseph, London, 1968).

Andrew, Christopher, and Vasili Mitrohkin, *The Mitrohkin Archive II: The
KGB and the World* (Allen Lane, London, 2005).

Anene, J.C., 'Jaja of Opobo', in K.O.Dike (ed.), *Eminent Nigerians of the
Nineteenth Century: A Series of Studies Originally Broadcast by the Nigerian
Broadcasting Corporation* (Cambridge University Press, 1960), pp. 17–25.

Apter, Andrew, *The Pan-African Nation: Oil and the Spectacle of Culture in
Nigeria* (University of Chicago Press, 2005).

Arnold, Guy, *Africa: A Modern History* (Atlantic Books, London, 2005).

Awolowo, Obafemi, *The Path to Nigerian Freedom* (Faber & Faber, London,
1947).

Bagehot, Walter, 'The Danger of Lending to Semi-civilized Countries', in
Norman St John Stevas (ed.), *The Collected Works of Walter Bagehot*,
vol. 10 (The Economist, London, 1978), pp. 419–23.

Baker, Raymond W., *Capitalism's Achilles Heel: Dirty Money and how to
Renew the Free-market System* (John Wiley and Sons, New York, 2005).

Barraclough, Geoffrey, *An Introduction to Contemporary History* (1964; Pelican edn, London, 1967).

Bates, Robert H., *Markets and States in Tropical Africa* (University of California Press, Los Angeles, 1981).

———, *When Things Fell Apart: State Failure in Late-century Africa* (Cambridge University Press, 2008).

Bayart, Jean-François, 'Africa in the World: a History of Extraversion', *African Affairs*, 99, 395 (2000), pp. 217–67.

———, *The State in Africa* (1994; 2nd edn, Polity Press, Cambridge, 2009).

———, 'Les chemins de traverse de l'hégémonie coloniale en Afrique de l'ouest francophone: anciens esclaves, anciens combattants, nouveaux musulmans', *Politique africaine*, 105 (2007), pp. 201–40.

———, 'Hégémonie et coercition en Afrique sub-saharienne: la « politique de la chicotte »', *Politique africaine*, 110 (2008), pp. 123–52.

Bayart, Jean-François, Stephen Ellis and Béatrice Hibou, *The Criminalization of the State in Africa* (James Currey and the International African Institute, Oxford, 1999).

Benthall, Jonathan, and Jérôme Bellion-Jourdan, *The Charitable Crescent: Politics of Aid in the Muslim World* (I.B. Tauris, London, 2003).

Berendsen, Bernard (ed.), *Emerging Global Scarcities and Power Shifts* (KIT Publishers, Amsterdam, 2009).

Berman, Bruce, and John Lonsdale, *Unhappy Valley: Conflict in Kenya and Africa* (2 vols, James Currey, London, 1992).

Blundo, Giorgio, and Jean-Pierre Olivier de Sardan (eds), *Etat et corruption en Afrique: une anthropologie comparative des relations entre fonctionnaires et usagers* (Karthala, Paris, 2007).

Bobbitt, Phillip, *The Shield of Achilles: War, Peace and the Course of History* (Penguin, London, 2002).

Boone, Catherine, 'Property and Constitutional Order: Land Tenure Reform and the Future of the African state', *African Affairs*, 106, 425 (2007), pp. 557–86.

Booth, James, *Writers and Politics in Nigeria* (Hodder & Stoughton, London, 1981).

Brague, Rémi, *The Law of God: The Philosophical History of an Idea* (trans. Lydia G. Cochrane, University of Chicago Press, 2007).

Bretton, Henry L., *Power and Stability in Nigeria: The Politics of Decolonization* (Frederick A. Praeger, New York, 1962).

———, *Power and Politics in Africa* (Longman, London, 1973).

Breytenbach, Breyten, 'Mandela's Smile: Notes on South Africa's Failed Revolution', *Harpers Magazine* (December 2008), pp. 39–48.

Brzezinski, Zbigniew, *Out of Control: Global Turmoil on the Eve of the Twenty-first Century* (Charles Scribner's Sons, New York, 1993).

Buchan, James, *Frozen Desire: The Meaning of Money* (Farrar, Straus, and Giroux, New York, 1997).

Burns, Alan, *In Defence of Colonies* (Geo. Allen & Unwin, London, 1957).

Cain, Peter, and A.G. Hopkins, *British Imperialism: Innovation and Expansion* (Longman, London etc., 1993).

Callaway, Helen, and Dorothy O. Helly, 'Crusader for Empire: Flora Shaw/Lady Lugard', in Nupur Chaudhuri and Margaret Strobel (eds), *Western Women and Imperialism: Complicity and Resistance* (Indiana University Press, Bloomington and Indianapolis, 1992), pp. 79–97.

Castells, Manuel, *End of Millennium* (1998; 2nd edn, Blackwell, Oxford, 2000).

Chabal, Patrick, and Jean-Pascal Daloz, *Africa Works: Disorder as Political Instrument* (James Currey and the International African Institute, Oxford, 1999).

Chakrabarty, Dipesh, *Provincializing Europe: Postcolonial Thought and Historical Difference* (Princeton University Press, 2000).

Codesria Bulletin, 1 & 2 (2004).

Cohen, Stanley, 'Politics and Crime: Spot the Difference', *British Journal of Sociology*, 47, 1 (2001), pp. 1–21.

Comaroff, Jean and John L. (eds), *Modernity and its Malcontents: Ritual and Power in Postcolonial Africa* (Chicago University Press, 1993).

Cookey, S.J.S., *King Jaja of the Niger Delta: His Life and Times, 1821–1891* (NOK publishers, New York, 1974).

Cooley, John K., *Unholy Wars* (2001; new edn, Pluto Press, London, 2002).

Cooper, Frederick, *Africa since 1940: The Past of the Present* (Cambridge University Press, 2002).

Cooper, Robert, 'The Post-modern State', in Mark Leonard (ed.), *Re-Ordering the World: The Long-term Implications of 11 September* (The Foreign Policy Centre, London, 2002), pp. 11–20.

Coquery-Vidrovitch, Catherine, 'De la périodisation en histoire africaine: peut-on l'envisager?', *Afrique et histoire*, 2 (2004), pp. 31–65.

Cotula, Lorenzo, Sonja Vermeulen, Rebecca Leonard and James Keeley, *Land Grab or Development Opportunity? Agricultural Investment and International Land Deals in Africa* (IIED, FAO and IFAD, Rome, 2009).

Crocker, W.R., *Australian Ambassador: International Relations at First Hand* (Melbourne University Press, Carlton, Victoria, 1971).

Darwin, John, *After Tamerlane: The Global History of Empire* (Allen Lane, London, 2007).

Davidson, Basil, *The Black Man's Burden: Africa and the Curse of the Nation-state* (James Currey, London, 1992).

De Boeck, Filip, comment in 'Ethnographic Sorcery', *African Studies Review* 51, 3 (2008), p. 143.

De Haan, Arjan, *Will China Change International Development as We Know It?* (ISS Working Paper 475, Institute of Social Studies, The Hague, 2009).

De Soto, Hernando, *The Mystery of Capital: Why Capitalism Triumphs in the West and Fails Everywhere Else* (Basic Books, New York, 2000).

De Waal, Alex, 'Mission without End? Peacekeeping in the African Political Marketplace', *International Affairs*, 85, 1 (2009), pp. 99–113.

Du Maine de la Josserie, Julien-Pierre, 'Idée de la Côte occidentale de Madagascar, depuis Ancouala au nord, jusqu'à Mouroundava désigné par les Noirs sous le nom Menabe', *Annales des voyages, de la géographie, et de l'histoire*, XI (1810), pp. 20–52.

Duffield, Mark, *Global Governance and the New Wars: The Merging of Development and Security* (Zed Books, London and New York, 2001).

Easterly, William, *The White Man's Burden: Why the West's Efforts to Aid the Rest Have Done so much Ill and so little Good* (Penguin Books, New York etc., 2006).

Eboh, Simeon O., 'Law and Order in the Society: the Nigerian Experience', *The Nigerian Journal of Theology*, 18 (2004), pp. 18–35.

Ellis, Stephen, 'Africa and International Corruption: the Strange Case of South Africa and Seychelles', *African Affairs*, 95, 379 (1996), pp. 165–96.

———, 'How to Rebuild Africa', *Foreign Affairs*, 84, 5 (2005), pp. 135–48.

———, 'Government by Graft: the Roots of Corruption in Africa', *Current History*, 105, 691 (May 2006), pp. 203–8.

———,The Okija Shrine: Death and Life in Nigerian Politics', *Journal of African History*, 49, 3 (2008), pp. 445–66.

Ellis, Stephen, and Gerrie ter Haar, *Worlds of Power: Religious Thought and Political Practice in Africa* (Hurst & Co., London, 2004).

———, 'Religion and Politics: Taking African Epistemologies Seriously', *Journal of Modern African Studies*, 45, 3 (2007), pp. 385–401.

Ellis, William, *History of Madagascar* (2 vols, Fisher & Son, London and Paris, 1838).

Falola, Toyin, and Matthew M. Heaton, *A History of Nigeria* (Cambridge University Press, 2008).

Feinstein, Andrew, *After the Party: A Personal and Political Journey inside the ANC* (Jonathan Ball, Johannesburg, 2007).

Ferguson, James, *The Anti-politics Machine: 'Development', Depoliticization, and Bureaucratic Power in Lesotho* (Cambridge University Press, 1990).

———, *Global Shadows: Africa in the Neoliberal World Order* (Duke University Press, Durham, NC and London, 2006).

Friedman, Robert I., *Red Mafiya: How the Russian Mob has Invaded America* (Little, Brown, and Co., New York, 2000).

Frynas, Jedrzej George, and Manuel Paulo, 'A New Scramble for African Oil? Historical, Political and Business Perspectives', *African Affairs* 106, 423 (2007), pp. 229–51.

Fuglestad, Finn, *The Ambiguities of History: The Problem of Ethnocentrism in Historical Writing* (Oslo Academic Press, 2005).

Geffray, Christian, *La Cause des armes au Mozambique: anthropologie d'une guerre civile* (Karthala, Paris, 1990).

Gephart, Malte, *Contextualizing Conceptions of Corruption: Challenges for the International anti-Corruption Campaign* (Working Paper no. 115, German Institute of Global and Area Studies, Hamburg, 2009).

Geschiere, Peter, *The Perils of Belonging: Autochthony, Citizenship, and Exclusion in Africa and Europe* (University of Chicago Press, 2009).

Geschiere, Peter, et al. (eds), 'Autochthony and the Crisis of Citizenship', special number of *African Studies Review*, 49, 2 (2006).

Gevisser, Mark, *Thabo Mbeki: The Dream Deferred* (Jonathan Ball, Johannesburg, 2007).

Gewald, Jan-Bart, 'More than Red Rubber and Figures Alone: a Critical Appraisal of the Memory of the Congo Exhibition at the Royal Museum for Central Africa, Tervuren, Belgium', *International Journal of African Historical Studies*, 39, 3 (2006), pp. 471–86.

Gill, John, 'UK Looks Set to Benefit from Nigerian Student Boom', *Times Higher Education Supplement*, 11 December 2008.

Glenny, Misha, *McMafia: Seriously Organised Crime* (Vintage, London, 2009).

'Gouverner la mer: Etats, pirates, sociétés', special number, *Politique africaine*, 116 (2009).

Gowan, Peter, *The Global Gamble: Washington's Faustian Bid for World Dominance* (Verso, London and New York, 1999).

Gray, John, 'We Simply Do Not Know!', *London Review of Books*, 31, 22 (19 Nov. 2009).

Halper, Stefan, *The Beijing Consensus: How China's Authoritarian Model will Dominate the 21st Century* (Basic Books, New York, 2010).

Hargreaves, John D., *West Africa Partitioned* (2 vols, Macmillan, London, 1974).

Hatchard, John, 'Combating Transnational Crime in Africa: Problems and Perspectives', *Journal of African Law*, 50, 2 (2006), pp. 145–60.

Hegel, G.W.F., *Lectures on the Philosophy of World History* (1830; trans. and introduced by H.B. Nisbet and Duncan Forbes, Cambridge University Press, 1975).

Herbst, Jeff, *States and Power in Africa: Comparative Lessons in Authority and Control* (Princeton University Press, 2000).

Hibou, Béatrice (ed.), *The Privatisation of the State* (Hurst & Co., London, 2005).

Hochschild, Adam, *King Leopold's Ghost: A Story of Greed, Terror, and Heroism in Colonial Africa* (Houghton Mifflin, Boston, MA, etc., 1998).

Hopkins, A.G., 'The New Economic History of Africa', *Journal of African History*, 50, 2 (2009), pp. 155–77.

Human Security Centre, *Human Security Report 2005: War and Peace in the 21st Century* (Oxford University Press, New York, 2005).

Ikubaje, John, *Corruption and anti-Corruption: Revenue Transparency in Nigeria's Oil Sector* (Joe-tolalu and Associates, Lagos, 2005).

Ikuenobe, Polycarp, 'Moral Thought in African Cultures? A Metaphilosophical Question', *African Philosophy*, 12, 2 (1999), pp. 105–23.

Iliffe, John, *Africans: The History of a Continent* (1995; 2nd edition, Cambridge University Press, 2007).

International Crisis Group, *Somalia: To Move Beyond the Failed State* (Africa Report no. 147, Nairobi/Brussels, 23 December 2008).

Joly, Eva, *Est-ce dans ce monde-là que nous voulons vivre?* (Eds. Les Arènes, Paris, 2003).

Junger, Sebastian, 'Blood Oil', *Vanity Fair* (February 2007).

Kennedy, Paul, *The Parliament of Man: The United Nations and the Quest for World Government* (Penguin edn, London, 2007).

Klare, Michael, *Blood and Oil* (2004; Penguin edn, London, 2005).

Kourouma, Ahmadou, *En attendant le vote des bêtes sauvages* (Seuil, Paris, 1998).

Lal, Deepak, *Unintended Consequences: The Impact of Factor Endowments, Culture and Politics on Long-run Economic Performance* (The MIT Press, Cambridge, MA, 1998).

Large, Daniel, 'Beyond "Dragon in the Bush": the Study of China-Africa Relations', *African Affairs* 107, 426 (2008), pp. 45–61.

Le Sage, Andre, 'Africa's Irregular Security Threats: Challenges for U.S. Engagement', Institute for National Strategic Studies, National Defense University, Washington DC, *Strategic Forum*, 255 (May 2010).

Le Sueur, James D., *Between Terror and Democracy: Algeria since 1989* (Fernwood Publishing etc., Black Point, Nova Scotia etc., 2010).

Lewis, Peter M., *Growing Apart: Oil, Politics, and Economic Change in Indonesia and Nigeria* (University of Michigan Press, Ann Arbor, MI, 2007).

Lonsdale, John, 'States and Social Processes in Africa: a Historiographical Survey', *African Studies Review*, 24, 2–3 (1981), pp. 139–225.

———, 'Moral Ethnicity and Political Tribalism', in Preben Kaarsholm and Jan Hultin (eds), *Inventions and Boundaries: Historical and Anthropological Approaches to the Study of Ethnicity and Nationalism* (Occasional paper 11, International Development Studies, Roskilde University, 1994).

Louis, Wm. Roger, and Ronald Robinson, 'The U.S. and the End of British Empire in Tropical Africa', in Prosser Gifford and Wm. Roger Louis (eds), *The Transfer of Power in Africa: Decolonization, 1940–1960* (Yale University Press, New Haven and London, 1982), pp. 31–55.

Luckham, Robin, et al., *The Middle Classes and their Role in National Development* (CDD/ODI Policy Brief no. 3, Centre for Development and Democracy, Accra, 2005).

Lugard, Frederick D., 'Report by Sir F.D. Lugard on the Amalgamation of Northern and Southern Nigeria, and Administration, 1912–1919', in A.H.M. Kirk-Greene, (ed.), *Lugard and the Amalgamation of Nigeria: A Documentary Record* (Frank Cass, London, 1968), pp. 49–171.

Mamdani, Mahmood, *Saviors and Survivors: Darfur, Politics, and the War on Terror* (Pantheon Books, New York, 2009).

Mann, Gregory, *Native Sons: West African Veterans and France in the Twentieth Century* (Duke Univ. Press, Durham, NC, 2006).

Marshall, Ruth, *Political Spiritualities: The Pentecostal Revolution in Nigeria* (University of Chicago Press, 2009).

Mazower, Mark, *Dark Continent: Europe's Twentieth Century* (Penguin, London, 1998).

Mazzitelli, Antonio L., 'Transnational Organized Crime in West Africa: the Additional Challenge', *International Affairs*, 83, 6 (2007), pp. 1071–90.

Mbembe, Achille, 'A propos des écritures africaines de soi', *Politique africaine*, 77 (2000), pp. 16–43.

———, 'An Essay on the Political Imagination in Wartime', *Codesria Bulletin*, 2–4 (2000), pp. 6–21.

———, *On the Postcolony* (University of California Press, Berkeley, 2001).

Miller, Joseph C., *Way of Death: Merchant Capitalism and the Angolan Slave Trade, 1730–1830* (University of Wisconsin Press, Madison, WI, 1996).

———, 'History and Africa/Africa and History', *American Historical Review*, 104, 1 (1999), pp. 1–32.

Minear, Larry, Colin Scott and Thomas Weiss, *The News Media, Civil War, and Humanitarian Action* (Lynne Rienner, Boulder, CO and London, 1996).

Moyo, Dambisa, *Dead Aid: Why Aid isn't Working and how there is Another Way for Africa* (Allen Lane, London, 2009).

Mpondo, Simon, 'The Season of the Rains', in Gerald Moore and Ulli Beier (eds), *The Penguin Book of Modern African Poetry* (1963; 3rd edn, Penguin, Harmondsworth etc., 1984), pp. 49–50.

Nagbe, Moses, *Bulk Challenge* (Champion Publications, Cape Coast, Ghana, 1996).

Napoleoni, Loretta, *Modern Jihad: Tracing the Dollars behind the Terror Networks* (Pluto Press, London etc., 2003).

Nellor, David C., 'The Rise of Africa's "Frontier" Markets', *Finance & Development* (Sept. 2008), pp. 30–3.

Nicolson, I.F., *The Administration of Nigeria 1900–1960: Men, Methods and Myths* (Clarendon Press, Oxford, 1969).

Nkrumah, Kwame, *The Autobiography of Kwame Nkrumah* (Thomas Nelson, Edinburgh, 1957).

Nyiri, Pal, *Foreign Concessions: The Past and Future of a Form of Shared Sovereignty* (inaugural lecture, VU University Amsterdam, 2009).

Ogot, Bethwell A., 'The Historical Development of African Societies, 1500–1800', in UNESCO, *General History of Africa*, V (Heinemann/ Unesco/University of California Press, London etc., 1992), pp. 895–905.

Okonta, Ike, 'Nigeria: Chronicle of a Dying State', *Current History*, 104, 682 (May 2005), pp. 203–8.

Olupona, Jacob (ed.), *African Spirituality: Forms, Meanings and Expressions* (Crossroad publishing, New York, 2000).

Osaghae, E.E., 'The State of Africa's Second Liberation', *Interventions*, 7, 1 (2005), pp. 1–20.

Palan, Ronen, *The Offshore World: Sovereign Markets, Virtual Places, and Nomad Millionaires* (Cornell University Press, London and Ithaca, 2003).

Palan, Ronen, Richard Murphy and Christian Chavagneux, *Tax Havens: How Globalization really Works* (Cornell University Press, Ithaca, NY, 2010).

Patrick, Stewart, and Kaysie Brown, *Greater than the Sum of its Parts? Assessing 'Whole of Government' Approaches to Fragile States* (International Peace Academy, New York, 2007).

Peel, John, *Religious Encounter and the Making of the Yoruba* (Indiana University Press, Bloomington, IN, 2000).

Pfaff, William, 'Mac Bundy said he was "All Wrong"', *New York Review of Books*, LVII, 10 (10 June 2010), pp. 59–64.

Polanyi, Karl, *The Great Transformation* (1944; Octagon Books, New York, 1975).

Porteous, Tom, *Britain in Africa* (Zed Books, London etc., 2008).

Pritchett, Lant, and Michael Woolcock, 'Solutions when the Solution is the Problem: Arraying the Disarray in Development', *World Development*, 32, 2 (2004), pp. 191–212.

Prunier, Gérard, *From Genocide to Continental War: The 'Congolese' Conflict and the Crisis of Contemporary Africa* (Hurst & Co., London, 2009).

Ratha, Dilip, Sanket Mohapatra and Ani Silwal, *Migration and Development Brief 11*, (World Bank, Washington, DC, 3 November 2009).

Rennie, Namvula, 'The Lion and the Dragon: African Experiences in China', *Journal of African Media Studies*, 1, 3 (2009), pp. 379–414.

Reno, William, *Corruption and State Politics in Sierra Leone* (Cambridge University Press, 1995).

———, 'Anti-Corruption Efforts in Liberia: are they Aimed at the Right Targets?', *International Peacekeeping*, 15, 3 (2008), pp. 387–404.

Report of the Foster-Sutton Tribunal of Inquiry into Allegations of Improper Conduct by the Premier of the Eastern Region of Nigeria (Her Majesty's Stationery Office, London, 1957).

Rimmer, Douglas, 'Learning about Economic Development from Africa', *African Affairs*, 102, 408 (2003), pp. 469–91.

Rist, Gilbert (trans. Patrick Camiller), *The History of Development: From Western Origins to Global Faith* (1997; new edn, Zed Books, London etc., 2002).

Robinson, Ronald, 'Non-European Foundations of European Imperialism: Sketch for a Theory of Collaboration', in E.R.J. Owen and R.B. Sutcliffe (eds), *Studies in the Theory of Imperialism* (Longman, London, 1972), pp. 117–42.

Rodney, Walter, *How Europe Underdeveloped Africa* (Bogle-L'Ouverture, London, 1972).

Sahlins, Marshall, *Apologies to Thucydides: Understanding History as Culture and Vice Versa* (University of Chicago Press, 2004).

Sautman, Barry, and Yan Hairong, 'The Forest for the Trees: Trade, Investment and the China-in-Africa Discourse', *Pacific Affairs*, 81, 1 (2008), pp. 9–29.

Schama, Simon, *Rough Crossings: Britain, the Slaves and the American Revolution* (BBC Books, London, 2005).

Schatz, Sayre P., *Development Bank Lending in Nigeria: The Federal Loans Board* (Nigerian Institute of Social and Economic Research and Oxford University Press, Ibadan and London, 1964).

Seaford, Richard, *Money and the Early Greek Mind: Homer, Philosophy, Tragedy* (Cambridge University Press, 2004).

———, Presidential address to the Classical Association, 'World without Limits', *Times Literary Supplement*, 19 June 2009.

Shaxson, Nicholas, *Poisoned Wells: The Dirty Politics of African Oil* (Palgrave Macmillan, New York etc., 2007).

Sirleaf, Ellen Johnson, *This Child Will be Great: Memoir of a Remarkable Life by Africa's First Woman President* (HarperCollins, New York, 2009).

Smith, Daniel J., *A Culture of Corruption: Everyday Deception and Popular Discontent in Nigeria* (Princeton University Press, 2007).

Smith, Robert A., *The Emancipation of the Hinterland* (The Star Magazine and Advertising Services, Monrovia, 1964).

Smith, Stephen W., 'Nodding and Winking', *London Review of Books*, 32, 3 (11 Feb. 2010), pp. 10–2.

Smithies, Arthur, 'Memorial: Joseph Alois Schumpeter, 1883–1950', *American Economic Review*, 40, 4 (1950), pp. 628–48.

Snow, Philip, *The Star Raft: China's Encounter with Africa* (Weidenfeld and Nicolson, London, 1988).

Soares de Oliveira, Ricardo, *Oil and Politics in the Gulf of Guinea* (Hurst & Co., London, 2007).

———, 'Business Success, Angola-style: Postcolonial Politics and the Rise and Rise of Sonangol', *Journal of Modern African Studies*, 45, 4 (2007), pp. 595–619.

Sogge, David, *State Weakness: Seen from Another Perspective*, Working Paper 64 (Fundacion para las Relaciones Internacionales y el Dialogo Exterior, Madrid, 2008).

Stiglitz, Joseph, *Globalization and its Discontents* (W.W. Norton & Co., New York, 2002).

Suret-Canale, Jean, 'La Guinée dans le système colonial', *Présence africaine*, 29 (1959–60), pp. 9–44.

Talbott, Strobe, *The Russia Hand: A Memoir of Presidential Diplomacy* (Random House, New York, 2002).

Ter Haar, Gerrie, *Halfway to Paradise: African Christians in Europe* (Cardiff Academic Press, 1998).

Thoumi, Francisco E., 'The Rise of Two Drug Tigers: The Development of the Illegal Drugs Industry and Drug Policy Failure in Afghanistan and Colombia', in F. Bovenkerk and M. Levi (eds), *The Organized Crime Community: Essays in Honor of Alan A. Block* (Studies of Organized Crime no. 6, Spring Science and Business, New York, 2007), pp. 125–48.

Tilly, Charles, 'War Making and State Making as Organized Crime', in Peter Evans, Dietrich Rueschemeyer and Theda Skocpol (eds), *Bringing the State Back In* (Cambridge University Press, 1985), pp. 169–87.

Toulabor, Comi M., *Le Togo sous Eyadema* (Karthala, Paris, 1986).

Toulmin, Camilla, *Climate Change in Africa* (Zed Books, London and New York, 2009).

Tull, Dennis, and Andreas Mehler, 'The Hidden Costs of Power-sharing: Reproducing Insurgent Violence in Africa', *African Affairs*, 104, 416 (2005), pp. 375–98.

Uche, Chibuike, 'Bank of England versus the IBRD: Did the Nigerian Colony Deserve a Central Bank?', *Explorations in Economic History*, 34, 2 (1997), pp. 220–41.

United Nations Conference on Trade and Development, *World Investment Report 2008* (UN, New York and Geneva, 2008).

United Nations Office on Drugs and Crime, *Cocaine Trafficking in West Africa: The Threat to Stability and Development (with Special Reference to Guinea-Bissau)* (UNODC, Vienna, 2007).

————, *Transnational Trafficking and the Rule of Law in West Africa: A Threat Assessment* (UNODC, Vienna, 2009).

————, *The Role of Organized Crime in the Smuggling of Migrants from West Africa to the European Union* (UNODC, Vienna, forthcoming).

United States Senate, Permanent subcommittee on investigations of the Committee on Governmental Affairs, *Private Banking and Money Laundering: A Case Study of Opportunities and Vulnerabilities* (US Government Printing Office, Washington DC, 2000).

Vellut, Jean-Luc, et al., *Het Geheugen van Congo: De koloniale tijd* (Koninklijk Museum voor Midden-Africa, Tervuren, 2005).

Weitz, Eric D., 'From the Vienna to the Paris System: International Politics and the Entangled Histories of Human Rights, Forced Deportations, and Civilizing Missions', *American Historical Review*, 113, 5 (2008), pp. 1313–43.

Wetenschappelijke Raad voor het Regeringsbeleid, *Minder pretentie, meer ambitie: ontwikkelingshulp die verschil maakt* (WRR and Amsterdam University Press, The Hague and Amsterdam, 2010).

Wiredu, Kwasi, 'Modes of Thought in African Philosophy', in John Middleton (editor-in-chief), *Encyclopaedia of Africa South of the Sahara* (4 vols, Charles Scribner's Sons, New York, 1997), 3, p. 171.

World Bank, *World Development Report, 2007: Development and the Next Generation* (The World Bank, Washington DC, 2006).

Wrong, Michaela, *It's Our Turn to Eat: The Story of a Kenyan Whistleblower* (Fourth Estate, London, 2009).

York, Peter, *Dictators' Homes* (Atlantic Books, London, 2005).

Young, Crawford, 'The End of the post-Colonial State in Africa? Reflections on Changing African Political Dynamics', *African Affairs*, 103, 410 (2004), pp. 23–49.

Zachary, G. Pascal, 'The Coming Revolution in Africa', *The Wilson Quarterly*, 32, 1 (2008), pp. 50–66.

Zartman, I. William (ed.), *Collapsed States: The Disintegration and Restoration of Legitimate Authority* (Lynne Rienner, Boulder, CO, 1995).

Zolo, Danilo, *Victors' Justice: From Nuremburg to Baghdad* (2006; English translation by M.W. Weir, Verso, London, 2009).

INDEX